Currency Swaps

A Self-Study Guide to Mastering and Applying Currency Swaps

Coopers & Lybrand

PROBUS PUBLISHING COMPANY
Chicago, Illinois
Cambridge, England

ISBN 1-55738-590-4

Printed in the United States of America

BB

1 2 3 4 5 6 7 8 9 0

Contents

Preface   v

Foreword   vii

Introduction   ix

1. The swap mechanism
What is a currency swap?   1
The terminology of currency swaps   9
What does a currency swap do?   *150 minutes*   19

Self-Study Exercises   *30 minutes*   39

2. Using currency swaps
Risk management with currency swaps   45
Return management with currency swaps:
      arbitrage with cash instruments   71
Return management with currency swaps:
      arbitrage with LTFX   *180 minutes*   91

Self-Study Exercises   *90 minutes*   95

3. Trading currency swaps
Dealing procedures   115
Swap documentation   116
The primary market: banks   122
The primary market: brokers   134
The secondary market: assignment   *90 minutes*   136

Self-Study Exercises   *30 minutes*   139

4. Pricing and valuing swaps
Price and valuation 147
Valuing generic curency swaps 150
Valuing a swap structure *190 minutes* 165

Self-Study Exercises *60 minutes* 173

5. Currency swap risk and regulation
Credit risk in currency swaps 183
Risk capital requirements for swaps 197
Managing credit risk on currency swaps 204
Regulation of the conduct of business 208
    in swaps in the UK *120 minutes*

Self-Study Exercises *45 minutes* 215

Glossary 225

How to mark the self-study questions 235

Preface

Since its inception in the early 1980s the swaps market has experienced phonomenal growth and is now a market of over US$3 trillion in size. This exponential growth means that swaps are now used by most financial institutions and corporate treasuries. At present there are only 70 swaps houses recognised by the International Swaps Dealers Association (ISDA)—largely major players in the international capital markets. Yet, as demand for these products continues to increase, the market will surely experience further growth in both the size and in the number of players. Innovation in the marketplace may be dominated currently by a few sophisticated derivatives houses, but many more organizations are involved in the day-to-day activity.

A professional guide to understanding swaps is essential for the various participants—be they management, trainee traders, back office support, system designers, accountants, or corporate treasurers seeking to use swaps in asset management. The Workbook Series on Derivatives is an excellent and muchneeded contribution to helping those with an interest in swaps to understand the variety and complexity of today's market.

John S. Spences
Deputy Chief Executive
Barclays de Zoete Wedd
November 1992

Foreword

In October 1991 we published *The Financial Jungle—a guide to financial instruments* to help promote the understanding of financial instruments and to identify the risks and benefits to both designers and users. Our sponsorship of the Workbook Series on Derivatives continues this theme.

New, increasingly sophisticated and complex swaps products are being designed all the time. The pace of change has been so rapid that many supporting personnel as well as senior management have struggled to keep step with the risk, accounting, tax, and regulatory implications of these innovative products. Examples abound on what happens when organizations trade financial instruments without fully understanding how they are put together.

It is vital that the designers understand the accounting and tax implications of the financial instruments they are seeking to promote. Equally, it is important for the users of instruments to comprehend their economic rationale and effect to ensure all risks are identified before transactions are completed. We believe these workbooks are part of the answer. They are well structured and easy to follow guides on how swaps are designed and how they work. Divided into four volumes—*Interest Rate Swaps, Currency Swaps, Equity Swaps, and Swaps and Financial Engineering*—they are invaluable study aids.

Phil Rivett
Chairman, Securities and Commodities Group

Paul Reyniers
Chairman, Financial Risk Management Group

Coopers & Lybrand
November 1992

Introduction

The currency swap was the original swap instrument. Indeed, in one form or another, its history can be traced back to the 16th century. Since the inter-war years, extensive use of currency swaps has been made by central banks as a means of supplying each other with additional foreign exchange reserves in times of crisis. However, the currency swap in its modern form only emerged in 1976, although a market in the instrument was slow to develop until the announcement of a deal between the World Bank and IBM in 1981 sealed its respectability.

The proximate reason for the development of the currency swap was the need to solve defects in earlier techniques, such as parallel and back-to-back loans, which were devised to circumvent exchange controls, specifically, in the UK. However, the abolition of UK controls, specifically, in 1979 (which inaugurated a wave of deregulation in other countries) did little to undermine the emerging market in currency swaps. The growth liberalisation of domestic markets and dramatic advances in telecommunications created new international opportunities for borrowers and lenders, not least, access to wider capital markets and arbitrage possibilities between imperfectly integrated domestic markets which could be used to reduce borrowing costs or enhance investment returns. However, in an environment of increasingly volatile interest and exchange rates, the realisation of new opportunities required techniques to efficiently manage the increased risks. By enabling a borrower to fund in one currency and then temporarily switch into another at a fixed exchange rate, the currency swap provided a key tool of risk management.

In terms of market size, currency swaps are now overshadowed by single-currency interest rate swaps (outstanding amounts came to $807m and $3,065m, respectively, at end-1991). The slower growth of the market in currency swaps, which is illustrated in the table below, reflects a number of facts:

■ given the exchange of principal amounts which usually takes place through a currency swap and the consequently greater credit exposure involved (in the form of delivery risk), their use is limited to the hedging of currency risk and arbitrage, and they have not been used for taking currency risk;

■ delivery risk and the complexity which intermediaries face in trying to hedge currency swaps has precluded them from becoming an actively-traded instrument like interest rate swaps;

■ because of the greater delivery risk, heavier risk capital requirements have been imposed on currency swaps than interest rate swaps; increasing credit concerns and the introduction of the Basle capital adequacy regime probably explains much of the slowdown in the currency swap market in 1990;

Currency swaps

- currency swaps remain a capital market instrument, whereas interest rate swaps have developed a large money market sector: short-term currency risk is instead managed with foreign swaps.

| US$bn | New currency swaps | | | outstanding currency swaps (end-year) |
	involving the US dollar	involving other currencies	total	
1983			5*	
1984			10*	
1985			20*	
1986				
1987	76.9	9.6	86.5	183.7
1988	103.8	20.5	124.3	
1989	132.4	45.7	178.1	
1990	131.2	81.6	212.8	
1991	244.2	84.1	328.3	807.2

However, despite smaller volumes, the currency swap cannot be said to be less important than the interest rate swap. While the interest rate swap integrates the money and capital markets in the same currency, the currency swap integrates different currencies into a global market for savings.

The importance of the currency swap is also demonstrated in the fact that the market appears to have adjusted to the general increase in credit concerns and new capital adequacy requirements without serious difficulties. Maturities have tended to shorten (the weighted average maturity of interbank swaps fell from six to three years between 1987 and 1991) and some previously-active intermediaries (typically US banks) have scaled back their involvement, but the severe contraction of the market predicted by some commentators has not occurred.

The resilience of the currency swap market has also demonstrated the prudent approach which intermediaries have adopted without official encouragement, the fact that currency swaps are used for hedging or arbitrage against underlying assets and liabilities rather than risk-taking and the generally high quality of currency swap end-users. These fundamental strengths have been reflected in a pick-up in growth in 1991 and the continued development of the market, not least, in terms of the range of currencies covered (shown in the diagram below).

Currency composition of outstanding currency swaps at end-1991

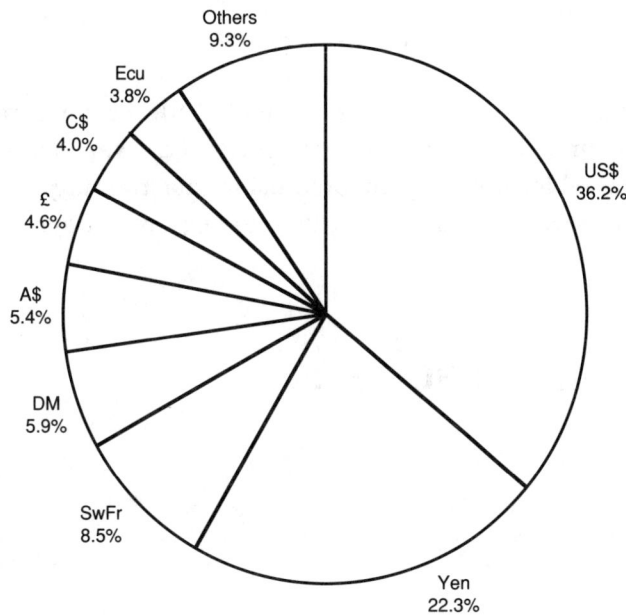

Source: ISDA

How to use this workbook

The importance of currency swaps has not been reflected in the published literature on the subject. Much of what has been published is cursory, simplistic and unsystematic. The purpose of this workbook is to provide the reader with a thorough grounding in currency swaps for the novice and layman. Having completed the workbook, the reader should be in a position to talk confidently and credibly to experienced market practitioners.

Those intending to use this workbook should be familiar with basic interest rate concepts and arithmetic, including forward-forward interest rates. However, the workbook ignores unnecessary technical complications in the form of alternative interest rate conventions. Knowledge of these conventions is vital in swap transactions, but is not specific to swaps and can be gained from a wider number of other sources.

This workbook is designed as a self-study programme. It has therefore been structured to guide the reader systematically through the subject and provides practical examples and case studies throughout to illustrate key points. The sources of market information used by experienced swaps practitioners are summarised and examples have been included from both screen-based information services and market publications.

A set of questions and answers is provided at the end of each section to enable the reader to test and monitor progress. To further facilitate the planning of study time, an estimate for the time needed to complete each chapter and set of exercise is given. Instructions for marking the exercise are set out at the back of the workbook. Both the timing and marking system are based on actual tests given to a representative sample of readers.

The workbook has been designed primarily for those with little or no experience of swaps, particularly where there is an urgent need to know. Experienced swap dealers and sales staff, however, may also find it valuable, not only in organising the training of their junior staff, but also when making swaps presentations to clients who require a degree of familiarisation with the subject.

Other workbooks in the series:

Interest Rate Swaps
Equity Swaps
Swaps and Financial Engineering

For further information on the workbook series, please call Probus Publishing at 1-800-PROBUS-1 or 1-312-868-1100.

1 The swap mechanism

What is a currency swap?

Definition:	**A currency swap is a contract which commits two counterparties to exchange, over an agreed period, two streams of interest payments in different currencies and, at the end of the period, to exchange the corresponding principal amounts at an exchange rate agreed at the start of the contract.**

An example

Consider a currency swap which commits:

■ Bank UK to pay Bank US, over a period of *two years*, a stream of *US dollar interest* on US$17m: interest payments are calculated at a US interest rate agreed at the time the swap is negotiated;

■ in exchange, Bank US to pay Bank UK, over the same period, a counterstream of *sterling interest* on £10m: interest payments are calculated at a UK interest rate agreed at the time the swap is negotiated;

■ Bank UK and Bank US also to exchange, at the end of the two-year period, the *principal amounts* of US$17m and £10m on which interest payments are being made: this exchange will take place at a £/$ exchange rate of 1.7000, which is agreed at the start of the swap.

This example is illustrated in Diagram 1.

Diagram 1: A currency swap

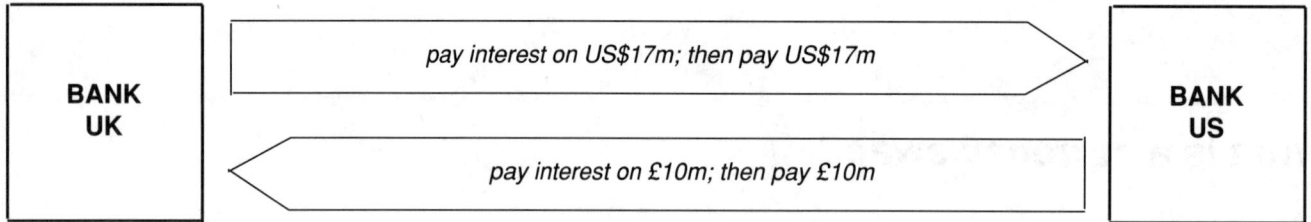

BANK UK

pay interest on US$17m; then pay US$17m

pay interest on £10m; then pay £10m

BANK US

The structure of the swap in terms of the sequence of cash flows is elaborated in Diagram 2.

Diagram 2: Sequence of payments in a currency swap

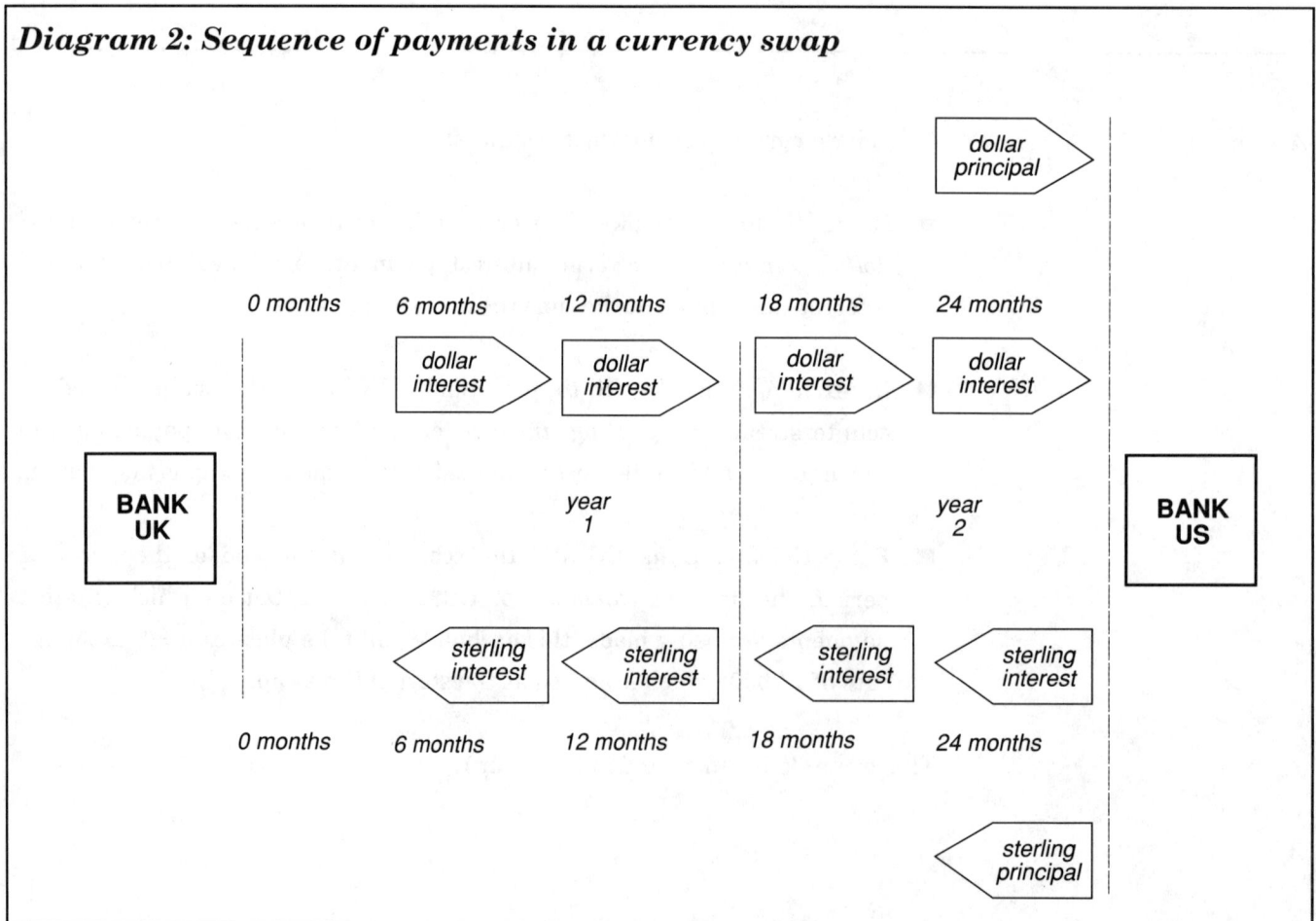

dollar principal

| 0 months | 6 months | 12 months | 18 months | 24 months |

dollar interest | dollar interest | dollar interest | dollar interest

BANK UK

year 1

year 2

BANK US

sterling interest | sterling interest | sterling interest | sterling interest

| 0 months | 6 months | 12 months | 18 months | 24 months |

sterling principal

There are several general points about currency swaps to note from this example:

■ Currency swaps differ from interest rate swaps[1] in that:
  — currency swaps involve an exchange of payments in *two currencies*.
  — currency swaps involve, not only exchanges of interest, but usually also an exchange of *principal* amounts.

■ Currency swaps impact on the *balance sheets* of the swap counterparties, but only when there is an exchange of principal amounts at maturity. A currency swap is therefore classed as an **off-balance sheet** instrument. In contrast, the transfers of principal amounts which took place under the **parallel** and **back-to-back loans** from which currency swaps originated were seen as coincidental loans and, as loans, were placed on the balance sheet[2]. By tightly linking transfers of principal amounts, swaps are classified as future exchanges (contingent liabilities) and so avoid being seen as outstanding loans.

■ Although currency swaps are off-balance sheet instruments, they are not **derivatives** (although they are often classified as such, alongside interest rate swaps). This is because there is an *eventual* movement of principal, whereas a derivative is defined as an instrument whose performance is *derived* from the behaviour of the price of a commodity, but which does not actually require that commodity to be bought or sold.

■ Bank UK and Bank US are undertaking the currency swap because, at maturity, Bank UK will have an amount of US dollars which it wishes to exchange for sterling and Bank US will have an amount of sterling which it wishes to exchange for US dollars, and both wish to avoid *currency risk*. In the currency swap, Bank UK and Bank US commit to exchange the principal amounts at the end of the swap, at an exchange rate fixed at the start of the swap. This rate will probably be the *spot exchange rate* prevailing at the start of the swap, but not necessarily: it is in fact subject to negotiation between the counterparties. By fixing the future exchange rate, the banks hedge each other against currency risk.

■ Like interest rate swaps, the interest payments exchanged through currency swaps can be calculated using:

— a *fixed* interest rate (eg, reflecting bond yields) versus a *floating* interest rate index (eg, Libor).

— two *floating* interest rate indexes (eg, three-month and six-month Libor).

■ In contrast to interest rate swaps, currency swaps can also exchange interest calculated using two *fixed* interest rates.

■ Like the exchange rate, the interest rates used in currency swaps are set by *negotiation* between the counterparties. It is possible, therefore, for those rates to be different from market levels.

■ The principal amount of US dollars to be paid at maturity by Bank UK and the principal amount of sterling to be paid in exchange by Bank US might be acquired:

— as *earnings* accumulated from business operations. Thus, Bank UK might be a UK bank earning dollars and seeking to repatriate them into sterling. Bank US might be a US bank earning sterling and seeking to repatriate them into dollars.

— through *previous borrowings* which are still outstanding. Thus, Bank UK might have an outstanding sterling borrowing and Bank US an outstanding dollar borrowing, but both now require a liability in the other currencies.

■ Although a currency swap only requires an exchange of principal at maturity, principal amounts can be exchanged at the *start* of the swap as well. This is the structure which is normally presented as a currency swap, but is in fact something more. A currency swap with an initial exchange of principal amounts is a combination of a risk (eg, a foreign currency borrowing) and a hedge (the currency swap). In this respect, it is similar to a foreign exchange swap, which is a combination of a risk (an outright forward foreign exchange transaction) and a hedge (an equal and opposite spot foreign exchange transaction). Currency swaps with an initial exchange of principal are undertaken where the swap is associated with a new borrowing or where at least one of the swap counterparties wishes to acquire a principal amount of one of the currencies being swapped.

In the example above, a currency swap with an initial exchange of principal would involve:

- UK Bank selling a principal amount of sterling to US Bank at the start of the swap, in exchange for a principal amount of US dollars.

- This exchange would be at an exchange rate fixed at the start of the swap, probably (but not always) the spot exchange rate.

- The sterling sold by UK Bank and the dollars sold by US Bank in the initial exchange would be *borrowed* by those banks specifically for swapping into the other currency.

- At maturity, this exchange would be reversed. This re-exchange would be at the original exchange rate: the swap is therefore said to be a **par swap**, meaning that both exchanges of principal are for equal amounts. Thus, US Bank would pay the same sterling amount back to UK Bank as it received in the initial exchange and would receive back its original amount of dollars.

- The sterling principal repaid to UK Bank by US Bank at maturity would be used by UK Bank to repay its original sterling borrowing. The sterling interest received by UK Bank from Bank US during the life of the swap would be used to service the interest due on the sterling borrowing. US Bank would use the dollar repayment it receives from UK Bank at maturity to repay its original dollar borrowing and the dollar interest received from UK Bank to service the interest due on that borrowing. In other words, through a currency swap, each counterparty services the debt of the other.

A currency swap involving an initial exchange of principal is illustrated in Diagram 3. It is important to note that, if there is an initial exchange of principal, the borrowings which are undertaken to fund this initial exchange are *separate* from the swap itself, although the initial exchange would be part of the currency swap documentation. In the example, UK Bank and US Bank would borrow from parties who would not be involved in the swap and indeed may have no knowledge of the swap. Currency swaps first emerged in a form which involved an initial exchange of principal: they were originally devised as an improvement on *parallel* and *back-to-*

Diagram 3: Sequence of payments in a currency swap involving an initial exchange of principal

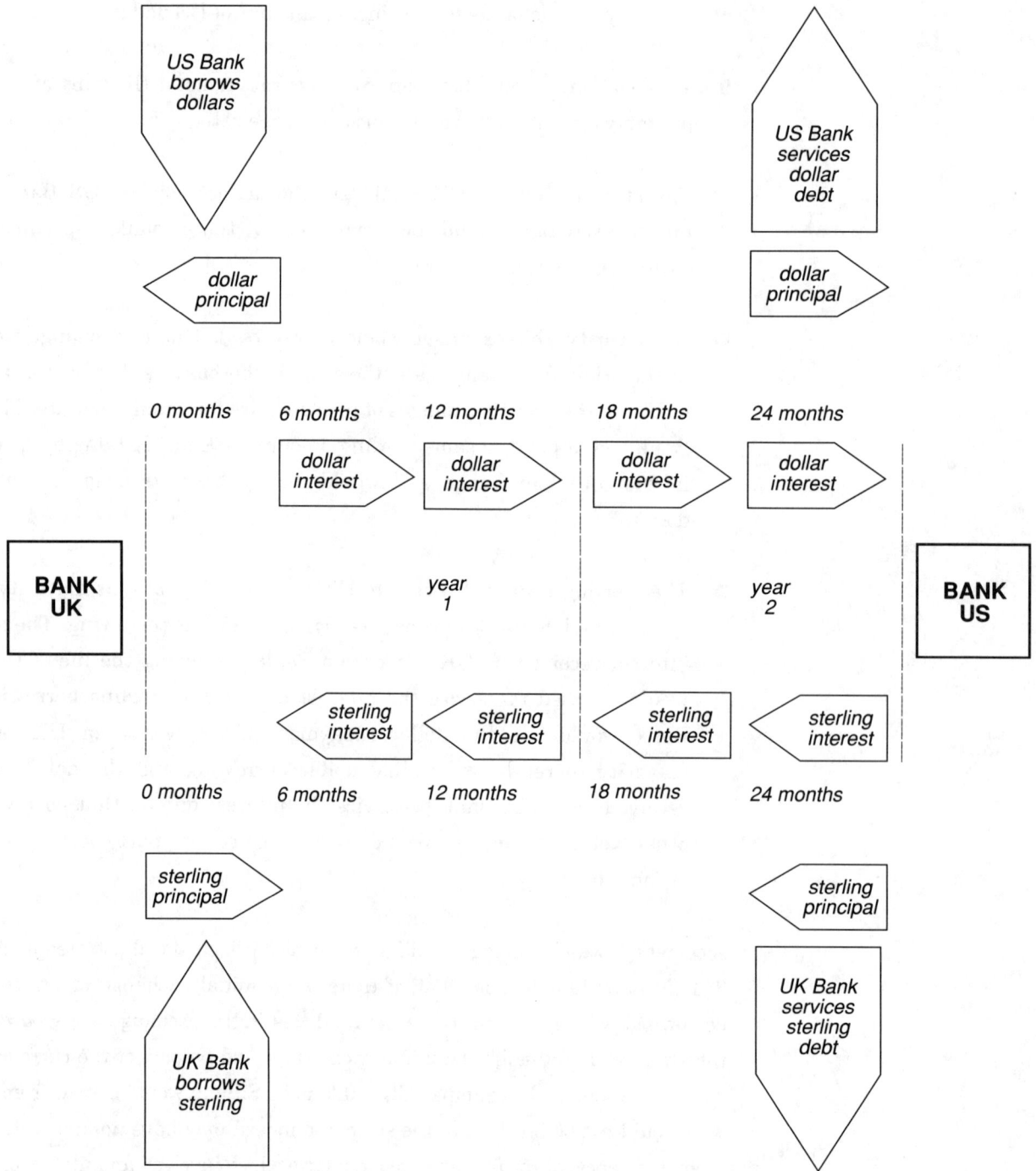

back loans. As noted already, currency swaps lock together the opposite transfers of principal amounts and so qualify them as exchanges rather than coincidental opposite loans.

■ It is possible to construct a currency swap with *no exchange of principal*, even at maturity. As noted already, an initial exchange of principal is anyway unnecessary. Instead of an exchange of principal at maturity, a *net settlement amount* could be paid by whichever counterparty is *paying* the currency which appreciates over the life of the swap. In a currency swap with an exchange of principal at maturity, the counterparty paying the appreciating currency has foregone the exchange rate gain by committing to receive it at an exchange rate fixed at the start of the swap. In a swap without an exchange of principal at maturity, this surrender of exchange rate gain is achieved by the payment of the net settlement amount by that counterparty. In the example used earlier, assume sterling appreciates against the dollar over the life of the swap. A net settlement amount would be paid at maturity by US Bank to UK Bank. If sterling depreciates against the dollar, US Bank should receive a net settlement amount from UK Bank. The practice of paying net settlement amounts is called **alternate performance**.

■ As with interest rate swaps, it is market practice to try to *net* individual exchanges (of interest and principal) through currency swaps. However, because different currencies are exchanged, netting of interest payments is less common in currency swaps than in interest rate swaps. In order to net opposite payments in different currencies, the value of cash flows in one currency have to be translated into the other, usually into US dollars.

Analysing currency swaps

Currency swaps involve flows of interest and principal. This can be difficult to illustrate. The convention used in this Workbook is to represent streams of interest payments with horizontal arrows to and from counterparties and exchanges of principal with semi-circular arrows. An example is set out in Diagram 4.

Diagram 4: Illustrating a currency swap

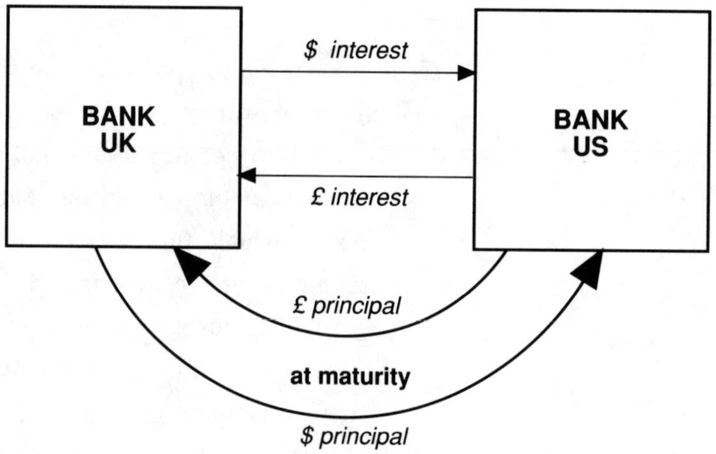

If swap counterparties exchange principal at the start of the swap, as well as at maturity, the swap would be as illustrated in Diagram 5. Note that the initial exchange of principal is represented by the *upper* semi-circular arrows and the final exchange by the *lower* ones.

Diagram 5: Illustrating a currency swap with an initial exchange of principal

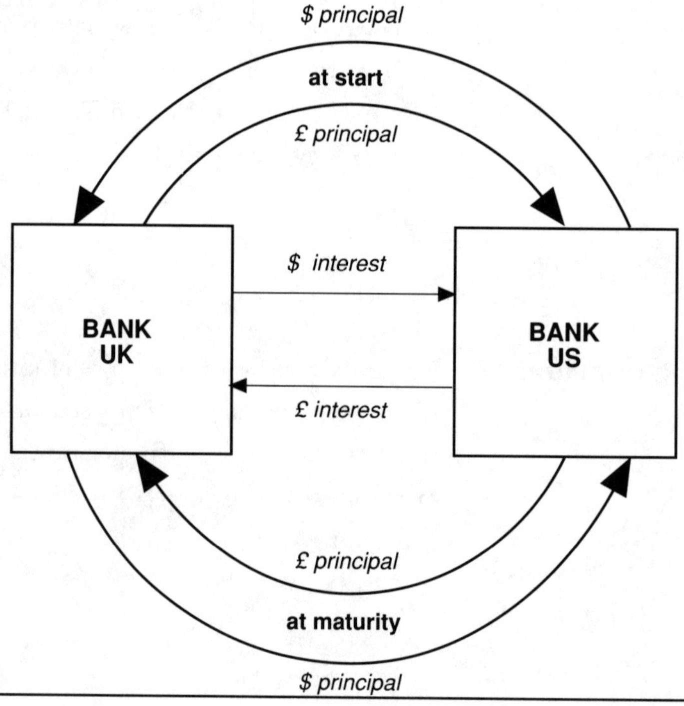

The terminology of currency swaps

Currency swap

The term **currency swap** is used generically in this Workbook to describe all interest rate swaps involving two currencies. However, the strict application of the term is limited to swaps involving the exchange of two fixed-interest streams, in other words, **fixed-against-fixed** swaps between currencies.

Diagram 6: A currency swap

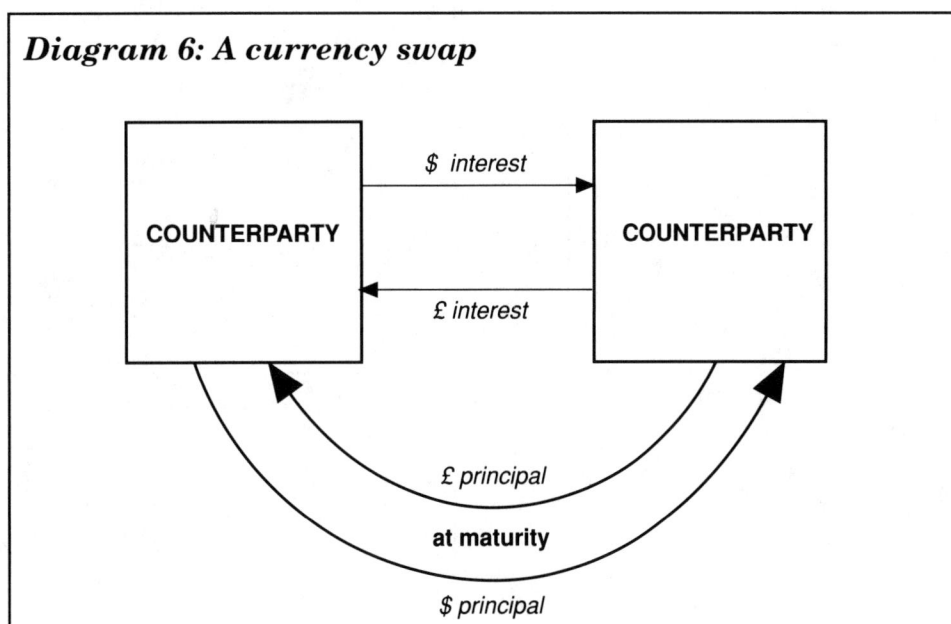

COUNTERPARTY → $ interest → COUNTERPARTY

COUNTERPARTY ← £ interest ← COUNTERPARTY

£ principal

at maturity

$ principal

Cross-currency swap

Cross-currency swaps involve an exchange of interest streams in different currencies, of which at least one is at a *floating* rate of interest. These instruments therefore enable a swap into both:

■ a different *currency*;

■ a different *interest rate basis*.

As regards interest rate bases, cross-currency swaps can be:

■ **fixed-against-floating**, in other words, cross-currency **coupon** swaps: see Diagram 7.

■ **floating-against-floating**, in other words, cross-currency **basis** swaps: see Diagram 8.

Diagram 7: A cross-currency coupon swap

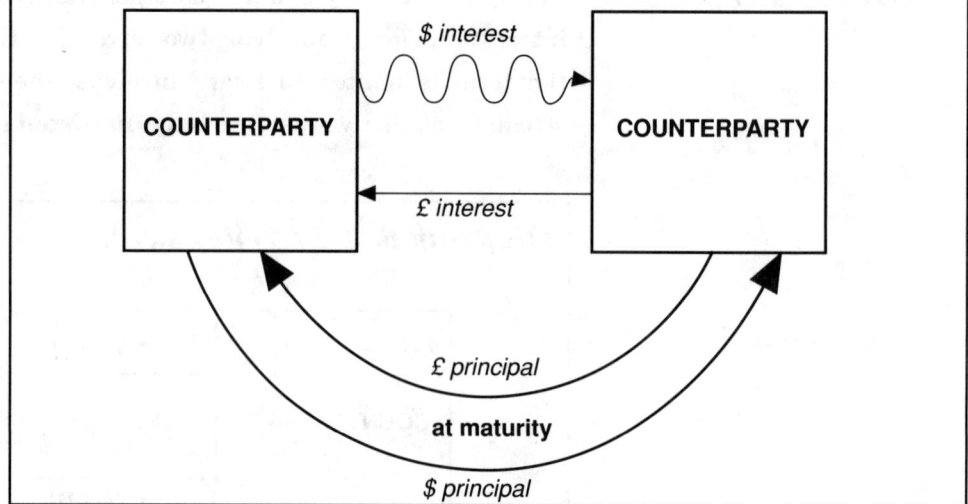

Diagram 8: A cross-currency basis swap

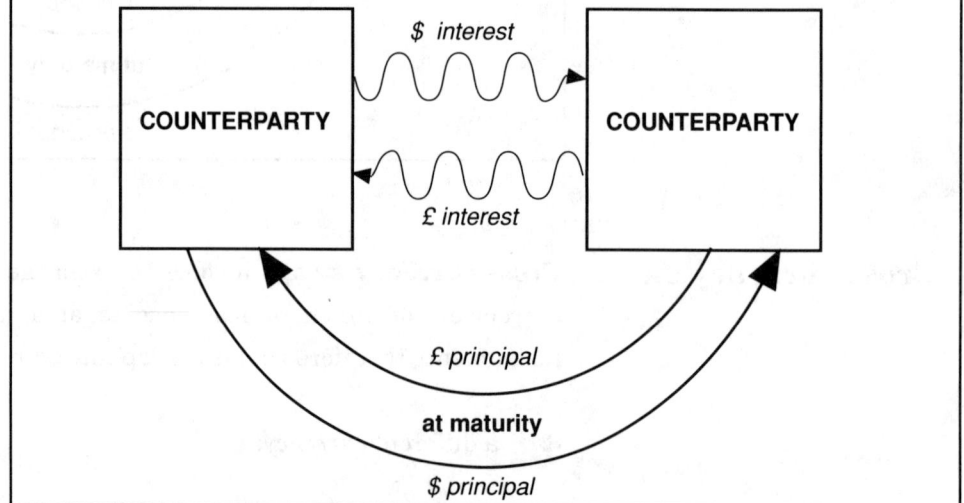

Table 1: Types of currency swap

Type of swap	Interest rate basis
currency swap	fixed-against-fixed
cross-currency coupon swap	fixed-against-floating
cross-currency basis swap	floating-against-floating

Cash swap

This term is sometimes used to describe currency swaps involving an initial exchange of principal.

Generic swap

Generic is a term used to describe the simplest of any type of financial instrument (the so-called **straight** or **plain vanilla** versions). Specifically, a generic currency swap has:

■ a constant *notional principal amount*;

■ an exchange of *fixed-against-floating* interest: in other words, a generic swap is a simple type of *cross-currency coupon swap*.

■ a constant *fixed interest rate*;

■ a flat *floating interest rate* (ie, no margin over the index): typically, the floating interest rate would be *US dollar Libor*;

■ regular *payment* of fixed and floating interest: payments need not be simultaneous, but netting means they usually are;

■ an immediate (or spot) *start* to the swap;

■ no special *risk features* (eg, a combination with an option).

All the more complex (**non-generic**) types of currency swap can be constructed from the generic instrument, by combining generic swaps within complicated structures or by adding derivative instruments like futures and options. This Workbook is limited to generic swaps in order to provide a clear introduction to the subject of currency swaps. Non-generic swaps are covered separately in the *IFR Self-Study Workbook* on *Financial Engineering with Swaps*, which is part of the *Swaps Series*.

Asset swap

Where interest streams exchanged through a currency swap are funded with interest received on specific assets, particularly where the assets are bought and sold as part of the same package with the swap, the swap is called an **asset swap**. It is important to note that an asset swap does not involve any change in the swap mechanism itself. The term simply identifies the *purpose* of the swap, rather than its structure. It is therefore possible to have asset swaps which are also coupon or basis swaps. Where an asset swap is sold as a package together with an asset, the swap and the asset itself remain otherwise separate instruments in that they can, and usually are, contracts between different sets of counterparties. Asset swaps are described in detail in the *IFR Self-Study Workbook* on *Financial Engineering with Swaps*, which was mentioned earlier.

Given the existence of the term 'asset swap', it would seem logical for currency swaps which are identified with specific *liabilities* rather than assets to be called **liability swaps**. However, the term is virtually never used for currency swaps, although it is very occasionally used to describe interest rate swaps.

Cocktail swap

In practice, it can be difficult to swap directly between some currencies, particularly where non-dollar floating interest is required. In such cases, the desired swap is achieved indirectly by going through a series of swaps involving an intermediate currency. The structure, which is called a **cocktail swap**, is illustrated in Diagram 9. This is similar to the way in which illiquid 'cross rates' (exchange rates between two non-dollar currencies) are constructed in the foreign exchange market: one non-dollar currency would be bought against dollars and then the dollars sold for the other non-dollar currency, with the dollar providing a common link, which cancels itself out. The link in currency swaps is typically *six-month US dollar Libor*, reflecting the fact that, in the markets in Eurodeposits which ultimately provide floating-rate funds, Eurodollars are very liquid, whereas most other currencies are generally illiquid. There can be a very considerable number of legs to a cocktail swap. These might include both currency and interest rate swaps.

As well as to construct swaps into non-dollar floating interest, cocktail swaps are also often created by swap intermediaries hedging their exposure to less liquid currency swaps. Cross-currency basis swaps between two non-dollar currencies were often the product of a cocktail of a cross-currency coupon swap between fixed-interest dollars and floating-interest currency on the one hand and a coupon swap in a third currency on the other.

Diagram 9: A cocktail swap

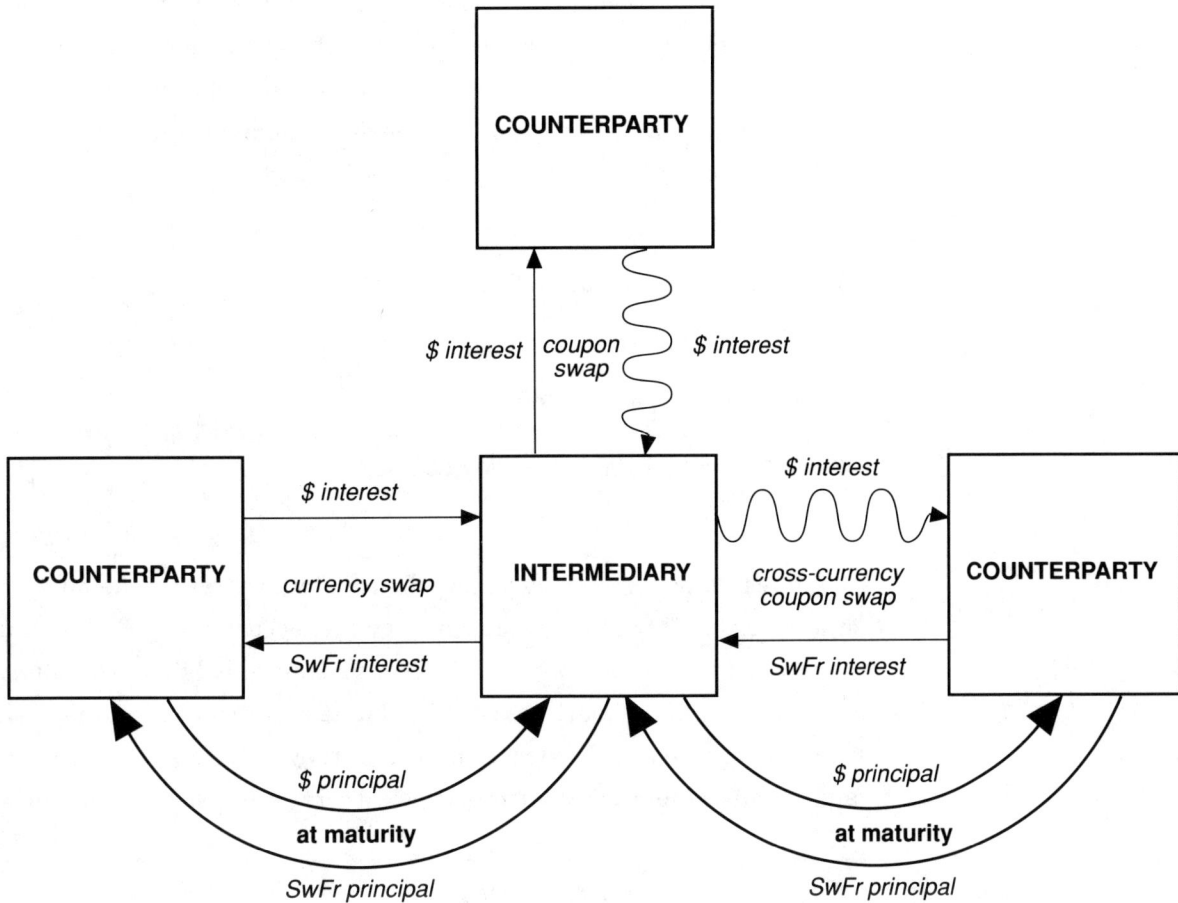

Differential swap

Sometimes known as a **diff swap** or **quanto swap**. This is a very special type of cross-currency basis swap (floating-against-floating) which does not involve any exchange of principal, even at maturity. Both streams of interest payments through a diff swap are calculated with reference to the same notional principal amount of the *same currency* and both streams of interest are actually paid in this currency. For example, a $/DM diff swap would typically involve an exchange of interest at six-month Deutsche mark Libor for interest at six-month US dollar Libor. Both Libor indexes would be applied to the same notional principal amount of, say, Deutsche mark and both interest streams would also be paid in Deutsche marks. In other words, the swap would exchange six-month US dollar Libor paid in Deutsche marks for six-month Deutsche mark Libor also paid in Deutsche marks. If six-month US dollar Libor was fixed at 5% per annum and six-month Deutsche mark Libor at 10% per annum, a diff swap for a notional principal amount of DM150m would entail an interest payment, for a period of 182 days, of:

$$\frac{5}{100} \times \frac{182}{360} \times 150{,}000{,}000 = \text{DM3,791,667}$$

against a counterpayment of:

$$\frac{10}{100} \times \frac{182}{360} \times 150{,}000{,}000 = \text{DM7,583,333}$$

As interest is paid in one currency, the counterparty using the diff swap with an asset or liability in the same currency avoids currency risk. For example, if counterparty Z is swapping out of a Deutsche mark liability or counterparty A out of a Deutsche mark asset, the interest stream into which they are swapping remains in Deutsche mark and they therefore avoid currency risk (and because there is no currency risk, there is no need for an exchange of

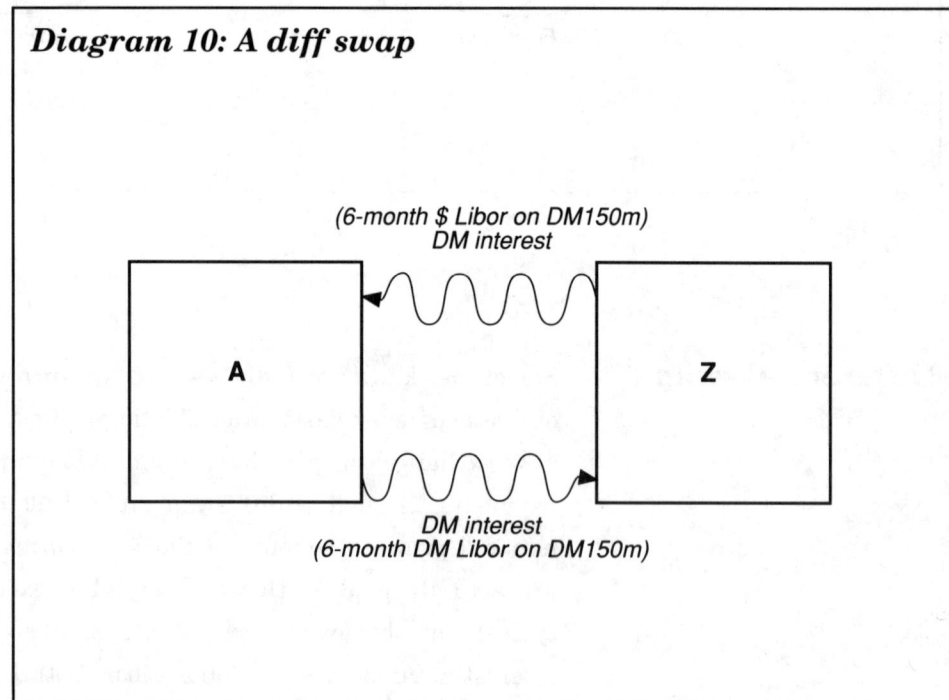

Diagram 10: A diff swap

(6-month $ Libor on DM150m)
DM interest

A   Z

DM interest
(6-month DM Libor on DM150m)

principal). Both counterparties are exposed to interest rate risk in the form of possible adverse changes in the *differential* between dollar and Deutsche mark Libors (this risk gives diff swaps their name). One counterparty, however, may have to accept currency risk: this is typically the bank providing the diff swap. A diff swap therefore can be an interest rate swap to one counterparty and a cross-currency basis swap to the other. In effect, a diff swap can unbundle interest rate and currency risk. This unbundling can make it difficult to hedge the currency risk in a diff swap. The cost of the hedge is usually charged as a margin over one of the Libors being swapped.

Circus swap

A circus swap is a simple form of cocktail swap, composed of a cross-currency coupon swap (fixed-against-floating) and a single-currency coupon swap, where both floating interest streams are calculated at the same Libor. These swaps are combined to replicate either:

■ a currency swap (fixed-against-fixed);

■ a cross-currency basis swap (floating-against-floating).

Diagram 11: A circus swap (replicating a currency swap)

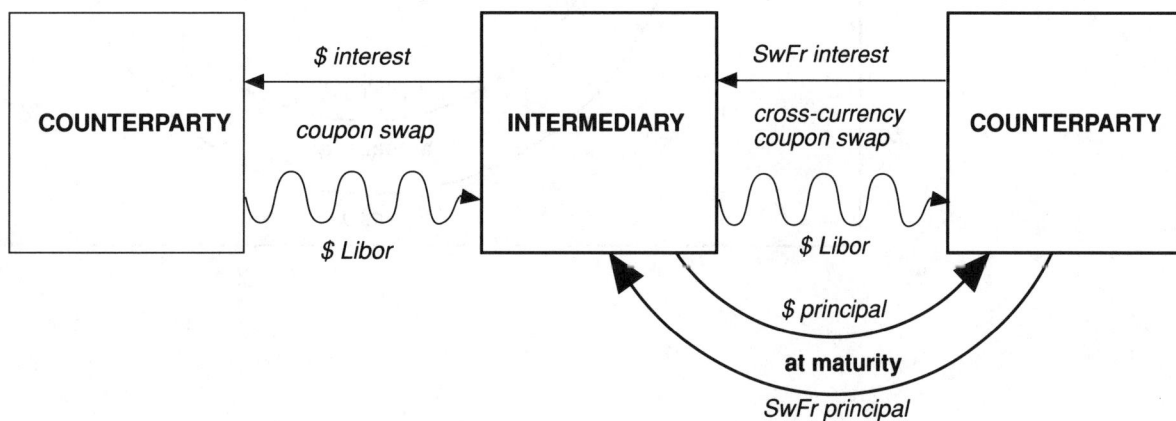

Currency swaps

For example, a circus swap might consist of a cross-currency swap between Swiss franc fixed interest and US dollar six-month Libor on the one hand and a US dollar coupon swap on the other hand. This produces a Swiss franc/US dollar currency swap. See Diagram 11.

Counterparties to a currency swap

In the case of single-currency coupon swaps, it is usual to distinguish counterparties in terms of who *pays* and who *receives* fixed-interest payments (the convention is to assume that the floating interest rate is six-month Libor). In the case of currency swaps, the relationship of the counterparties is complicated by the exchange of currencies. It is therefore prudent to describe each counterparty to a currency coupon swap in terms of *both* the types of interest and the currencies it pays and receives, eg, 'I pay six-month US dollar Libor against three-year sterling fixed-interest'.

Diagram 12: Counterparties to a cross-currency coupon swap

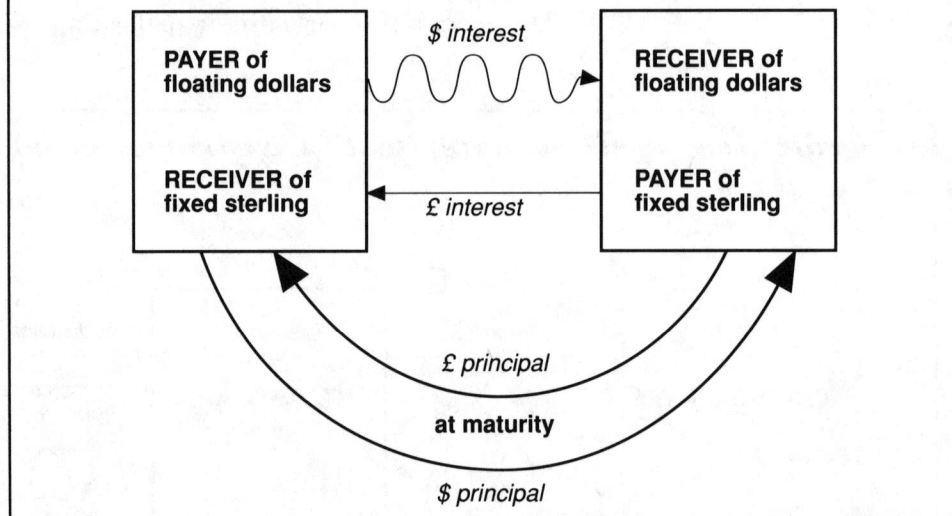

PAYER of floating dollars / RECEIVER of fixed sterling

$ interest

RECEIVER of floating dollars / PAYER of fixed sterling

£ interest

£ principal at maturity

$ principal

How currency swap prices are quoted

As noted already, it has become a convention in the markets in most single-currency coupon swaps to use *six-month Libor* as the standard index for the floating interest rate. The same is true of cross-currency swaps. It is therefore possible to discuss the 'price' of cross-currency coupon swaps solely in terms of their fixed interest rates. However, there is also the question of which currency should be the standard for six-month Libor. As noted already, the convention is in fact to use six-month *US dollar* Libor.

Cross-currency basis swaps also usually have six-month US dollar Libor as one of their floating-interest rate indexes, which allows them to be quoted in terms of the *margin* over or under Libor in the non-dollar currency being swapped. For example, a £/$ cross-currency basis swap might be quoted as *+10*, meaning the swap is between US dollar Libor on the one hand and sterling Libor plus 10 basis points on the other.

Currency swaps are generally quoted in terms of **all-in** prices, ie, as absolute annual percentage interest rates. Swap intermediaries may quote two all-in prices for each currency swap, eg, *6.86–6.96%*. This is a **two-way** price, meaning a dual quotation consisting of a *buying* and a *selling* price for each instrument. However, the terms 'buying' and 'selling' can be ambiguous in the case of swaps, so they should be substituted by the terms **paying** and **receiving**. Specifically:

■ in cross-currency coupon swaps, paying and receiving are taken as referring to fixed interest and, as noted, the convention is to assume the floating interest is at six-month US dollar Libor, unless otherwise specified;

■ in cross-currency basis swaps, both sides of the swap should be specified;

■ in fixed-against-fixed (true currency) swaps both sides of the swap should also be specified.

Which side of a two-way price is being paid and which is being received may not seem immediately obvious. However, it only needs to be remembered that the intermediary quoting the prices will be aiming to make a profit, if two swaps are transacted simultaneously at both prices. This means the intermediary should pay the *lower* fixed rate through one swap and should receive the *higher* fixed rate through the other, thereby earning the **dealing** spread between the two rates. For example, in the case of the earlier quote of 6.86–6.96%, the quoting dealer will hope to receive a fixed rate of 6.96% per annum and pay a fixed rate of 6.86%, earning a spread of 10 basis points per annum on every matching pair of swaps. The objective which underlies two-way price quotes is illustrated in the diagram below.

Diagram 13: Two-way swap prices

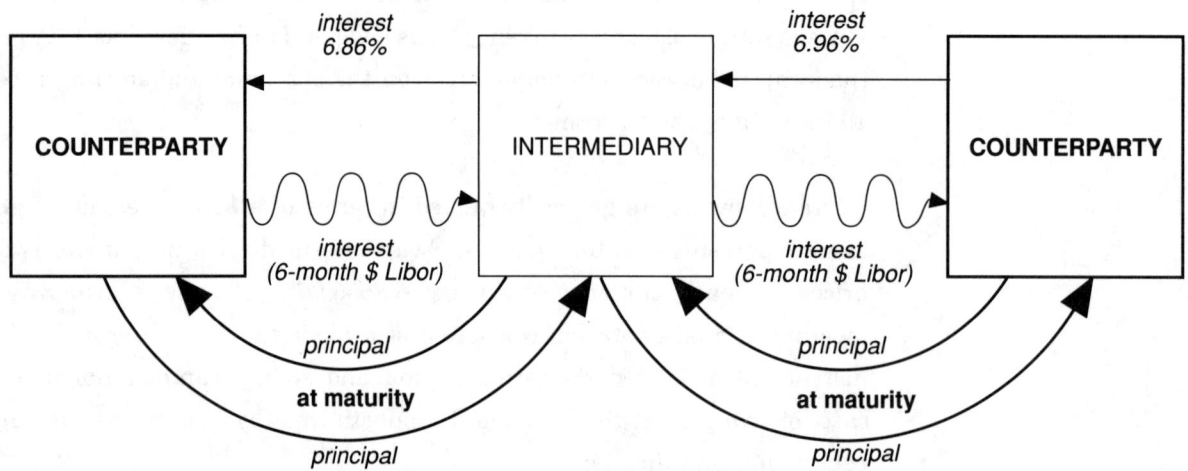

What does a currency swap do?

Currency swaps and risk

Each counterparty in a currency swap is committed to pay the other counterparty a stream of interest plus a principal amount in one currency, in exchange for receiving from the other a counterstream of interest plus a principal amount in another currency. It has been explained that the exchange of principal at maturity is made at an exchange rate agreed at the start of the swap: usually the *spot exchange rate* prevailing at that time. Between the agreement of the exchange rate and the exchange itself, the spot rate between the two currencies will change. By having committed to a currency swap and the increasingly historic exchange rate which it entails, the counterparty *paying* the currency which *appreciates* during the life of the swap foregoes a foreign exchange profit, by having fixed the cost to itself of the depreciating countercurrency at the historic exchange rate. On the other hand, the counterparty *receiving* the currency which appreciates during the life of the swap avoids a foreign exchange loss by having fixed the cost to itself of the appreciating countercurrency at the historic exchange rate. In other words, a currency swap creates an exposure to *currency risk*.

An example

Consider the £/$ currency swap with an initial exchange of principal used in the example at the start. This was negotiated at 1.7000, which was the prevailing spot exchange rate. At maturity, US Bank paid £10m to UK Bank and received $17m. If sterling had appreciated to 1.8000 by maturity, US Bank would have foregone $18m and an extra $1m, while UK Bank would have avoided paying the equivalent.

If a currency swap involves *floating* interest, the amount of interest to be exchanged will change as the floating-interest rate index is periodically reset during the life of the swap. The interest paid through the swap might increase or the interest received might decrease or both (in the case of basis swaps), the net effect of which would be to reduce the overall profitability of the swap, or to create or increase a loss. In other words, besides exposure to currency risk, a currency swap can also create exposure to *interest rate risk*.

However, if a currency swap involves the exchange of *fixed interest* only (in other words, it is a true currency swap), the amounts of interest paid through the swap do not change, by definition, and there is therefore no interest rate risk. In this case, a currency swap merely changes the currency in which counterparties make net interest payments and only creates an exposure to currency risk.

The currency and interest rate risks created by a currency swap can also be created by borrowing and lending *cash* instruments in different currencies. A currency swap, therefore, performs *off-balance sheet* an equivalent function to that performed by cash instruments *on-balance sheet*. This can be seen from the swap in Diagrams 14a–b. UK Bank — as the payer of dollar interest and principal, and receiver of sterling interest and principal — is exposed to the same currency and interest rate risks as if it had borrowed through the creation of a dollar liability (eg, issuing a dollar bond) and lent through the creation of a sterling asset (eg, investing in a sterling bond). On the other hand, US Bank — as the payer of sterling interest and principal, and receiver of dollar interest and principal — is exposed to the same currency and interest rate risks as if it had borrowed through the creation of a sterling liability (eg, issuing a sterling bond) and lent through the creation of a dollar asset (eg, investing in a dollar bond).

Diagram 14a: A currency swap with an initial exchange of principal

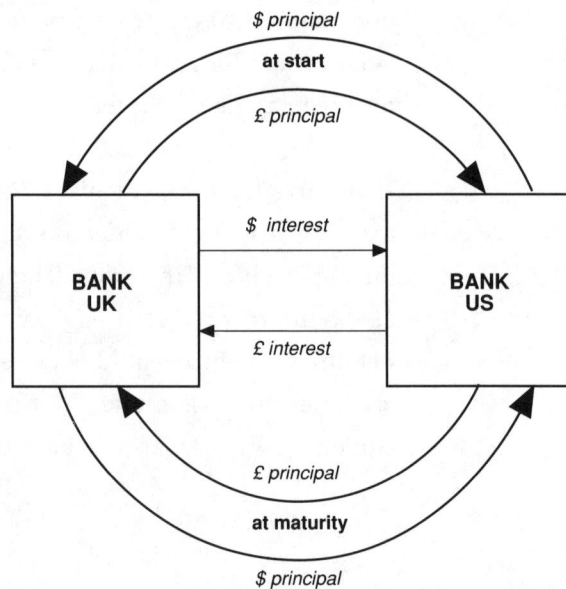

$ principal
at start
£ principal

$ interest

BANK UK

BANK US

£ interest

£ principal
at maturity
$ principal

Diagram 14b: Replicating a currency swap with cash instruments

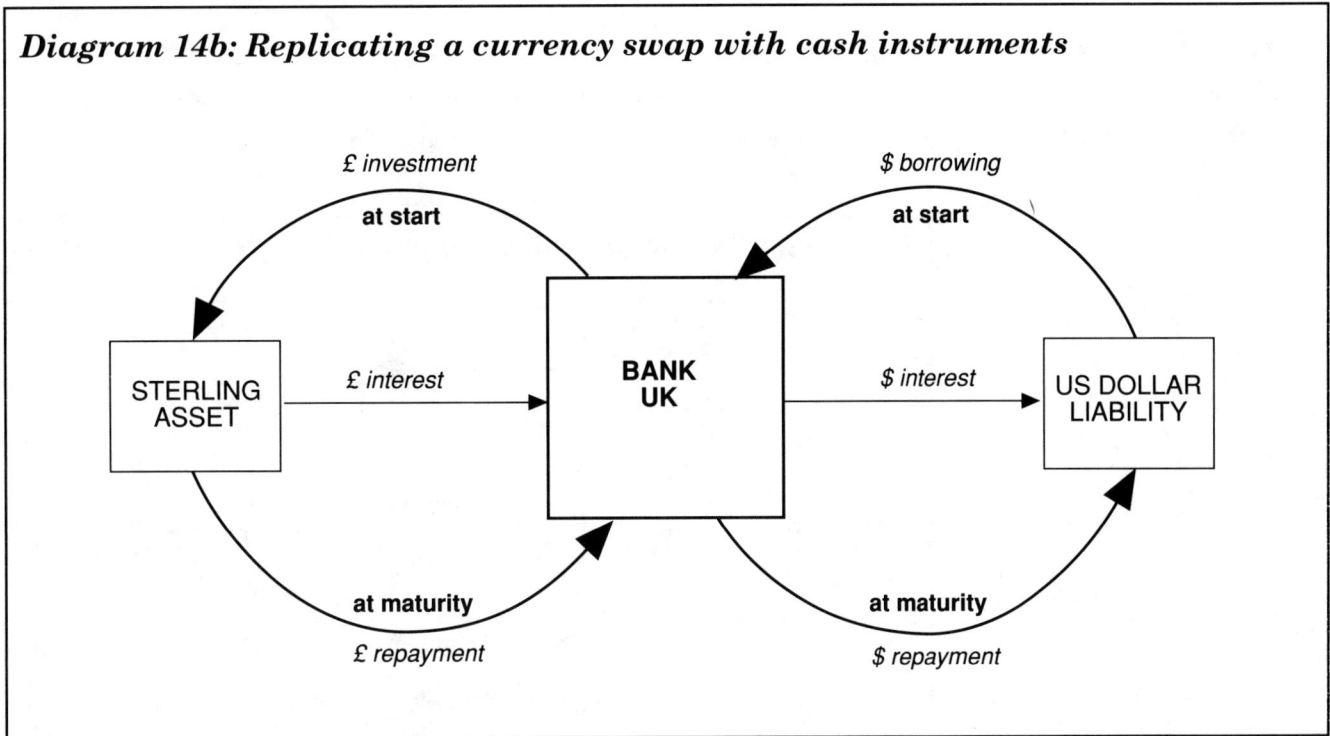

Currency swaps and forward foreign exchange

Currency swaps are not the only type of financial instrument that creates currency risk. The same risk exposure is also offered by *forward foreign exchange transactions*. There are two basic types of forward foreign exchange transaction with which currency swaps can be compared:

- **outright forward** foreign exchange transactions. Where outright forwards are applied for longer-term periods, they are usually referred to as **long-term foreign exchange (LTFX).**

- **foreign exchange swaps**.

In practice, the LTFX and foreign exchange swap markets are liquid out to three to five years at most, depending on the currencies involved, whereas currency swaps are available out to 10 years and beyond, again depending on the currencies involved. Currency swaps also tend to be available in much larger amounts than LTFX. This reflects the limitations on the liquidity of the Eurodeposit markets which underlie forward foreign exchange and the fact that currency swaps are priced in the capital markets (see *Part Four* on *Pricing and Valuing Currency Swaps*).

Currency swaps and outright forward foreign exchange

While a currency swap performs a similar *function*, in creating currency risk, to an outright forward foreign exchange transaction, there are important *structural* differences. These are described in Table 2.

Diagram 15a: A currency swap

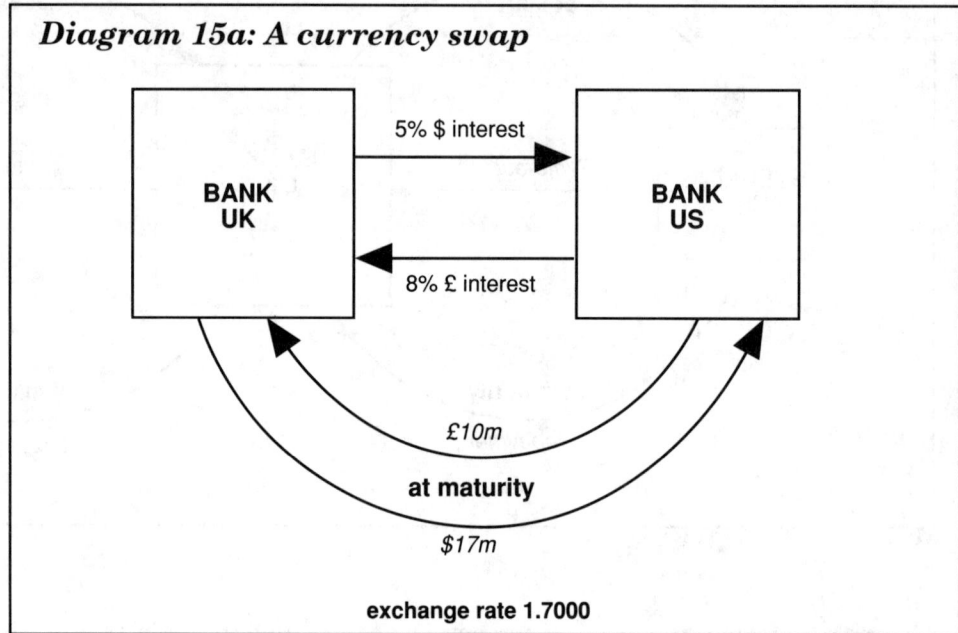

BANK UK → 5% $ interest → BANK US

BANK UK ← 8% £ interest ← BANK US

£10m
at maturity
$17m

exchange rate 1.7000

Diagram 15b: An outright forward foreign exchange transaction

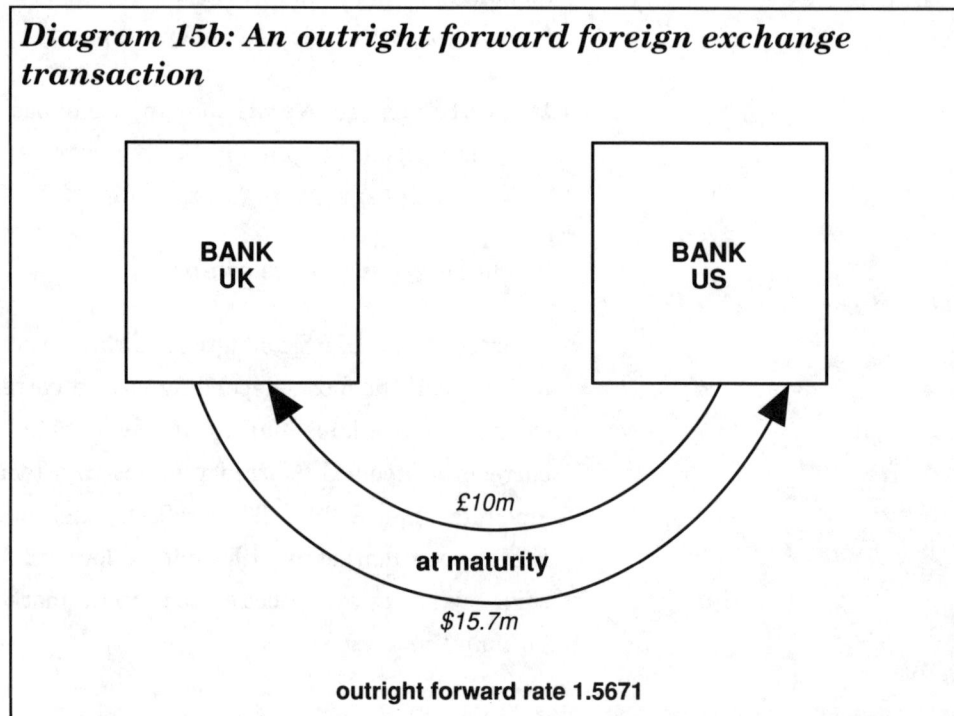

BANK UK   BANK US

£10m
at maturity
$15.7m

outright forward rate 1.5671

The forward exchange rate at which principal amounts of currency are exchanged in an outright forward transaction is different from the spot exchange rate. The differential between spot and forward rates reflects the difference between the *interest rates* on the two currencies being exchanged (the pricing of forward foreign exchange rates is explained in *Box 1*). In contrast, currency swaps usually exchange principal amounts at the spot exchange rate. However, currency swaps also exchange *interest* cash flows on the principal amounts being swapped, whereas outright forwards do not exchange interest. In other words, both types of transaction take account of interest rate differentials between the currencies being swapped, but do so in different ways:

- outright forward foreign exchange transactions reflect interest rate differentials in the *exchange rate*;

- currency swaps actually exchange *interest cash flows* and leave the exchange rate unchanged over the life of the swap.

Table 2: Comparing currency swaps and outright forwards

Currency swaps (see Diagram 15a)	Outright forwards (LTFX) (see Diagram 15b)
Involves exchange of interest *and* principal amounts of currencies.	No interest amounts are exchanged, only *principal* amounts at maturity.
The exchange of principal amounts takes place at an exchange rate agreed at the start of the swap, usually (but not necessarily) the *spot exchange rate*.	The exchange of principal amounts at maturity takes place at the *forward exchange rate* prevailing at the start of the swap: this is usually different from the spot rate.
For example, a currency swap might involve an exchange over the life of the swap of streams of dollar and sterling interest, and the exchange at maturity of principal amounts of $17m and £10m, corresponding to the spot £/$ exchange rate of 1.7000 prevailing at the start of the swap.	*For example, an outright forward might take place at a forward £/$ exchange rate of 1.5671 agreed at the start of the swap. The simplest equivalent outright forward to a currency swap would involve an exchange at maturity of principal amounts of £10m and $15.671m.*

■ the *timing* of cash flows in outright forward foreign exchange transactions and currency swaps is very different. A currency swap involves a series of exchanges (interest during the life of the swap and principal at maturity), whereas an outright forward involves just one exchange (principal at maturity). The difference in the basic cash flow profiles through the two instruments is illustrated in Table 3.

Table 3: Comparing cash flows in currency swaps and outright forwards

	Currency swap		Outright forward		
	UK Bank receives sterling at 8%pa	UK Bank pays dollars at 5%pa	UK Bank receives sterling at forward rate	UK Bank pays dollars at forward rate	Forward exchange rate
Year	£m	$m	£m	$m	£/$
1	+0.800	−0.850	—	—	—
2	+0.800	−0.850	—	—	—
3	+0.800	−0.850	—	—	—
	+10.000	−17.000	+10.000	−15.671	1.5671
Total	+12.400	−19.550	+10.000	−15.671	—

■ while currency swaps and outright forwards differ in terms of the timing of cash flows, the fact that the differential between the spot and forward exchange rates in outright forwards is mirrored in differences between interest cash flows in currency swaps means that the two instruments have equal *net present values*. This is shown in Table 4. Note that a normal yield-to-maturity is used to discount the cash flows in the currency swap, but **zero-coupon interest rates** are used to discount the cash flows in the outright forward[3]. In both cases, the net present values of the two currencies imply an exchange rate of 1.7000.

Box 1: Forward foreign exchange rates

Assume a bank commits to buying one currency in exchange for another at a date in the future and at an exchange rate fixed now. For example, assume the bank commits to buy US dollars against Deutsche marks in exactly one year's time. In order to be able to quote a forward exchange rate at which it is certain of at least breaking even, the bank must hedge its currency risk (if the bank waited to sell the dollars for Deutsche marks until it received them in a year's time, the dollar might depreciate against the Deutsche mark in the meantime). In order to hedge, the bank could undertake the following sequence of transactions:

- borrow dollars for a year;Eurobonds

- sell the dollars for Deutsche marks in the spot market;

- invest the Deutsche marks for a year;

- at the end of the year, use the Deutsche marks received back from its investment to pay for the dollars which it has agreed to buy forward;

- use the dollars bought forward to repay the dollar borrowing made at the start.

The forward exchange rate (in terms of Deutsche marks per dollar) is simply the ratio of the number of Deutsche marks sold forward to the number of dollars bought forward. The number of Deutsche marks sold forward is equal to the total return on the original investment of Deutsche marks and is given by:

$$\text{Deutsche mark investment} \left(1+ \frac{\text{interest rate}_{DM} \times \text{day count}}{100 \times \text{annual basis}}\right)$$

The forward amount of dollars is the total to be paid back on the borrowing and is given by:

$$\text{dollar borrowing} \left(1+ \frac{\text{interest rate}_{\$} \times \text{day count}}{100 \times \text{annual basis}}\right)$$

The forward exchange rate is therefore given by:

$$\frac{\text{Deutsche mark investment} \left(1+ \frac{\text{interest rate}_{DM} \times \text{day count}}{100 \times \text{annual basis}}\right)}{\text{dollar borrowing} \left(1+ \frac{\text{interest rate}_{\$} \times \text{day count}}{100 \times \text{annual basis}}\right)}$$

Given that the number of Deutsche marks invested per dollar borrowed is given by the spot $/DM exchange rate, this equation can be simplified to:

$$\text{spot \$/DM rate} \left[\frac{\left(1 + \dfrac{\text{interest rate}_{DM} \times \text{day count}}{100 \times \text{annual basis}}\right)}{\left(1 + \dfrac{\text{interest rate}_{\$} \times \text{day count}}{100 \times \text{annual basis}}\right)} \right]$$

For example, if the spot $/DM exchange rate is 1.5000, 12-month dollar Libor is 5% per annum and 12-month Deutsche mark Libor is 10% per annum, the forward exchange rate is:

$$1.5000 \left[\frac{\left(1 + \dfrac{10 \times 365}{100 \times 360}\right)}{\left(1 + \dfrac{5 \times 365}{100 \times 360}\right)} \right] = 1.5724$$

It can be seen that the differential between forward and spot exchange rates — the so-called **forward points** — reflects the differential between the interest rates on the two currencies being swapped and is given by:

$$\text{spot \$/DM rate} \left[\frac{\left(1 + \dfrac{\text{interest rate}_{DM} \times \text{day count}}{100 \times \text{annual basis}}\right)}{\left(1 + \dfrac{\text{interest rate}_{\$} \times \text{day count}}{100 \times \text{annual basis}}\right)} - 1 \right]$$

In the example above, the forward points are given by:

$$1.5000 \left[\frac{\left(1 + \dfrac{10 \times 365}{100 \times 360}\right)}{\left(1 + \dfrac{5 \times 365}{100 \times 360}\right)} - 1 \right] = 0.0724$$

The forward exchange rate is often called the **outright forward rate**, in order to distinguish it from the forward points.

Table 4: Comparing the net present values of currency swaps and outright forwards

Currency swap

Year	Dollars paid at 5% US$m	Yield-to-maturity %pa	Present value at 5% US$m	Sterling received at 8% £m	Yield-to-maturity %pa	Present value at 8% £m
1	−0.85	3.0	−0.810	+0.80	6.0	+0.741
2	−0.85	4.0	−0.771	+0.80	7.0	+0.686
3	−0.85	5.0	−0.734	+0.80	8.0	+0.635
	−17.00	5.0	−14.685	+10.00	8.0	+7.938
net present value			−17.000	net present value		+10.000

exchange rate of NPVs = \$17.000/£10.000 = 1.7000

Outright forward

Year	Dollars paid US$m	Zero-coupon interest rate %pa	Present value at 3-year zero-coupon interest rate US$m	Sterling received £m	Zero-coupon interest rate %pa	Present value at 3-year zero-coupon interest rate £m
1	—	—	—	—	—	—
2	—	—	—	—	—	—
3	—	—	—	—	—	—
	−15.671	5.216	−13.454	+10.0	8.111	+7.914
net present value			−13.454	net present value		7.914

exchange rate of NPVs = \$13.454/£7.914 = 1.7000

Currency swaps

It may seem at first glance that the cash flow differences between currency swaps and outright forwards could be bridged by constructing a simple series of outright forwards (one for each exchange of interest and one for the exchange of principal amounts at maturity). However, the cash flows through a series of outright forwards will generally not be the same as those through the corresponding currency swap, because forward rates tend to be different for each transaction date, whereas the exchange rate in currency swaps is constant. Table 5 demonstrates the difference between a currency swap and a series of outright forward transactions, both involving the three-year forward purchase of £10m against dollars. Note that the currency swap exchanges at 1.7000 and the outright forward at a range of different exchange rates.

Table 5: Comparing currency swaps and outright forwards

	Currency swap			Outright forwards		
	UK Bank receives sterling at 8%pa	UK Bank pays dollars at 5%pa	Exchange rate	UK Bank receives sterling at forward rate	UK Bank pays dollars at forward rate	Forward exchange rate
Year	£m	$m	£/$	£m	$m	£/$
1	+0.800	−0.850	—	+0.800	−1.322	1.6519
2	+0.800	−0.850	—	+0.800	−1.284	1.6055
3	+0.800	−0.850	—	+0.800	−1.254	1.5671
	+10.000	−17.000	1.7000	+10.000	−15.671	1.5671
	+12.400	−19.550	—	+12.400	−19.531	—

Better approximations between currency swaps and outright forwards are possible. In order to better match the cash flows on currency swaps and outright forwards, there are two possibilities. Either:

■ an outright forward can be restructured into the equivalent of a fixed-against-fixed currency swap. This special type of outright forward transaction is called a **par forward**, which is actually a series of outright forwards packaged into a single transaction with each exchange of currencies at the same average (par) forward exchange rate. As such, par forwards produce a constant stream of cash flows up to maturity, just like a currency swap. Of course, the par forward rate is an average of market forward exchange rates and so diverges from the spot rate usually employed in currency swaps. Par forwards are described in *Box 2*. Table 6 illustrates the cash flows through a currency swap and an equivalent par forward transaction. The par forward can only replicate a fixed-against-fixed currency swap, because only this type of swap makes interest payments which are known in advance;

Table 6: Comparing currency swaps and par forwards

	Currency swap			Par forward		
	UK Bank receives sterling at 8%pa	UK Bank pays dollars at 5%pa	Exchange rate	UK Bank receives sterling at forward rate	UK Bank pays dollars at forward rate	Par exchange rate[4]
Year	£m	$m	£/$	£m	$m	£/$
1	+0.800	−0.850	—	+0.800	−1.294	1.6180
2	+0.800	−0.850	—	+0.800	−1.294	1.6180
3	+0.800	0.850		+0.800	1.294	1.6180
	+10.000	−17.000	1.7000	+10.000	−16.180	1.6180
	+12.400	−19.550	—	+12.400	−20.062	—

Currency swaps

■ a currency swap can instead be restructured into the equivalent of an outright forward. This special type of currency swap is called a **zero-coupon fixed-against-fixed currency swap**, which is a currency swap involving no interest payments (in other words, it has zero coupons), just an exchange of principal amounts at maturity, as in an outright forward. The principal amounts to be exchanged are calculated by compounding to maturity the interest payments which would have been made through a normal fixed-against-fixed swap. In effect, the normal interest payments are reinvested and paid as part of the principal amounts exchanged at maturity. The calculation is illustrated in Table 7. The zero-coupon swap which matches an outright forward must be fixed-against-fixed, otherwise the size of future interest payments could not be known in advance and therefore the necessary compounding calculations could not be performed.

Table 7: Calculation of zero-coupon currency swap cash flows

	Dollar cash flows			Sterling cash flows		
Year	[1] Normal swap at 5%pa	[2] Column [1] compounded to maturity at 5%pa	[3] Zero-coupon swap	[1] Normal swap at 8%pa	[2] Column [1] compounded to maturity at 8%pa	[3] Zero-coupon swap
1	−5	−5.51	—	−8	−9.33	—
2	−5	−5.25	—	−8	−8.64	—
3	−5	−5.00	—	−8	−8.00	—
	−150	−150.00	−170.76	−100	−100.00	−125.97
	—	−170.76	−170.76	—	−125.97	−125.97

Box 2: Par forwards

A par forward contract commits a bank to a series of forward foreign exchange transactions at the same fixed outright forward exchange rate. It is used to smooth out cash flows for customers having to hedge a stream of future foreign currency payments or receipts. Because of varying differences between the interest rates of different tenors on currencies being swapped, there is usually a different outright rate for each forward date. The par forward rate is essentially an average of these individual outright forward rates.

However, the par forward rate is not just a straight average of individual outright rates. The average has to be adjusted for cash flow differences with individual forward rates. For example, take the par forward £/$ transaction illustrated in Table 6 in the main text. This is for a series of three annual forward purchases of £10m against dollars. The outright forward rates for the three forward dates are:

Date of transaction	Outright rate
End-year 1	1.6519
End-year 2	1.6055
End-year 3	1.5671
Average	1.6082

The arithmetic average of these rates is 1.6082. If UK Bank were to buy £/$ forward at this average rate, rather than at individual outright rates, it would pay less dollars in year 1 and more dollars in years 2 and 3:

Date of transaction	Outright rate	Average rate	Net gain/loss
End-year 1	1.6519	1.6082	+0.0437
End-year 2	1.6055	1.6082	−0.0027
End-year 3	1.5671	1.6082	−0.0411

If UK Bank hedges its par forward with a series of individual outright forwards at the rates listed above, it will have surplus dollars in year 1 and dollar deficits in years 2 and 3. In fact, the surplus in year 1 is so large that it more than covers the deficits in years 2 and 3. UK Bank ends up with surplus dollars to invest in all three years, although in decreasing amounts:

Date of transaction	Net gain/loss	Surplus/deficit on £10m	Cumulative surplus/ deficit on £10m
End-year 1	+0.0437	+$437,000	+$437,000
End-year 2	−0.0027	−$27,000	+$410,000
End-year 3	−0.0411	−$41,100	+$369,000

In effect, Bank UK has $369,000 to invest for the whole three years, $41,000 to invest for years 2 and 3, and $27,000 to invest over year 1. The schedule of investment of these surpluses is:

Investment periods	Surpluses for investment	Zero-coupon interest rates	Repayment plus return
3 years	$369,000	5.330%	$431,204
2 years	$41,000	4.101%	$44,432
1 year	$27,000	3.000%	$27,810

In view of the net interest gain, the par forward rate at which Bank UK would break even can be higher than the arithmetic average (more generous in terms of dollars paid per pound sterling). In effect, the par forward rate can be subsidised. The amount of the subsidy should be the same for each forward transaction. The answer is in fact $158,376, which corresponds to an exchange rate subsidy of:

$$\frac{\$158,376}{1.6082 \times \text{£10m}} = 0.0098$$

giving a par forward rate of:

1.6082 + 0.0098 = 1.6180

Currency swaps and foreign exchange swaps

Foreign exchange swaps involve a spot and a reverse forward foreign exchange transaction. As the two transactions are opposites, a foreign exchange swap is intrinsically hedged against currency risk. In terms of *function*, as noted earlier, foreign exchange swaps are similar to currency swaps with an initial exchange of principal amounts: in both cases, the initial exchange hedges the currency risk on the re-exchange at maturity. However, there are important differences in *structure* between a foreign swap and a currency swap. These differences are described in Table 8. Foreign exchange swaps are described in *Box 3*.

Table 8: Comparing currency and foreign exchange swaps

Currency swap *(see Diagram 16a)*	Foreign exchange swap *(see Diagram 16b)*
Involves exchanges of both interest *and* principal amounts.	No interest is exchanged, only *principal* amounts of currencies (at the start and at maturity of the swap).
Exchanges of principal are usually made at the *spot exchange rate* prevailing at the start of the swap. This means that the same amounts are exchanged at maturity as at the start of the swap.	The initial exchange of principal amounts is made at the prevailing spot exchange rate and re-exchange at the *forward exchange rate* also prevailing at the start of the swap. As spot and forward exchange rates are usually different, the amounts of principal exchanged at maturity are usually different from the amounts exchanged at the start of the swap.
For example, a currency swap might involve an exchange and subsequent re-exchange of principal amounts of $17m and £10m, as well as the exchange over the life of the swap of streams of dollar and sterling interest amounts. The exchange and re-exchange of principal amounts is made at the same initial £/$ rate of 1.7000.	*For example, a foreign exchange swap might involve an initial exchange of $17m and £10m, and a re-exchange at maturity of $15.671m and £10m. These exchanges take place, respectively, at spot £/$ exchange rate of 1.7000 and the contemporary forward £/$ rate of 1.5671.*

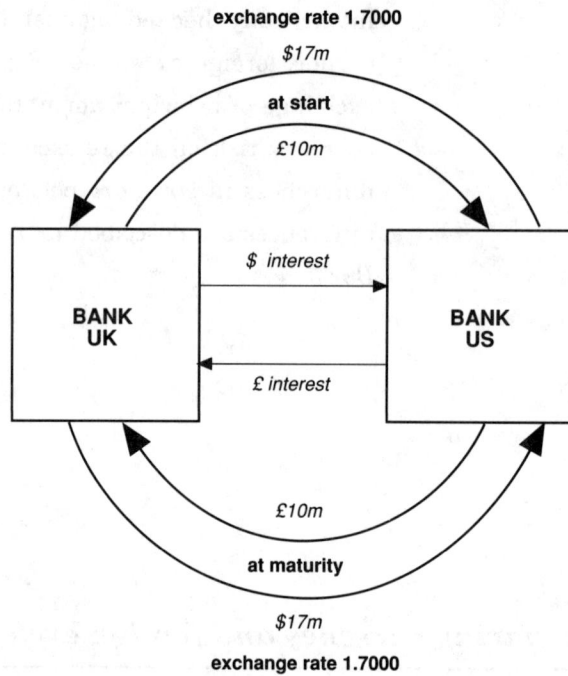

Diagram 16a: A currency swap with initial exchange of principal

exchange rate 1.7000
$17m
at start
£10m

BANK UK

$ interest

£ interest

BANK US

£10m
at maturity
$17m
exchange rate 1.7000

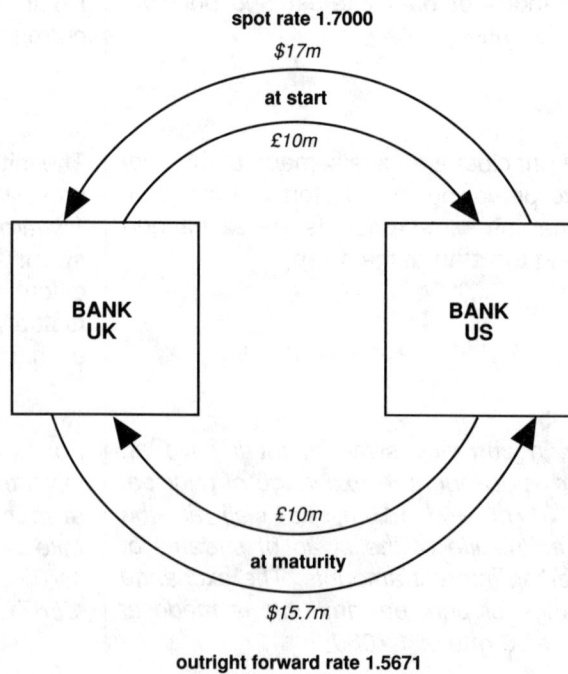

Diagram 16b: A foreign exchange swap

spot rate 1.7000
$17m
at start
£10m

BANK UK

BANK US

£10m
at maturity
$15.7m
outright forward rate 1.5671

Box 3: Foreign exchange swaps

A foreign exchange swap is a combination of:

■ a *spot* foreign exchange transaction;

■ the reverse *outright forward* foreign exchange transaction.

For example, sterling can be sold against dollars spot and bought back forward. Foreign exchange swaps therefore allow currencies to be temporarily exchanged: currencies are often said to be 'borrowed' or 'lent through the swap'. In the example above, dollars are being borrowed and sterling lent through the swap by Bank UK.

The amount of base currency (sterling or, if sterling is not involved, the dollar) in a swap is the same in both legs of the transaction. For example, in a swap, if £10m was sold against dollars spot, the same £10m would be bought back against dollars forward. The amount of dollars varies instead.

As the spot and reverse outright forward transactions in a swap effectively hedge each other, the exchange of currencies through a swap is without currency risk. Foreign exchange swaps therefore provide a means of **covered interest arbitrage**: exploiting interest rate differentials between currencies which are not offset by the differential between their spot and forward exchange rates.

Because the spot and forward legs of swaps hedge each other, there is no dealing spread between the spot exchange rate in the spot leg and the spot exchange rate component of the forward leg (remember that an outright forward is composed of the spot exchange rate and the forward points: see *Box 1*). This makes foreign exchange swaps cheaper to use as currency hedges than outright forwards.

Given that the same spot rate is used in both legs of a swap, it can be seen that the differential between the spot and outright forward rates of a swap is equal to the forward points, which in turn are equal to the interest rate differential between the currencies being swapped. The forward points in a swap are called the **swap rate**. If the outright forward rate is lower than the spot rate, the counterparty buying the base currency spot and selling it forward will make a loss equal to the swap rate and is said to 'pay the points'. On the other hand, the counterparty selling the base currency spot and buying it forward will make a profit equal to the swap rate and is said to be 'make the points'.

Although individual foreign exchange swaps are different in structure to individual currency swaps, it is possible to use foreign exchange swaps to replicate cross-currency basis swaps (floating-against-floating). Specifically, a series of foreign exchange swaps, in which each swap is rolled over at its maturity, has the same structure and function as a cross-currency basis swap. As future levels of floating-interest rate indexes are unknown, the price of future foreign exchange swaps (which will reflect future interest rate differentials) and the future prices of basis swaps are both unknown. The cash flows through foreign exchange and cross-currency basis swaps are compared in Diagram 17.

Although the two instruments are identical, cross-currency basis swaps are often preferred to a series of foreign exchange swaps in that:

■ cross-currency swaps avoid the dealing spread which would have to be paid on each foreign exchange swap;

■ the interest cash flows through a currency swap are constant.

Diagram 17: Comparing cross-currency basis swaps and foreign exchange swaps

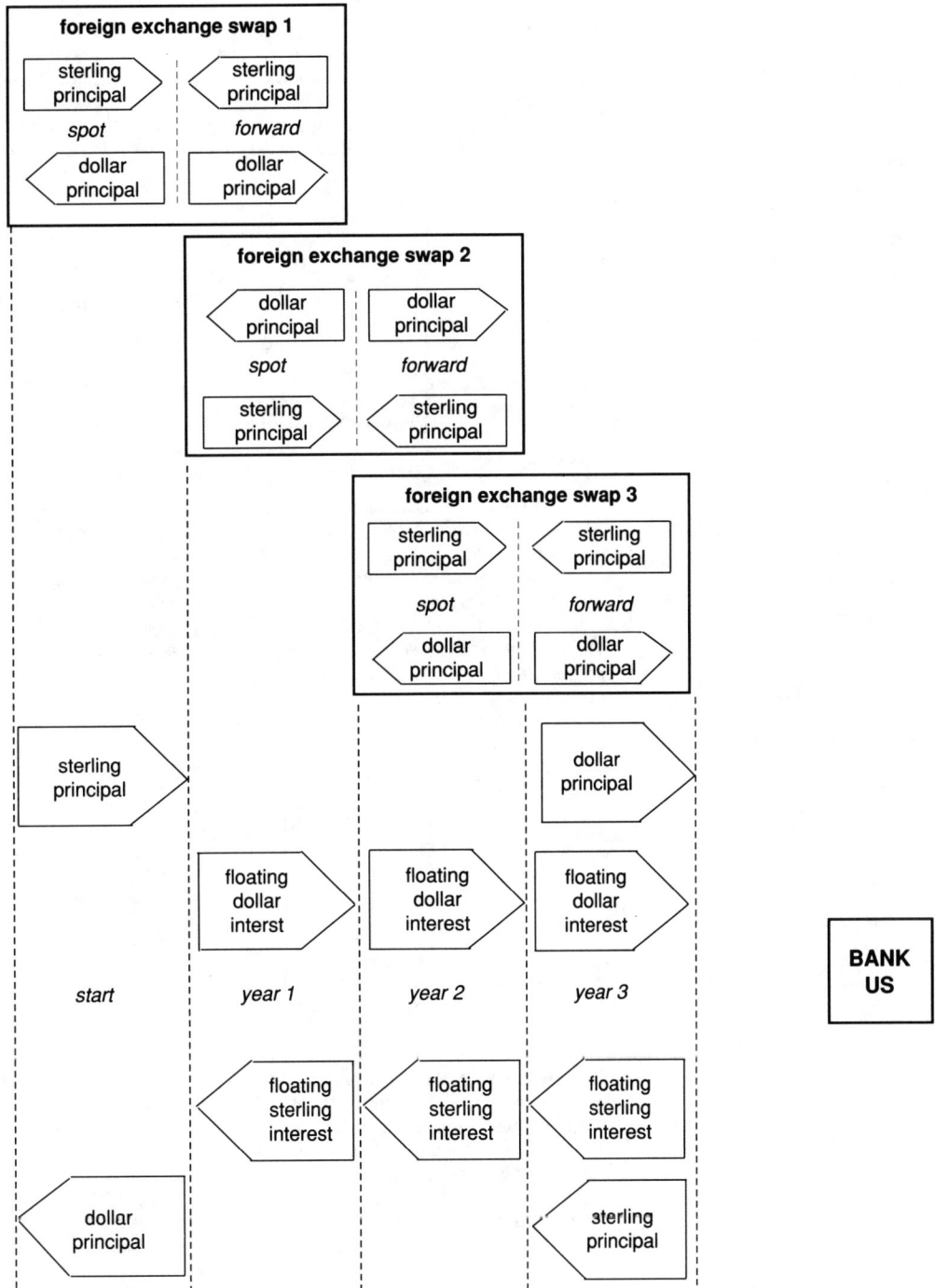

Notes

1. The term **interest rate swap** is applied to exchanges of interest in the *same currency*. Currency swaps involve exchanges of interest and principal in different currencies. Some currency swaps are, however, sometimes identified by the composite term 'cross-currency interest rate swap': see the later section on terminology.

2. The **parallel loan** originated as a means of circumventing exchange controls in the UK. In the 1970s, UK companies buying US dollars to make overseas investments were required to pay a tax, the so-called *dollar premium*. However, dollars borrowed abroad were exempt. A ready source of dollars was provided by US banks seeking sterling funds to expand their UK operations, but lacking a retail deposit base. Parallel loans matched the two sides, by arranging for a UK company to lend sterling to the UK subsidiary of a US company, while the US company lent dollars to the US subsidiary of the UK company.

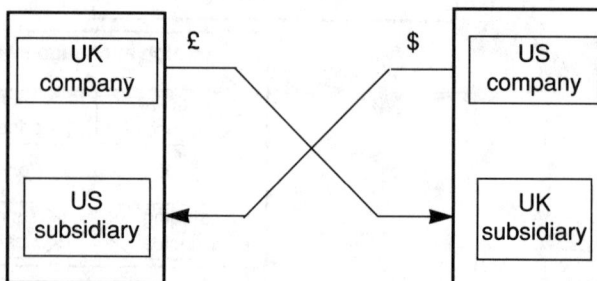

The parallel loan had two basic drawbacks:
— the loans were legally two separate transactions, since there were two distinct sets of borrowers and lenders, which meant that there was no *right of offset*, meaning that, if one of the counterparties defaulted, the other had to continue to honour its entire obligations to the defaulter;
— the transactions impacted on the balance sheet like conventional loans.

These shortcomings led to the development of the **back-to-back loan**. In this type of transaction, the parent company of a UK group would lend sterling to the parent company of a US group and, in exchange, the US parent would lend dollars to the UK parent (creating a cross-border transaction). The parents would then on-lend the funds to their own overseas subsidiaries.

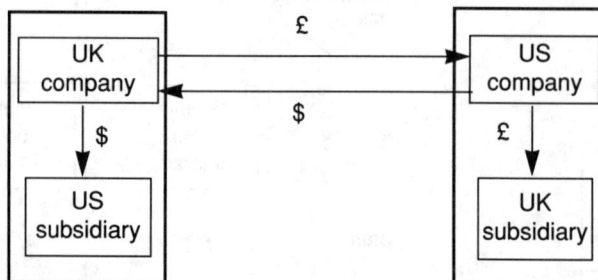

The direct linking of the two parent companies was meant to ensure that the loans were legally part of one transaction, with a right of offset in the event of default by one of the counterparties. Moreover, as the loans were supposed to be contingent upon each other, back-to-back loans were meant to be classed as exchanges, rather than as coincidental loans, and so be kept off the balance sheet. In practice, the legal and accounting treatment of back-to-back loans is ambiguous. There are still two separate sets of rights and obligations, despite the fact that there are only two counterparties for both loans. The legal uncertainty is increased by the cross-border structure. Currency swaps offer much greater certainty on this point and also provide a much more flexible structure.

3. Yield-to-maturity is the average rate of return or cost of funds on a regular series of future cash flows. For single future cash flows, such as occur in an outright forward transaction, the appropriate measure is a zero-coupon yield as this assumes a cash flow at maturity only.

4. See *Box 2* for an explanation of how the par forward rate is calculated.

Self-Study Exercises: <u>Questions</u>　Part 1

Assume in all questions that all interest rates are quoted on the same basis in terms of day count, annual basis and compounding conventions.

Question 1.1:　In what ways does a currency swap differ from an interest rate swap?

Question 1.2:　Why might currency swaps be classed as *off-balance sheet,* but not *derivative* instruments?

Question 1.3:　If there is an exchange of principal through a currency swap at maturity, what exchange rate is used?

Question 1.4:　Why might there be an exchange of principal at the start of a currency swap?

Question 1.5:　Which interest rate provides a common benchmark for many currency swaps?

Question 1.6:　Match the types of swap named in the left-hand column with the descriptions listed in the right-hand column.

A	currency swap	1	fixed-against-floating interest
B	cross-currency coupon swap	2	a fixed-against-floating currency swap combined with an interest rate swap
C	cross-currency basis swap	3	fixed-against-fixed interest
D	cocktail swap	4	floating-against-floating interest
E	circus swap	5	a fixed-against-dollar Libor currency swap combined with a dollar coupon swap

Question 1.7: If a $/DM currency swap is negotiated at an exchange rate of 1.4500 and is settled by alternate performance, rather than by exchange of principal, which counterparty should pay if the $/DM spot rate is 1.4400 by maturity?

Question 1.8: What are the main differences between currency swaps and LTFX? What are the main similarities?

Question 1.9: What LTFX instruments operate like currency swaps? What special type of currency swap operates like LTFX?

Question 1.10: What type of currency swap could be replicated with foreign exchange swaps?

Self-Study Exercises: <u>Answers</u>   Part 1

Answer 1.1:   A currency swap differs from an interest rate swap in that:

■ currency swaps, but not interest rate swaps, involve an exchange of payments in *two currencies*;

■ currency swaps, but not interest rate swaps, can involve an exchange of *principal amounts*.

Answer 1.2:   Currency swaps are *off-balance sheet* instruments, because they impact on the balance sheets of the swap counterparties only if and when there is an exchange of principal amounts. However, currency swaps are not *derivative* instruments. A derivative is defined as an instrument whose performance is derived from the behaviour of the price of a commodity, but which does not actually require that commodity to be bought or sold, whereas a currency swap can involve an exchange of principal amounts of currencies.

Answer 1.3:   An exchange of principal through a currency swap usually takes place at an exchange rate *negotiated* between the swap counterparties. In practice, this will usually be the *spot exchange rate* which prevailed at the start of the swap.

Answer 1.4:   There would be an exchange of principal at the start of a currency swap if:

■ one or both of the swap counterparties needed to acquire a principal amount of one of the currencies being swapped;

■ both swap counterparties were swapping the proceeds of new borrowings into each other's currency.

Answer 1.5:   Cross-currency swaps (fixed-against-floating or floating-against-floating) are often quoted in terms of the fixed interest rate of the non-dollar currency being swapped against six-month US dollar Libor.

Answer 1.6:

A	Currency swap	3 fixed-against-fixed interest
B	Cross-currency coupon swap	1 fixed-against-floating interest
C	Cross-currency basis swap	4 floating-against-floating interest
D	Cocktail swap	2 a fixed-against-floating currency swap combined with an interest rate swap
E	Circus swap	5 a fixed-against-dollar Libor currency swap combined with a dollar coupon swap

Answer 1.7: The payer of dollars and receiver of Deutsche marks pays a net amount in settlement of the currency swap. By having committed to a currency swap and the increasingly historic exchange rate which it entails (1.4500), the counterparty paying the currency which appreciates (ie, dollars) foregoes a foreign exchange profit on the swap by having fixed the cost to itself of the appreciating countercurrency (ie, Deutsche marks) at the historic exchange rate.

Answer 1.8: The main *differences* between currency swaps and LTFX are structural:
- currency swaps can involve exchanges of interest and principal amounts of currencies: in LTFX, no interest amounts are exchanged;
- in currency swaps, the exchange of principal amounts takes place at an exchange rate agreed at the start of the swap, usually (but not necessarily) the *spot exchange rate*: in LTFX, the exchange of principal amounts at maturity takes place at the *forward exchange rate* prevailing at the start of the swap;
- both instruments take account of interest rate differentials between the currencies being swapped: LTFX reflects interest rate differentials in the difference between the spot and *forward exchange rates*; currency swaps actually exchange *interest* cash flows and leave the exchange rate unchanged over the life of the swap.

The main *similarities* between currency swaps and LTFX are functional:
- both instruments create foreign exchange risk and can therefore be used to hedge or take currency risk;

- while currency swaps and LTFX differ in terms of the timing of cash flows, the fact that the differential between the spot and forward exchange rates in LTFX is mirrored, in currency swaps, in differences between interest cash flows means that the two instruments have equal *net present values*.

Answer 1.9: The special type of LTFX instrument which operates like a currency swap is a *par forward*. A par forward is actually a series of outright forwards packaged into a single transaction with each exchange of currencies at the same average (par) forward exchange rate. As such, par forwards produce a constant stream of cash flows up to maturity, just like a currency swap. Of course, the par forward rate is essentially an average of forward exchange rates and so diverges from the spot rate usually employed in currency swaps. The par forward can only replicate a fixed-against-fixed currency swap, because only this type of swap makes interest payments which are known in advance.

The special type of currency swap which operates like LTFX is a *zero-coupon fixed-against-fixed currency swap*. This is a currency swap involving no interest payments (in other words, it has zero coupons), just an exchange of principal amounts at maturity, as in an outright forward. The principal amounts to be exchanged are calculated by compounding to maturity the interest payments which would have been made through a normal fixed-against-fixed swap. In effect, the normal interest payments are reinvested and paid as part of the principal amounts exchanged at maturity. The zero-coupon swap which matches an outright forward must be fixed-against-fixed, otherwise the size of future interest payments could not be known in advance and therefore the necessary compounding calculation could not be performed.

Answer 1.10: Foreign exchange swaps can be used to replicate *cross-currency basis swaps* (floating-against-floating). Specifically, a *series* of foreign exchange swaps, in which each swap is rolled over at its maturity, has the same structure and function as a cross-currency basis swap. As future levels of floating interest rate indexes are unknown, the price of future foreign exchange swaps (which will reflect future interest rate differentials) and the future prices of basis swaps are both unknown.

2 Using currency swaps

Risk management with currency swaps

Managing currency risk and interest rate risk

In *Part One*, it was explained that a currency swap creates an exposure to the risk of change in both:

- exchange rates

- interest rates

Currency swaps could therefore be used to *take risk* positions based upon expectations about the direction in which exchange rates or interest rates or both will move in the future. However, in practice, currency swaps are not originated for the purpose of taking currency risk. This is because the exchange of principal amounts which usually occurs in currency swaps entails too much credit risk and limits the liquidity of the instrument, which makes it difficult to open and close positions. Currency swaps are therefore used exclusively to *hedge* currency risks (by providing equal and opposite currency risk). On the other hand, currency swaps are used to take and hedge *interest rate risk*. Like interest rate swaps, currency swaps can swap between either:

- fixed and floating interest streams;

- two floating interest streams, each calculated using a different interest rate index;

- and (unlike interest rate swaps) two fixed interest streams.

An example

A UK airline, with mainly sterling revenues, has borrowed fixed-interest dollars in order to purchase aircraft from the US. It now expects the dollar to appreciate against sterling. A sustained rise in the dollar would increase the amount of sterling which the airline would need in order to buy the dollars required to repay the dollar borrowing. The sterling cost of dollar interest payments would also increase.

The airline could hedge its exposure to a dollar appreciation by putting on a £/$ currency swap. The currency swap would fix the rate at which the airline, at maturity, could exchange its accumulated sterling revenues for the dollars needed to repay its borrowing. Fixing the exchange rate hedges the currency risk in borrowing dollars and repaying from sterling income.

Assume that the UK airline, not only expects the dollar to appreciate, but also believes UK interest rates will fall. It could use a currency swap to take advantage of the expected fall in UK interest rates, at the same time as hedging against currency risk, by swapping from fixed-interest dollars into floating-interest sterling. Specifically, the UK airline would use a cross-currency coupon swap (fixed-to-floating).

The simplest structure for the currency swap in the example would be one *without* an initial exchange of principal. This is illustrated in Diagram 18. The stages in transacting this type of swap are:

■ at the start of the swap, the £/$ rate at which the principal amounts will be exchanged at maturity is agreed (probably, but not necessarily, the prevailing £/$ spot rate);

■ at the same time, the interest rates for the swap are also agreed;

■ over the life of the swap, the UK airline will pay a stream of sterling floating interest through the swap and will receive a counterstream of dollar fixed interest in exchange: the dollar interest received will be used to service the dollar borrowing; the sterling interest paid through the swap will be funded from earnings;

■ at maturity, the airline will pay a sterling principal amount through the swap and receive a dollar principal amount in exchange. The exchange is made at the £/$ rate agreed at the start of the swap. The airline will fund its payment of principal through the swap from accumulated sterling earnings from its business and will use the dollar principal it receives in exchange to repay its dollar borrowing.

Diagram 18: Managing currency and interest rate risk with a currency swap
(without an initial exchange of principal)

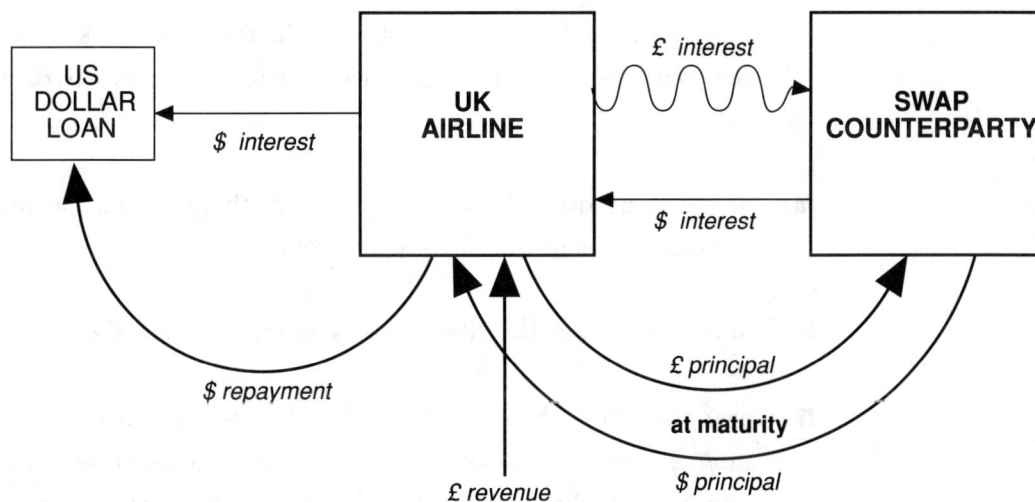

Currency swaps

The structure of the currency swap in the above example would have to be slightly more complicated, if it were necessary to make an *initial exchange* of principal amounts through the swap. An initial exchange would be required either where a swap counterparty needs to acquire a currency or to convert a new borrowing from one currency to another.

An example

In the above example an initial exchange of principal would be required where the swap counterparty to the UK airline needed to acquire a principal amount of dollars. In this case, the UK airline would simply acquire the dollars from the spot foreign exchange market. It would fund this spot purchase of dollars with the sterling received through the swap in the initial exchange of principal amounts. This set of transactions is illustrated in Diagram 19. The stages in transacting this type of swap are:

■ at the start of the swap, the UK airline buys dollars against sterling in the spot foreign exchange market;

■ the dollars purchased in the spot market are exchanged through the swap for sterling, at the same £/$ exchange rate at which the UK airline had to buy dollars against sterling in the spot market: the sterling received through the swap is used to fund the spot purchase of the dollars;

■ at the same time, the £/$ rate at which the principal amounts will be exchanged at maturity is fixed at the same spot rate;

■ at the same time, the interest rates for the swap are also agreed;

■ over the life of the swap, the UK airline will pay a stream of sterling interest through the swap and will receive a counterstream of dollar interest in exchange: the dollar interest received will be used to service the dollar borrowing; the sterling interest paid through the swap will be funded from earnings;

■ at maturity, the airline will pay a sterling principal amount through the swap and receive a dollar principal amount in exchange. The exchange is made at the £/$ rate agreed at the start of the swap. The airline will fund its payment of principal through the swap from accumulated sterling earnings from its business and will use the dollar principal it receives in exchange to repay its dollar borrowing.

Diagram 19: Managing currency and interest rate risk with a currency swap
(with an initial exchange of principal)

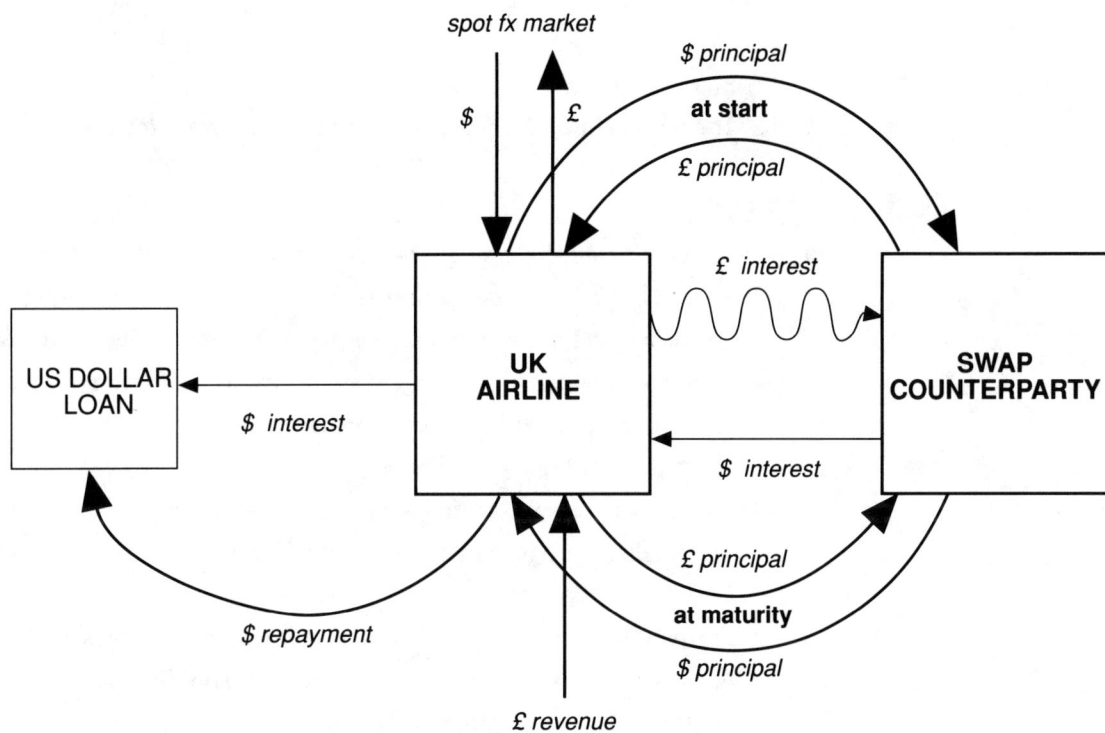

An example

The UK airline in the previous two examples may not have been able to borrow fixed-interest dollar funding. In this case, it might have borrowed sterling instead and exchanged them for dollars using a currency swap with an initial exchange of principal. This set of transactions is illustrated in Diagram 20. The stages in transacting this type of swap are:

- the UK airline borrows sterling;

- the sterling is immediately exchanged through the swap for dollars (the initial exchange of principal), which are then used to purchase aircraft;

- at the same time, the rate at which the principal amounts will be exchanged at maturity is fixed (probably, but not necessarily, at the prevailing £/$ spot rate);

- at the same time, the interest rates for the swap are also agreed;

- over the life of the swap, the UK airline will pay a stream of dollar interest through the swap and will receive a counterstream of sterling interest in exchange: the sterling interest it receives will be used to service its sterling borrowing; it could raise the dollar interest it pays through the swap from several sources:
  — accumulated dollar revenues;
  — converting accumulated sterling revenues into dollars in the spot foreign exchange market, as and when dollar interest payments are due;
  — converting projected sterling revenues into dollars in the forward foreign exchange market for each of the future dates on which dollar interest payments are due.

- at maturity, the airline will receive a sterling principal amount through the swap and pay a dollar principal amount in exchange. The exchange is made at the £/$ rate agreed at the start of the swap. The airline could use the same sources as above to fund the exchange of principal through the swap and will use the sterling it receives in exchange to repay its sterling borrowing.

Diagram 20: *Managing currency and interest rate risk — on a new borrowing — with a currency swap (with an initial exchange of principal)*

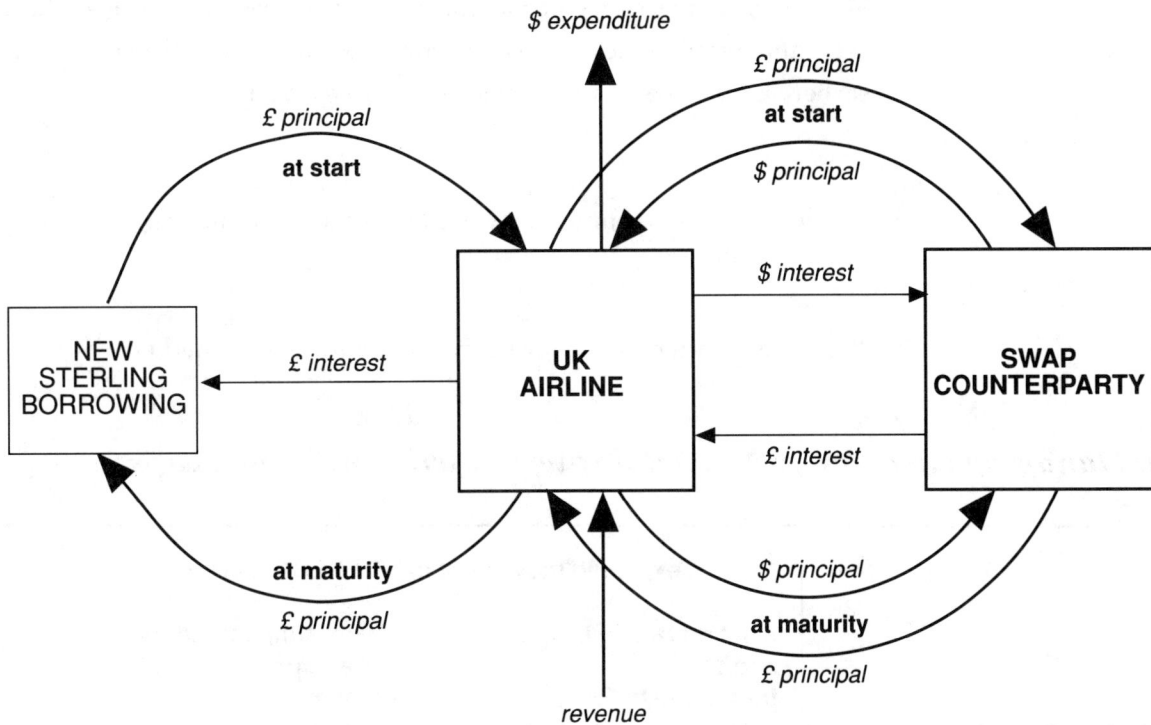

Deferred hedging

As well as anticipating exchange rate and interest rate changes, currency swaps can also be used reactively, to *lock in* unrealised profits which have arisen from past favourable changes in rates or to *stem* any further increase in unrealised losses from past unfavourable changes. In the first two examples above, it may be that the dollar depreciated subsequent to the airline's borrowing, thereby reducing the amount of sterling which would have to be sold at maturity in order to buy in the dollars needed to repay the dollar borrowing. The dollar depreciation would also reduce the cost of servicing the interest payments on the dollar borrowing. A currency swap from dollars into sterling would not only protect the airline against any future dollar appreciation, but would fix the gains from the previous dollar depreciation. This approach is simply deferred hedging.

Risk strategies

The various ways in which currency swaps can be used to hedge currency risk and simultaneously hedge or take interest rate risk, are summarised in Table 9. The structure of the currency swap required for each of these uses is then illustrated in the series of diagrams which follows. The swaps which have been illustrated do not involve an initial exchange of principal. As explained earlier, an initial exchange would be required either:

■   where a swap counterparty needed to acquire a currency;

■   to convert a new borrowing from one currency to another.

Table 9: *Managing currency and interest rate risk with currency swaps*

			expected movement in INTEREST RATES	
			existing rate to RISE and/or target rate to FALL	existing rate to FALL and/or target rate to RISE
existing currency to APPRECIATE	**target** currency to DEPRECIATE**		swap liabilities from fixed to floating or floating to floating	swap liabilities from fixed to fixed or floating to fixed
			do not swap currency of assets*	do not swap currency of assets*
existing currency to DEPRECIATE	**target** currency to APPRECIATE**		swap assets fixed to fixed or floating to fixed	swap assets fixed to floating or floating to floating
			do not swap currency of liabilities*	do not swap currency of liabilities*

(left axis label: **expected movement in EXCHANGE RATES**)

*   Use interest rate swaps instead.
**   Target currency is the currency into which a swap is being considered.

In Table 9, it is suggested that a currency swap should *not* be used where:

- the existing currency of a foreign-currency liability is expected to depreciate: depreciation would reduce the amount of domestic currency required to buy the foreign currency needed to repay the liability;

- the existing currency of a foreign-currency asset is expected to appreciate: appreciation would increase the domestic currency value of the asset;

- the currency into which a liability might be swapped is expected to appreciate: appreciation would increase the amount of domestic currency required to buy the foreign currency needed to repay the liability;

- the currency into which an asset might be swapped is expected to depreciate: depreciation would reduce the domestic currency value of the asset.

The use of currency swaps in these situations would mean giving up currency gains (the first two cases) or risking currency losses (the second two cases). However, doing nothing would mean foregoing lower interest rates on liabilities or higher interest rates on assets. The solution would be to use interest rate swaps, which change the interest rate basis of assets and liabilities, but not the currency.

Hedging liabilities

Take the case of a borrower with an unhedged fixed-interest liability in a foreign currency, where:

■ the foreign currency is expected to or has already started to appreciate against the domestic currency;

■ the interest rate on the domestic currency is expected to or has already started to fall.

The borrower faces an increase in the domestic currency cost of the repayment of debt principal. To hedge against this and, at the same time, benefit from falling domestic currency interest rates, the borrower could use a *cross-currency coupon swap* (fixed-against-floating) to:

■ swap the liability from the (appreciating) foreign currency into the (depreciating) domestic currency;

■ swap from foreign currency interest into (falling) domestic currency interest: the borrower would pay floating interest in domestic currency through the swap and in exchange receive fixed interest in foreign currency (which it would use to service the interest due on its foreign currency borrowing).

Diagram 21: Using a currency swap to hedge:
    — *a fixed-interest liability*
    — *in an appreciating currency*
    — *and benefit from a falling interest rate in domestic currency*

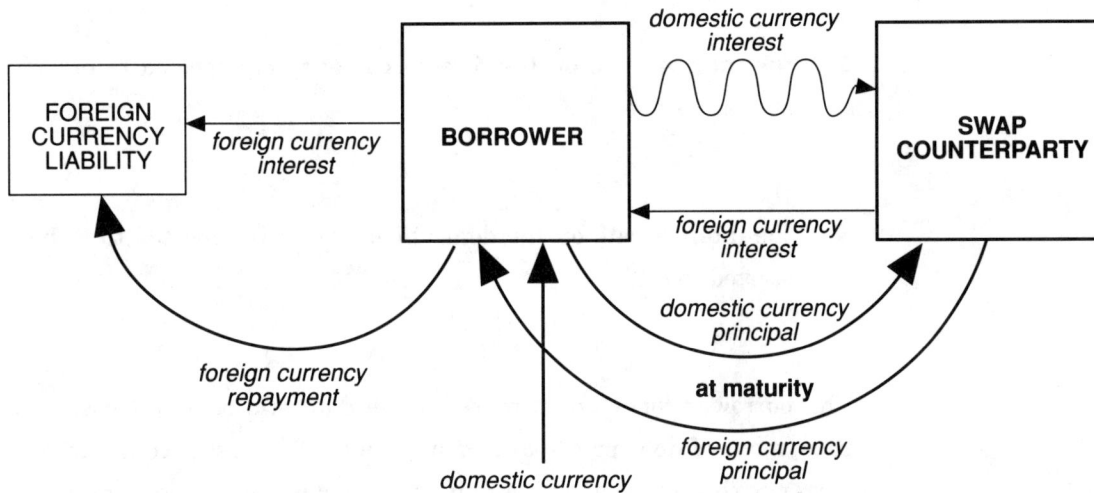

REMEMBER: *the foreign currency is expected to APPRECIATE*
               the domestic currency interest rate is expected to FALL

Take the case of a borrower with an unhedged floating-interest liability in a foreign currency, where:

■ the foreign currency is expected to or has already started to appreciate against the domestic currency;

■ the interest rate on the foreign currency is expected to or has already started to rise;

■ the interest rate on the domestic currency is expected to or has already started to fall.

The borrower faces an increase in the domestic currency cost of both the repayment of debt principal and payments of interest. To hedge against the currency risk, while avoiding rising foreign currency interest rates and, at the same time, benefiting from falling domestic currency interest rates, the borrower could use a *cross-currency basis swap* (floating-against-floating) to:

■ swap the liability from the (appreciating) foreign currency into the (depreciating) domestic currency;

■ swap from (rising) foreign currency interest into (falling) domestic currency interest: the borrower would pay floating interest in domestic currency through the swap and in exchange receive floating interest in foreign currency (which it would use to service the interest due on its foreign currency borrowing).

Diagram 22: Using a currency swap to hedge
— a floating-interest liability
— in an appreciating currency
— and benefit from a falling interest rate in domestic currency

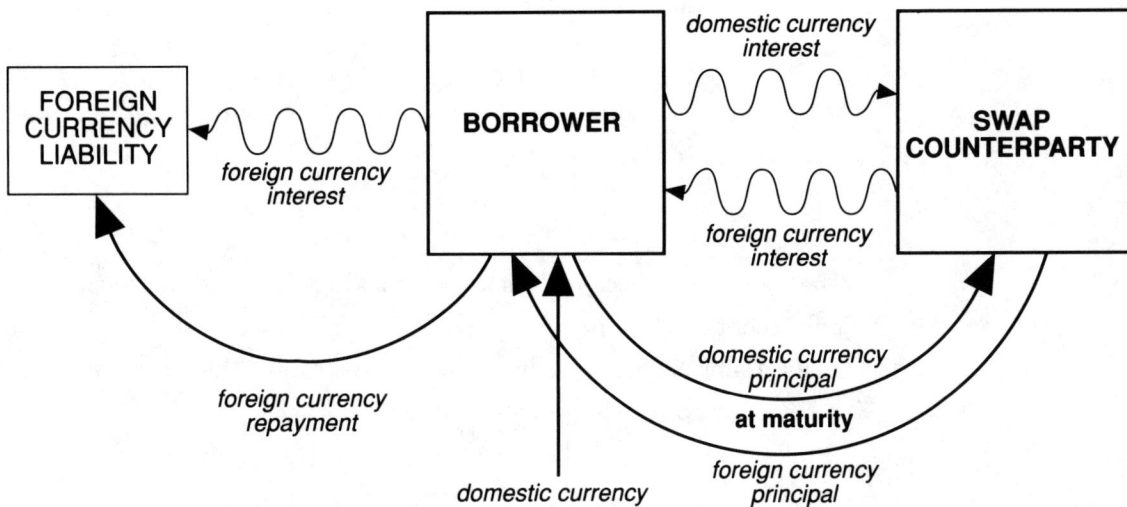

REMEMBER: *the foreign currency is expected to APPRECIATE*
the foreign currency interest rate is expected to RISE
the domestic currency interest rate is expected to FALL

Take the case of a borrower with an unhedged fixed-interest liability in a foreign currency, where:

■ the foreign currency is expected to or has already started to appreciate against the domestic currency;

■ the interest rate on the domestic currency is expected to or has already started to rise.

The borrower faces an increase in the domestic currency cost of the repayment of debt principal. To hedge against this and, at the same time, avoid rising domestic currency interest rates, the borrower could use a *currency swap* (fixed-against-fixed) to:

■ swap the liability from the (appreciating) foreign currency into the (depreciating) domestic currency;

■ swap from fixed foreign currency interest into fixed domestic currency interest: the borrower would pay fixed interest in domestic currency through the swap and in exchange receive fixed interest in foreign currency (which it would use to service the interest due on its foreign currency borrowing).

Diagram 23: Using a currency swap to hedge
   — a fixed-interest liability
   — in an appreciating currency
   — and avoid a rising interest rate in domestic currency

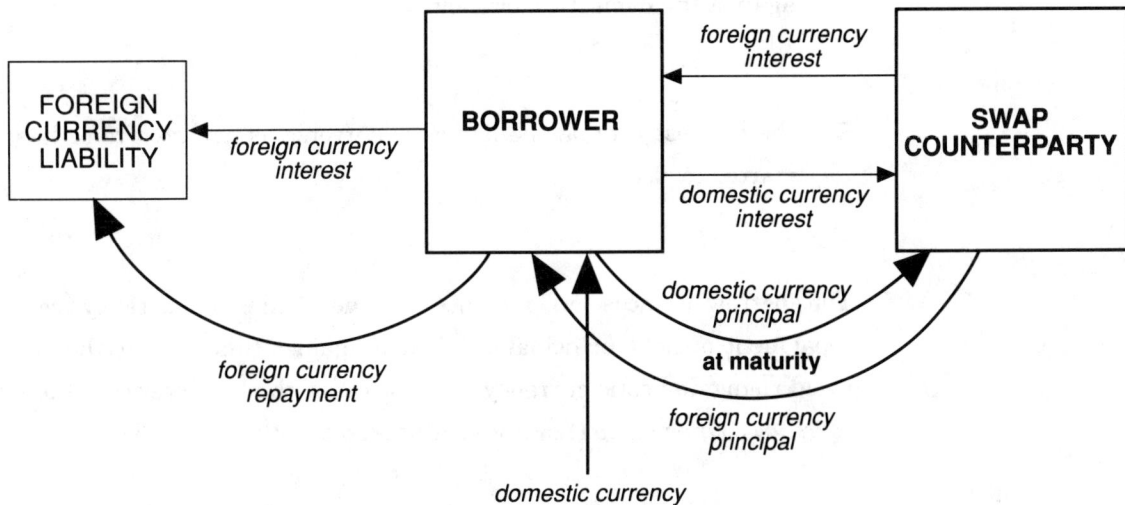

REMEMBER: *the foreign currency is expected to APPRECIATE*
   the domestic currency interest rate is expected to RISE

Take the case of a borrower with an unhedged floating-interest liability in a foreign currency, where:

■ the foreign currency is expected to or has already started to appreciate against the domestic currency;

■ the interest rate on the domestic currency is expected to or has already started to rise.

The borrower faces an increase in the domestic currency cost of the repayment of debt principal. To hedge against this and, at the same time, avoid rising domestic currency interest rates, the borrower could use a *cross-currency coupon swap* (floating-against-fixed) to:

■ swap the liability from the (appreciating) foreign currency into the (depreciating) domestic currency;

■ swap from foreign currency interest into fixed domestic currency interest: the borrower would pay fixed interest in domestic currency through the swap and in exchange receive floating interest in foreign currency (which it would use to service the interest due on its foreign currency borrowing).

Diagram 24: Using a currency swap to hedge
      — a floating-interest liability
      — in an appreciating currency
      — and avoid a rising interest rate in domestic currency

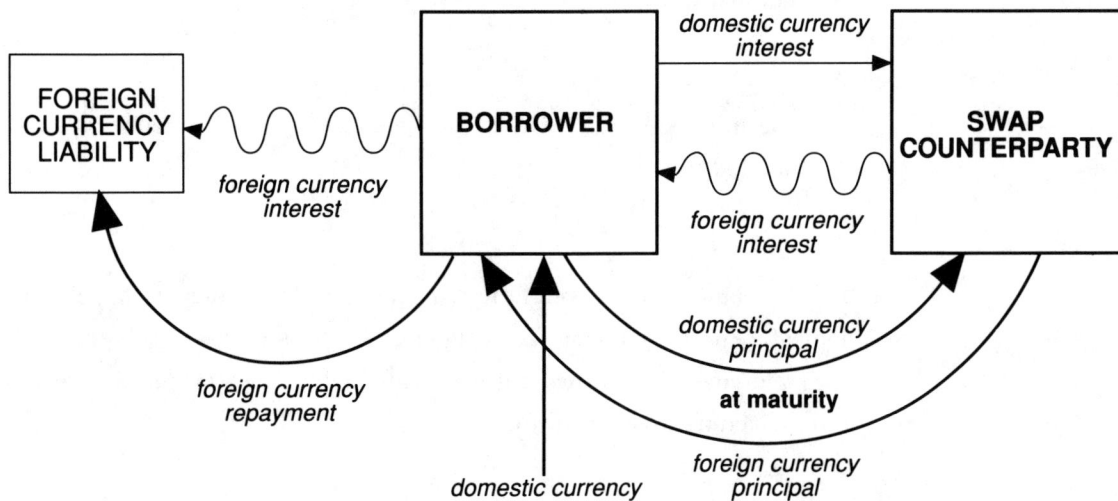

REMEMBER: the foreign currency is expected to APPRECIATE
                       the domestic currency interest rate is expected to RISE

Hedging assets

Take the case of an investor with an unhedged fixed-interest asset in a foreign currency, where:

■ the foreign currency is expected to or has already started to depreciate against the domestic currency;

■ the interest rate on the domestic currency is expected to or has already started to fall.

The investor faces a reduction in the capital value of its investment in domestic currency terms. To hedge against this and, at the same time, avoid falling domestic currency interest rates, the investor could use a *currency swap* (fixed-against-fixed) to:

■ swap the asset from the (depreciating) foreign currency into the (appreciating) domestic currency;

■ swap from foreign currency interest into fixed domestic currency interest: the investor would receive fixed interest in domestic currency through the swap and in exchange pay fixed interest in foreign currency (which it would fund from the interest received on its foreign currency asset).

Diagram 25: Using a currency swap to hedge
    — a fixed-interest asset
    — in a depreciating currency
    — and avoid a falling interest rate in domestic currency

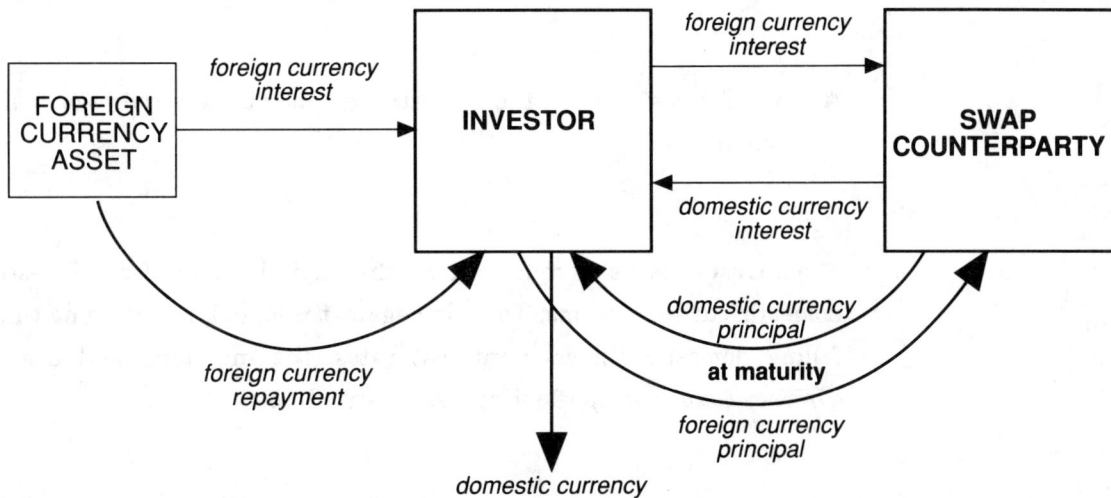

REMEMBER: *the foreign currency is expected to DEPRECIATE*
             the domestic currency interest rate is expected to FALL

Take the case of an investor with an unhedged floating-interest asset in a foreign currency, where:

■ the foreign currency is expected to or has already started to depreciate against the domestic currency;

■ the interest rate on the domestic currency is expected to or has already started to fall.

The investor faces a reduction in the capital value of its investment in domestic currency terms. To hedge against this and, at the same time, avoid falling domestic currency interest rates, the investor could use a *cross-currency coupon swap* (floating-against-fixed) to:

■ swap the asset from the (depreciating) foreign currency into the (appreciating) domestic currency;

■ swap from foreign currency interest into fixed domestic currency interest: the investor would receive fixed interest in domestic currency through the swap and in exchange pay floating interest in foreign currency (which it would fund from the interest received on its foreign currency asset).

Diagram 26: Using a currency swap to hedge
        — a floating-interest asset
        — in a depreciating currency
        — and avoid a falling interest rate in domestic currency

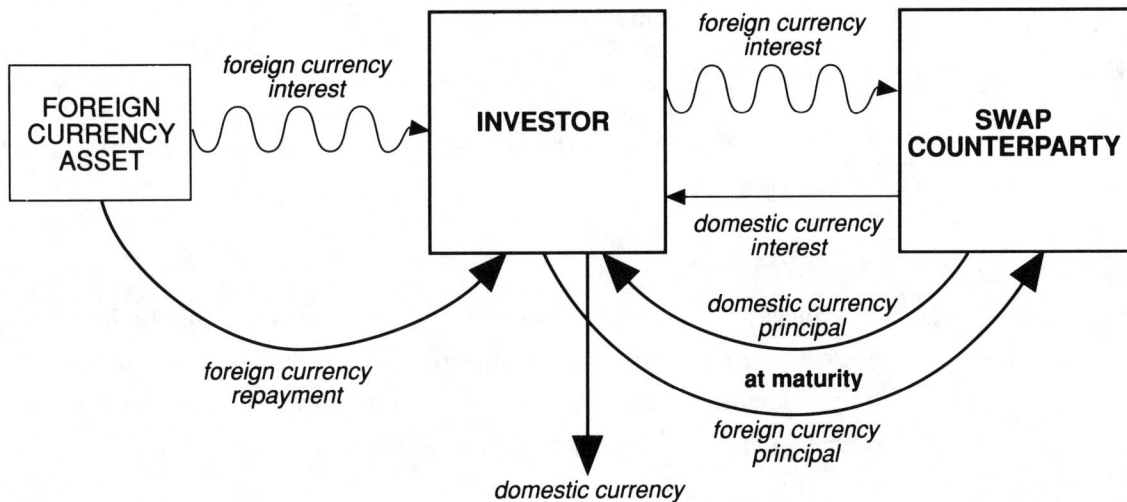

```
                                    foreign currency
       foreign currency                 interest
          interest
FOREIGN  ~~~~~~>    INVESTOR   ~~~~~~>    SWAP
CURRENCY                                 COUNTERPARTY
ASSET
                              <------
                          domestic currency
                              interest

      foreign currency       domestic currency
        repayment                principal

                              at maturity

                         foreign currency
                             principal
          domestic currency
```

REMEMBER: *the foreign currency is expected to DEPRECIATE*
                     the domestic currency interest rate is expected to FALL

Take the case of an investor with an unhedged fixed-interest asset in a foreign currency, where:

■ the foreign currency is expected to or has already started to depreciate against the domestic currency;

■ the interest rate on the domestic currency is expected to or has already started to rise.

The investor faces a reduction in the capital value of its investment in domestic currency terms. To hedge against this and, at the same time, benefit from rising domestic currency interest rates, the investor could use a *cross-currency coupon swap* (fixed-against-floating) to:

■ swap the asset from the (depreciating) foreign currency into the (appreciating) domestic currency;

■ swap from foreign currency interest into (rising) domestic currency interest: the investor would receive floating interest in domestic currency through the swap and in exchange pay fixed interest in foreign currency (which it would fund from the interest received on its foreign currency asset).

Diagram 27: Using a currency swap to hedge
— a fixed-interest asset
— in a depreciating currency
— and benefit from a rising interest rate in domestic currency

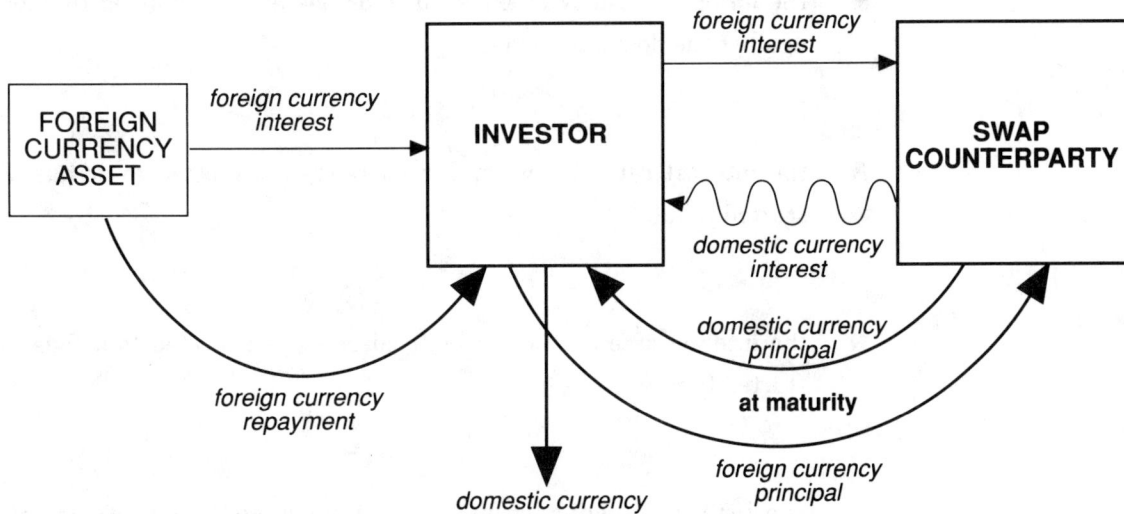

REMEMBER: the foreign currency is expected to DEPRECIATE
the domestic currency interest rate is expected to RISE

Take the case of an investor with an unhedged floating-interest asset in a foreign currency, where:

■ the foreign currency is expected to or has already started to depreciate against the domestic currency;

■ the interest rate on the foreign currency is expected to or has already started to fall;

■ the interest rate on the domestic currency is expected to or has already started to rise.

The investor faces a reduction in the capital value of its investment in terms of domestic currency. To hedge against this, while avoiding falling foreign currency interest rates and, at the same time, benefiting from rising domestic currency interest rates, the investor could use a *cross-currency basis swap* (floating-against-floating) to:

■ swap the asset from the (depreciating) foreign currency into the (appreciating) domestic currency;

■ swap from (falling) foreign currency interest into (rising) domestic currency interest: the investor would receive floating interest in domestic currency through the swap and in exchange pay floating interest in foreign currency (which it would fund from the interest received on its foreign currency asset).

Diagram 28: Using a currency swap to hedge
           — a floating-interest asset
           — in a depreciating currency
           — and benefit from a rising interest rate in domestic currency

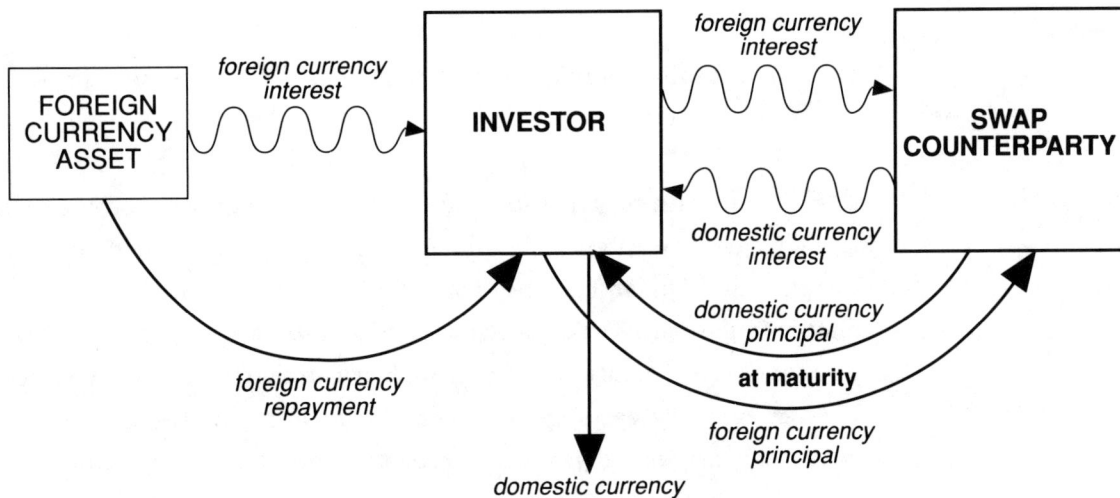

REMEMBER: *the foreign currency is expected to DEPRECIATE*
                       the foreign currency interest rate is expected to FALL
                       the domestic currency interest rate is expected to RISE

Hedging translation risk

Currency swaps can be used to help solve the problem of how to hedge **translation exposure**. This type of exposure arises from the need to account, in terms of the domestic currency of the parent company, for:

■ foreign currency assets and liabilities of overseas branches;

■ the unrealised foreign currency earnings of overseas subsidiaries.

The foreign currency assets and liabilities of overseas branches include foreign currency receivables which have not yet been paid to the parent company and foreign currency borrowings which are due to be repaid. These may be regarded as translational exposures to currency risk, at least until payments are actually made (when they become **transaction exposures**). Foreign currency earnings are generally regarded as translation exposures until they are actually paid over to the parent company. Until then, the domestic currency value of foreign currency assets, liabilities and earnings will be uncertain (and will be at risk). When payments are made or received, it is possible to use conventional hedges against currency risk.

It can be seen that a key factor in distinguishing translation from transaction exposure is the time delay between the valuation of foreign currency assets, liabilities and earnings, and their actual conversion into domestic currency. In other words, translation exposure is deferred transaction exposure. If this is a medium or long-term period, as explained in *Part One*, conventional currency hedges (forward foreign exchange) become awkward to apply. However, currency swaps are available for such periods.

Return management with currency swaps: arbitrage with cash instruments

Definition	**An arbitrage is a simultaneous sale and purchase of the same commodity at different prices to realise a profit.**

As in the case of interest rate swaps, the major incentive behind the establishment of the market in currency swaps has been arbitrage. The arbitrage opportunities are essentially the same in the case of both instruments: differences between the interest paid (received) through swaps and the interest received from (paid by) another instrument. In an arbitrage between a swap and a cash instrument, although different types of instrument are bought and sold, they represent the same commodity in the sense that they both generate interest calculated using the same type of interest rate. If one instrument pays a higher rate of interest than the other, there is an opportunity for arbitrage by arranging to receive the higher interest stream from one and simultaneously pay the lower interest stream through the other. Any change (up or down) in one interest stream will be matched by an equal but opposite change in the other — since they are both calculated using the same interest rate — but the arbitrage difference will remain unchanged. Efficient and competitive cash and derivatives markets should have access to the same price information and resources. Consequently, the two interest streams should be the same. In practice, these markets have not been entirely efficient nor competitive, and price discrepancies have occurred, giving rise to arbitrage opportunities. The basic principle is illustrated in Diagram 29.

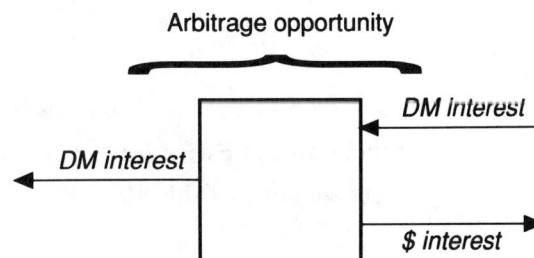

Diagram 29: Arbitrage with a currency swap

The key difference between arbitrages involving interest rate swaps and currency swaps is that an arbitrage involving a currency swap will generate profits in one currency, while the swap will leave the arbitrageur paying or receiving another currency. In the example illustrated in Diagram 1, arbitrage profits were made in Deutsche marks, while the swap was into US dollars. The arbitrage profits have to be converted into the other currency. This must be done in the forward foreign exchange market, if currency risk is to be avoided. This problem is discussed further in the examples presented below.

Arbitraging liabilities

The main opportunities for arbitrage with currency swaps are provided by new borrowing. This is often called **new issue arbitrage**, although the borrowing can be either new issues of debt securities or new bank loans. Currency swaps are not used to arbitrage *existing* liabilities (although, as explained in the previous section, they are used with existing liabilities for *risk management* purposes, such as locking in unrealised exchange rate gains and avoiding rising interest rates).

An example

Take two borrowers looking for new funds:

- A multilateral development bank, to be called *MDB*, has a policy of borrowing currencies with low interest rates such as the Swiss franc, but the scale and regularity of its borrowing quickly saturates demand in small bond markets. Investors soon start to require higher margins in order to take more MDB paper into their portfolios. However, MDB can more readily attract investors in the US, where its debt is a rarity.

- A US multinational industrial company, to be called *USCo*, which requires dollars, but faces strong competition from many other similar companies in the US dollar bond market. However, USCo may find it is a welcome rarity in the Swiss market, where its name is well known and respected.

Assume also that both borrowers require five-year funds and that they can borrow in the Swiss franc and US dollar fixed-income (bond) markets at the costs set out in Table 10.

Table 10: Cost of capital market funds

	Swiss franc bonds	US dollar bonds
MDB	6 1/2%	4%
USCo	7%	5 1/4%
differential	50bp	125bp

What is noticeable about the relative funding costs of the two borrowers is that MDB can fund itself more cheaply than USCo by 125bp in US dollars, but by only 50bp in Swiss francs. This difference in the relative pricing of the risk on the two borrowers by different currency sectors of the international capital market (for the reasons already explained) can be exploited using a currency swap. Basically, MDB borrows fixed-rate dollars and swaps the cost in a way which shares its advantage with USCo. Because the arbitrage requires a swap between currencies, a prerequisite for the deal is that MDB actually wants to end up with Swiss francs and USCo actually wants to end up with dollars. Assuming this is the case, the arbitrage requires the following steps, which are illustrated in Diagrams 30a–e.

Step 1   MDB and USCo each have to set a target for the all-in cost of funds they wish to produce from the swap. In this example, it is assumed that:

■ MDB is seeking a reduction in its cost of borrowing Swiss francs of at least 50bp from 6 1/2% to 6% per annum.

■ USCo would accept a reduction in its cost of borrowing dollars of 12.5bp from 5 1/4% to 5 1/8% per annum.

Step 2   MDB borrows fixed-rate US dollars by issuing a five-year Eurobond at 4% per annum and USCo borrows fixed-rate Swiss francs by issuing a five-year bond at 7% per annum[1].

Diagram 30a: New issue arbitrage (new issues)

Step 3 — MDB and USCo then swap the principal amounts they have borrowed for five years at a negotiated exchange rate (probably, but not necessarily, the prevailing spot exchange rate). Assume MDB borrowed $100m and USCo SwFr150m, and that they have exchanged these amounts at an agreed exchange rate of $/SwFr1.5000.

Diagram 30b: New issue arbitrage (exchange of principal)

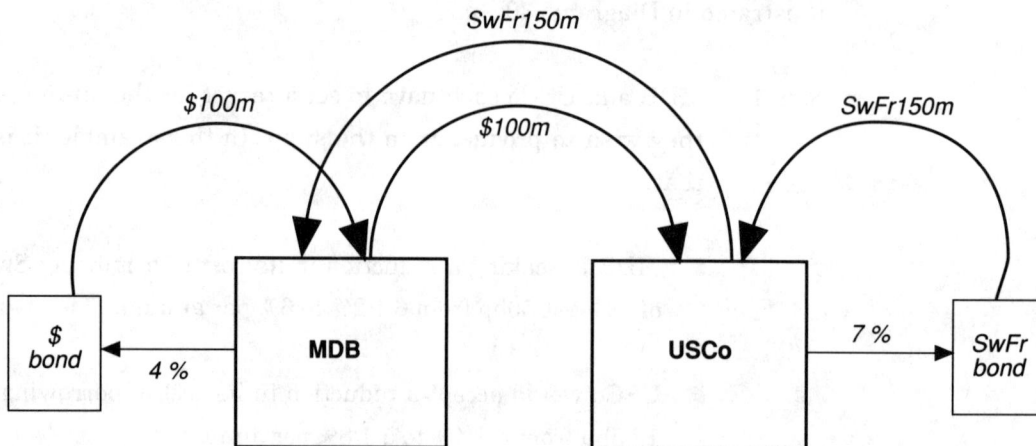

Step 4   During the life of the swap, MDB and USCo swap interest with each other. MDB would receive dollar interest from USCo which it would use to service the interest obligations on its original dollar borrowing. In exchange, USCo would receive Swiss franc interest from MDB which it would use to service the interest obligations on its original Swiss franc borrowing. In net terms, the swap would leave MDB paying fixed-rate Swiss franc interest to USCo and USCo paying fixed-rate US dollar interest to MDB. The interest rates paid and received in the swap are negotiated between the two counterparties at the start of the swap.

Diagram 30c: New issue arbitrage (exchange of interest)

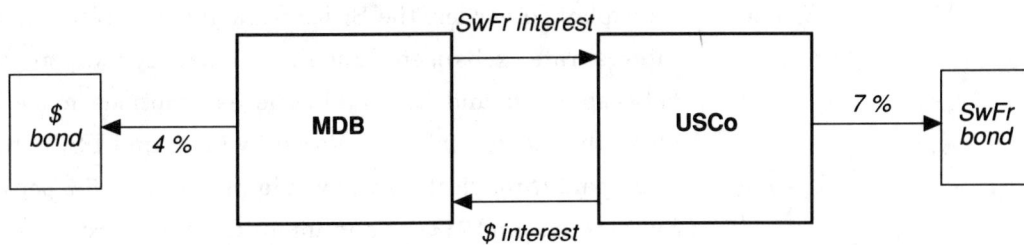

Step 5   At maturity, MDB and USCo would reverse the initial exchange of principal amounts. This re-exchange would be at the exchange rate agreed for the original exchange of principal, which was $/SwFr1.5000. Thus, MDB would repay SwFr150m to USCo and USCo would repay $100m to MDB. The two counterparties would use these amounts to repay their original borrowings.

Diagram 30d: New issue arbitrage (re-exchange of principal)

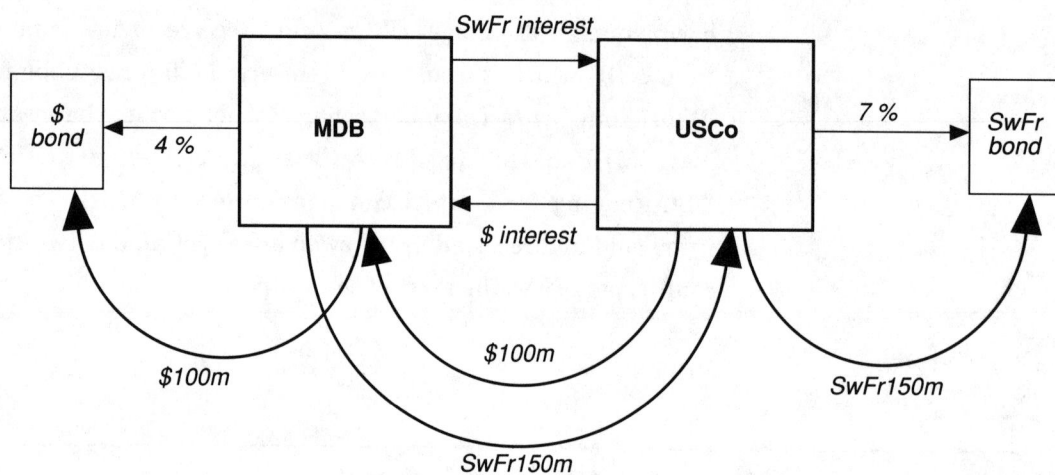

Step 6   As explained earlier, the Swiss franc interest rate and the dollar interest rate exchanged through the currency swap are negotiated between MDB and USCo. On the assumptions made in Step 1 about the cost of funds targets set by MDB and USCo, the interest rates paid through the swap would probably be 6% per annum for Swiss francs and 4% per annum for dollars (there are a number of possible combinations). This arithmetic is demonstrated in Diagram 30e and Table 11.

Table 11: Cash flows through the currency swap

| | MDB | | | | USCo | | |
| | bond issue | currency swap | | | currency swap | | bond issue |
year	$	$	SwFr		$	SwFr	SwFr
0	+ 100	− 100	+ 150		+ 100	− 150	+ 150
1	− 4	+ 4	− 9		− 4	+ 9	− 10.5
2	− 4	+ 4	− 9		− 4	+ 9	− 10.5
3	− 4	+ 4	− 9		− 4	+ 9	− 10.5
4	− 4	+ 4	− 9		− 4	+ 9	− 10.5
5	− 4	+ 4	− 9		− 4	+ 9	− 10.5
	− 100	+ 100	− 150		− 100	+ 150	− 150
net	− 20	+ 20	− 45		− 20	+ 45	− 52.5

Diagram 30e: New issue arbitrage (complete transaction)

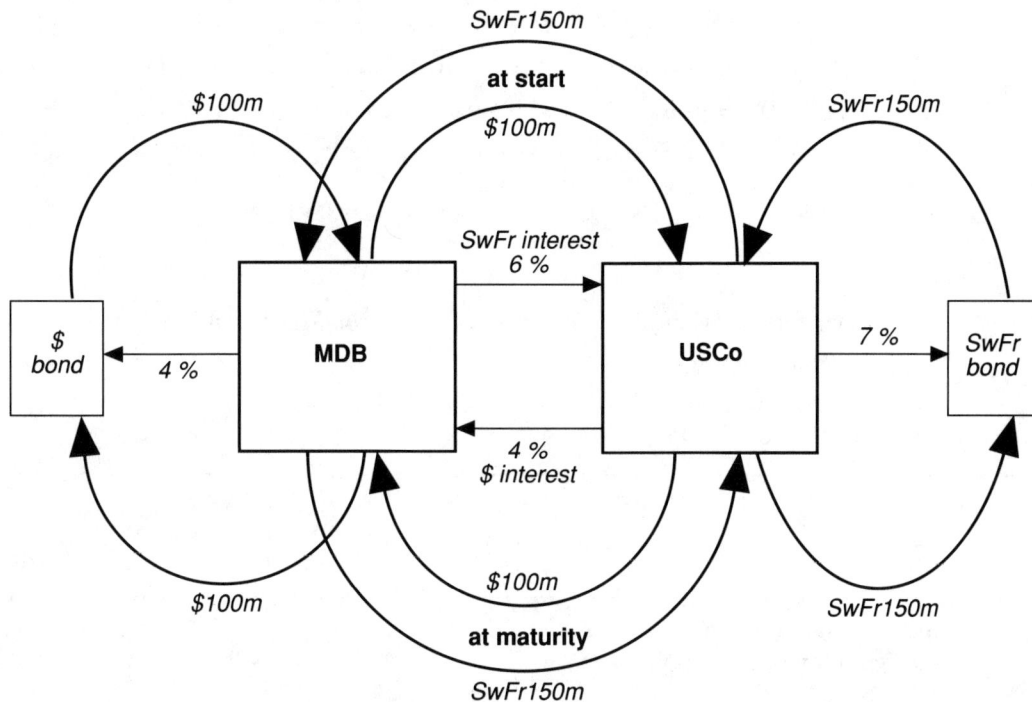

It can be seen from Diagram 30e and Table 11 that:

■ MDB will break-even in dollars, as it receives 4% per annum through the swap and pays 4% per annum on its bond, and so ends up paying a net cost of funds of 6% per annum in Swiss francs through the swap.

■ USCo will lose 100 basis points in Swiss francs between the 6% per annum received swap and 7% per annum paid on its bond, and so ends up paying a net cost of funds of 4% per annum in US dollars through the swap *plus* 100bp loss in Swiss francs.

In the case of USCo, the net cost of funds is not simply the sum of the 4% per annum paid in dollars and the 100bp loss in Swiss francs. The 100bp have to be converted from Swiss Francs to dollars using forward foreign exchange rates. A quick way of calculating the result is provided in the form of **basis conversion factors** between major currencies for standard maturities published and regularly updated on the *IFR Corporate Eye* service disseminated on *Telerate* pages 20221–20224. A page from this service setting out conversion factors for five-year funds is reproduced and explained in *Box 4*. The conversion factor from dollars to Swiss francs in the example is 1.086. The conversion factor from Swiss francs to dollars is therefore 0.921 (= 1/1.086). Thus, 92bp in dollars can be seen to be equivalent to 100bp in Swiss francs (= 0.921 x 100). USCo therefore ends up paying:

4.0% + 0.92% = 4.92% per annum in dollars

The calculation of the net cost of funds for MDB and USCo is summarised in Tables 12a and 12b.

Table 12a: Net cost of funds to MDB

	cash flows	$	$/SwFr conversion factor	SwFr
Payments	(a) fixed $ interest on bond	− 4.0%	—	—
	(b) fixed SwFr interest through swap	—	—	− 6.0%
Receipts	(c) fixed $ interest through swap	+ 4.0%	—	—
	(d) $ arbitrage profit (= a + c)	—	1.086	—
Net cost	fixed SwFr interest (= b + d)	—	—	− 6.0%

Table 12b: Net cost of funds to USCo

	cash flows	SwFr	SwFr/$ conversion factor	$
Payment	(a) fixed SwFr interest on bond	− 7.0%	—	—
	(b) fixed $ interest through swap	—	—	− 4.0%
Receipt	(c) fixed SwFr interest through swap	+ 6.0%	—	—
	(d) SwFr arbitrage profit (= a + c)	− 1.0%	0.921	− 0.92%
Net cost	fixed $ interest (= b + d)	− 1.0%	—	− 4.92%

Box 4: Basis conversion factors

As explained in the main text, a key difference between interest rate swaps and currency swaps is that an arbitrage involving a currency swap will generate profits/losses in one currency, while the swap will leave the arbitrageur paying or receiving another currency. For example, in the new issue arbitrage illustrated in the diagram below, counterparty A ends up paying 6.50% per annum in yen plus 25bp in dollars. Counterparty Z ends up paying US dollar Libor less 45bp in yen. The arbitrage profits/losses in one currency have to be converted into the other currency in the forward foreign exchange market. The net cost of swapped funds is not simply the sum of the dollar and yen rates, as one basis point in yen is not equivalent in value to one basis point in dollars.

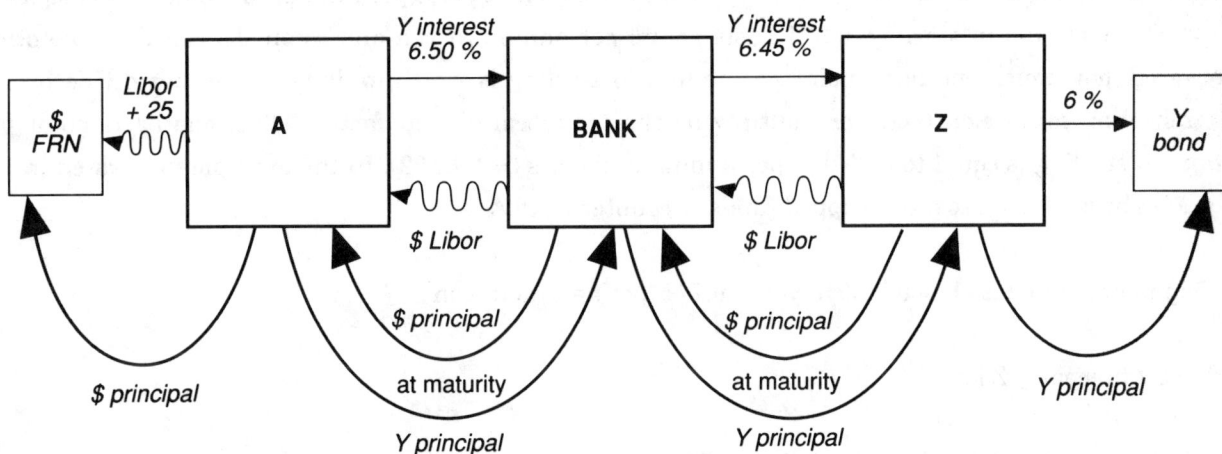

The outright forward rates needed to calculate the net cost of swapped funds are conveniently summarised in the form of **basis conversion factors** which are published and regularly updated on the *IFR Corporate Eye* service disseminated on *Telerate* screen pages 20221–20224. The number of basis points per annum profit/loss in one currency is simply multiplied by the appropriate conversion factor to give the equivalent number of basis points per annum in another currency. IFR publishes basis conversion factors between eight major currencies for standard maturities of 3, 5, 7 and 10 years. A page from this service, setting out conversion factors for five-year funds, is reproduced below.

```
15/01/93  16–16  GMT LAST UPDATE                                    P20222
[FIVE YEAR BASIS CONVERSION FACTORS]

            STG      YEN      DM      SFR      C$      ECU      A$
US$        1.102    0.971    1.007   1.086    1.066   1.059    1.109
           STG      0.850    0.922   0.855    0.933   0.927    0.971
                    YEN      1.084   1.006    1.098   1.090    1.142
                             DM      0.928    1.013   1.006    1.053
                                     SFR      1.091   1.084    1.135
                                              C$      0.994    1.040
                                                      ECU      1.047
                                                               A$
```

Using this page, it can be seen (from the top row) that one basis point per annum in US dollars is equal to 1.102bp per annum in sterling, 0.971 basis points per annum in yen and so on. To calculate the other way — eg, how much one basis point per annum in sterling is worth in dollars — either divide by the dollar/sterling conversion factor or multiply by the reciprocal of that factor. Thus, one basis point per annum in sterling is equal to 0.907bp per annum in dollars (= 1/1.102). In the example illustrated in the diagram above, the net cost of swapped funds to counterparty A is:

(− 25bp in dollars × 0.971) + 6.50% in yen = 6.74% per annum in yen

and to counterparty Z is:

(+ 45bp in yen × 1/0.971) + Libor in dollars = Libor less 46bp in dollars

To summarise, MDB has reduced the cost of its Swiss franc funding by 50bp from 6 1/2% on a direct bond issue to 6% per annum through the swap. USCo has reduced its cost of dollar funding by 33bp per annum from 5 1/4% on a direct bond issue to 4.92% per annum through the swap (beating its target). These gains can be seen as the result of MDB and USCo acting in concert. The two companies together saved 125bp by having MDB rather than USCo issue a dollar bond, but gave up 50bp by having USCo and not MDB issue a Swiss franc bond, producing a overall gain between them of approximately 75bp (this net figure is approximate because it is the sum of amounts in different currencies).

There are a number of points to note about new issue arbitrage:

■   The swap in this example is a true *currency swap* (fixed-against-fixed). Fixed-against-fixed currency swaps were used in the first new issue arbitrage transactions and they remain the most common instrument. The 1982 currency swap between the World Bank and IBM, which helped establish the market in currency swaps, was fixed-against-fixed.

■   Given the cost reductions which swap arbitrage can achieve, it is not surprising that swap opportunities are a crucial consideration in bond issuance. This is particularly true for major international borrowers such as the World Bank which need to diversify their sources of funding. Currency swaps allow borrowers to separate their *funding* decisions (liquidity management) from their *currency and interest risk* decisions (risk management). Thus, borrowers can fund in the large and efficient dollar market and then swap into their desired currency.

■   In the example above, it would be possible for the arbitrage to go ahead, even if MDB had no access to the Swiss franc bond market at all and/or USCo had no access to the dollar bond market (this is unlikely for borrowers of the calibre of MDB and USCo, but might be for other lesser names). After all, MDB does not have to enter the Swiss franc bond market: this is done by USCo. Equally, USCo does not have to enter the dollar bond market: this is done by MDB. All that is necessary is for MDB and USCo to have target figures in mind for their net cost of funds through the swap. Currency swaps are, therefore, not only a method of reducing funding cost, but also a means of gaining *access* to bond markets.

■ Currency swaps can also be used where access to a currency is incomplete, for example, where a borrowing would be too large to be accommodated in a small capital market such as that in Swiss francs. Funds can be raised in the dollar market in the size required and swapped into Swiss francs from counterparties which have previous issues outstanding in that currency.

■ In the example above, MDB issued dollar bonds and swapped into Swiss francs, while USCo issued Swiss franc bonds and swapped into dollars. In net terms, MDB ends up servicing Swiss franc debt and USCo ends up servicing dollar debt. However, MDB retains the dollar bonds it issued on its balance sheet and USCo retains its Swiss franc bonds on its balance sheet. The currency swap merely converts the cash flows on MDB's bonds from dollars into Swiss francs and the cash flows on USCo's bonds from Swiss francs into dollars. In effect, the swap creates **synthetic** bonds for MDB and USCo.

■ Because swaps allow one currency to be synthesised from another, they link the prices of bonds in different currencies. Unsatisfied demand for bonds in one currency, which might otherwise be reflected in higher prices, can be met by swapping from other currencies, thereby keeping prices in check. In other words, currency swaps encourage the *integration* of the international capital market.

■ In the example, MDB had an **absolute advantage** over USCo in that it could borrow both currencies more cheaply. However, it had more of an absolute advantage in dollars than in Swiss francs. The greater absolute advantage of MDB in dollars and the lesser absolute disadvantage of USCo in Swiss francs is described as MDB's **comparative advantage** in dollars and USCo's comparative advantage in Swiss francs. These comparative advantages mean that the reduction in the cost of borrowing achieved by having MDB borrow dollars for USCo was not entirely offset by the increase in the cost of borrowing entailed by having USCo borrow Swiss francs, so the swap as a whole offered net arbitrage profits.

■ Comparative advantage, as it operates in new issue arbitrage, was proposed by the early 19th century English political economist David Ricardo to explain international trade. Ricardo used a two-country two-good model of the world economy, in which one country was more efficient at producing both goods than the other (just as MDB in the example above can raise cheaper funds than USCo in both dollars and Swiss francs). Ricardo suggested that, if the 'efficient' country was not equally more efficient than the 'inefficient' country in producing both goods, it would be possible to realise an overall gain in welfare, if each country specialised in producing a different good and exchanged it for the other through trade. By specialising in its most efficient line of production, the efficient country should realise enough of a productivity gain to more than offset the loss of production through having the inefficient country produce the other good. The inefficient country minimises this loss by specialising in its *least inefficient* line of production (just as USCo borrowed in Swiss francs) and the efficient country maximises the offsetting gain by specialising in its *most efficient* line of production (just as MDB borrowed dollars). The efficient country is said to have an absolute advantage in the production of both goods, but a comparative advantage in the one it produces most efficiently, while the inefficient country has an absolute disadvantage in the production of both goods, but a comparative advantage in the one it produces least inefficiently. In the example above, MDB has a comparative advantage in dollar bonds and USCo has a comparative advantage in Swiss franc bonds.

■ New issue arbitrage against currency swaps is often undertaken in situations where each counterparty has an absolute advantage in one of the currencies being swapped, rather than just a comparative advantage. For example, MDB might be able to borrow dollars cheaper than USCo, but USCo might be able to borrow Swiss francs cheaper than MDB. This situation is not uncommon between different currency sectors of the international capital market (but does not occur within the same currency sector and is therefore not a source for new issue arbitrage against interest rate swaps).

Currency swaps

- In the early swap market, new issue arbitrages were arranged by investment banks acting as *agents* for swap counterparties. However, corporate counterparties have traditionally been reluctant to take on the credit risk of other non-banks and banks have for some time been required to participate in swaps as principal *intermediaries*. The structure of a new issue arbitrage swap is therefore slightly more complicated than in the example which has been demonstrated. One swap becomes two, one between the intermediary bank and each of the end-user counterparties. The intermediary bank acts like a swap dealer, charging for the credit and any other risks to which it is exposed, by taking a dealing spread between the interest streams it receives and the interest streams it pays. The structure of the new issue arbitrage swap demonstrated above would therefore probably be as illustrated in Diagram 31 below (assuming a 10bp spread to the intermediary bank taken in Swiss francs).

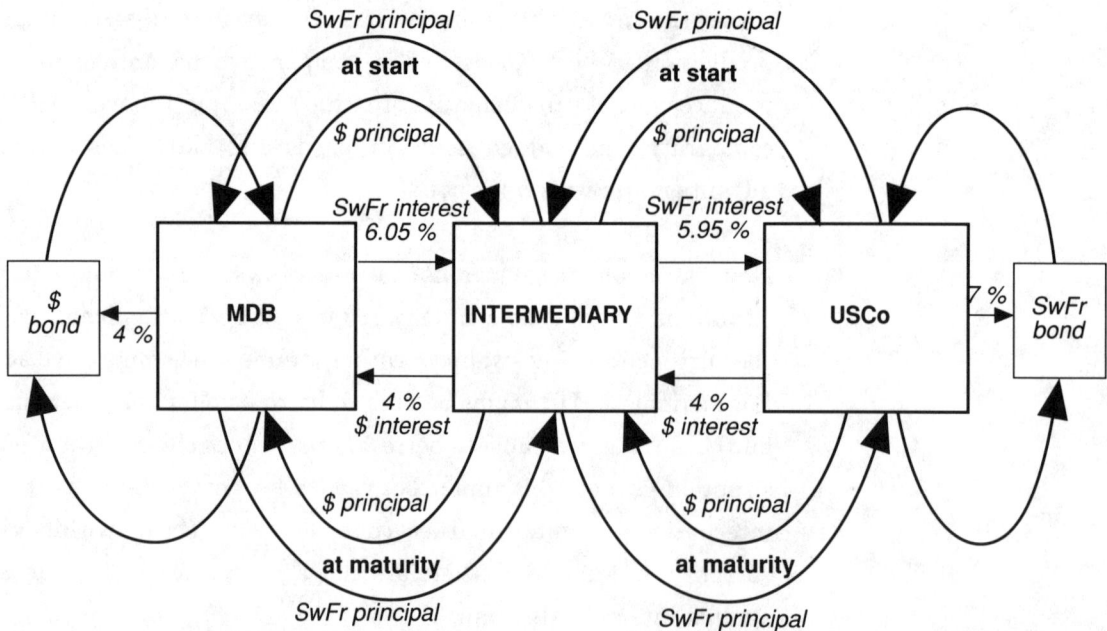

Diagram 31: New issue arbitrage with an intermediary

In the case of cross-currency coupon swaps (fixed-against-floating), the convention of using US dollar Libor as the standard interest rate for the floating side of the swap tends to produce the situation illustrated in Diagram 32, which leaves a residual exposure to currency risk for the end-users.

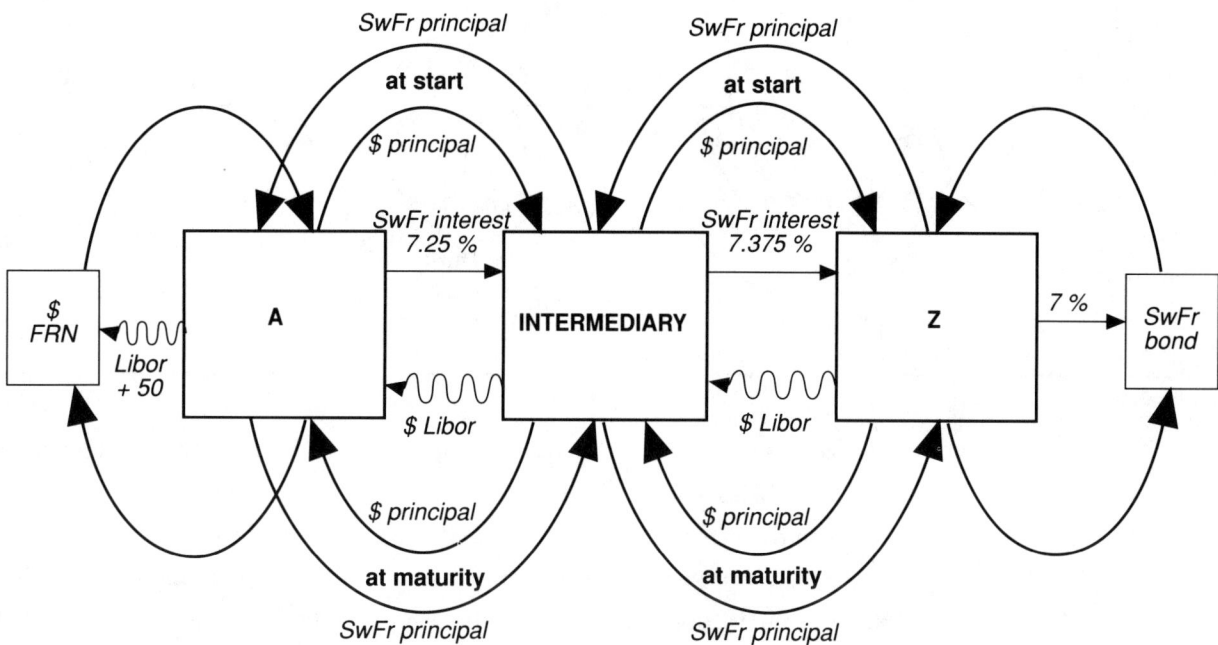

Diagram 32: Currency exposure in new issue arbitrage

It can be seen from the diagram that counterparty A receives dollar Libor through the swap, but pays out Libor + 1/2% on the FRN, thereby losing 50bp in dollars. Counterparty Z receives 7.375% per annum through the swap, but only pays 7% per annum on the bond, thereby earning 37.5bp in Swiss francs. This faces counterparty A with the problem of having to fund a deficit of 50bp in dollars and counterparty Z with converting 37.5bp in Swiss francs into dollars. Both counterparties will have to manage these cash flow problems in the forward foreign exchange market. In practice, however, it is usual for the intermediary bank to absorb these problems. This is done by restructuring the swap as illustrated in Diagram 33.

Diagram 33: Managing currency risk in new issue arbitrage

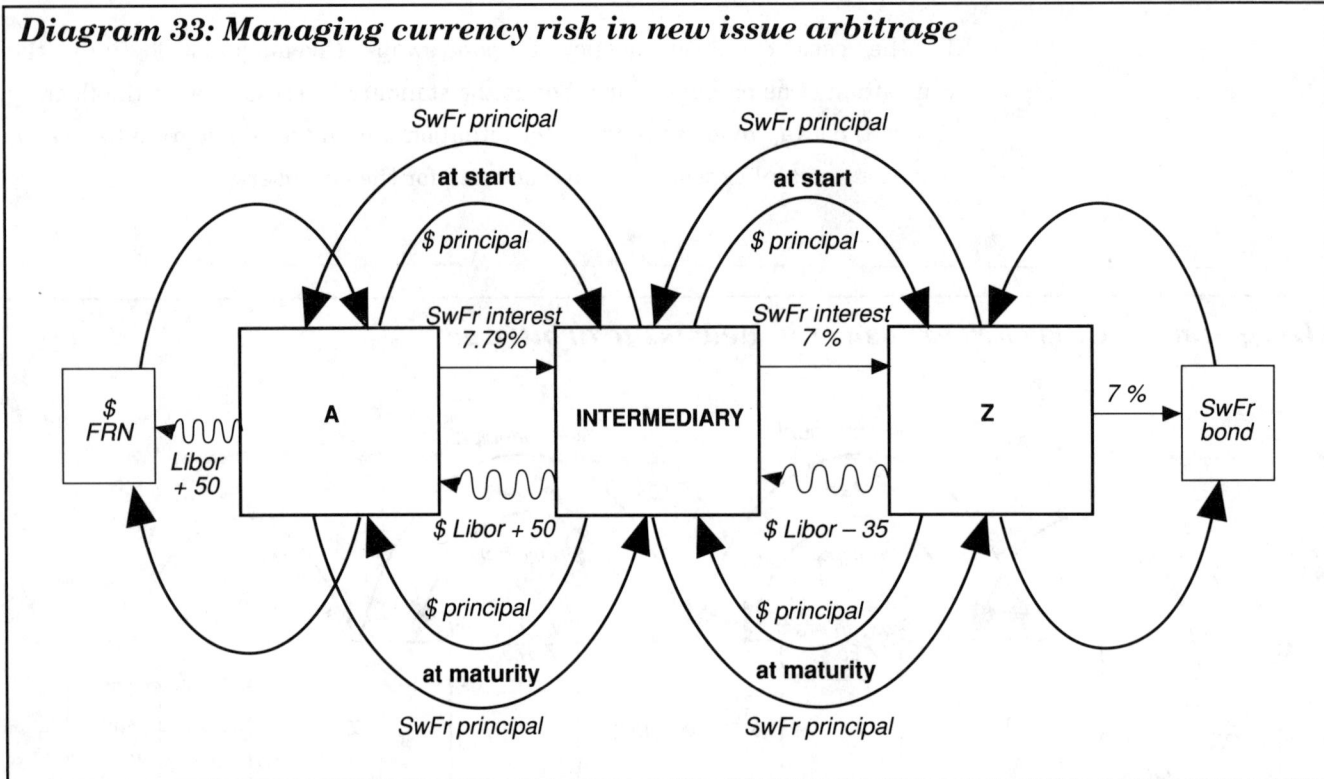

The restructured swap leaves the intermediary bank with the dollar deficit and the Swiss franc surplus. The bank will then handle the currency risk between the two cash flows. Note that the 50bp added to the Libor received by A through the swap will be compensated by an equivalent increase in the Swiss franc interest rate paid in the swap: using the basis conversion factors in Box 4, the equivalent is 54bp (= 50 x 1.086). The 37.5bp subtracted from the Swiss franc interest rate received by Z is compensated by an equivalent increase in dollar interest rate paid in the swap, which is about 35bp (= 37.5 x 0.921).

Arbitraging assets

Just as currency swaps can be used to arbitrage against cash liabilities and reduce the cost of funding, so it is also possible to use currency swaps to arbitrage cash assets and enhance the return on investments. There are a number of possible swaps. However, the most common are from fixed-interest assets in one currency into either fixed or floating-interest assets in another.

Diagram 34 illustrates a swap from fixed-interest Swiss francs into fixed-interest dollars using a currency swap (fixed-against-fixed). At the start, the investor pays a principal amount of dollars through the swap in exchange for Swiss francs, which are used to buy the Swiss franc bonds. The periodic Swiss franc interest received on the bond is then converted by the swap into dollars. At maturity, the principal amount of Swiss francs received when the bond is repaid are exchanged in the swap for dollars. The exchange rate used for the re-exchange is the one agreed at the start of the swap for the original exchange of principal amounts, thus avoiding any currency risk.

Diagram 34: Arbitrage with assets — using a currency swap to create a synthetic fixed-interest bond

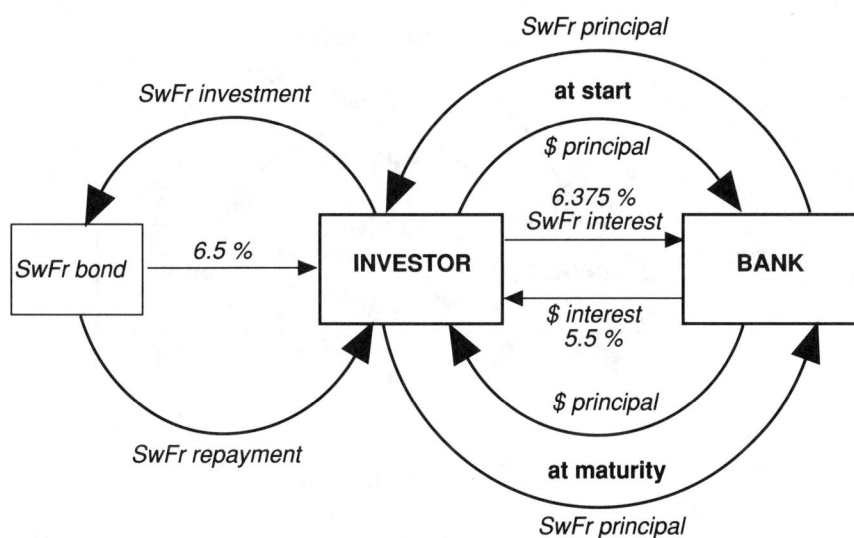

Receipts	fixed Swiss franc interest on asset	6.5%
	fixed dollar interest through swap	5.5%
Payments	fixed Swiss franc interest through swap	6.375%
Net receipts	fixed dollar interest	5.615%*

* Arbitrage gain is converted using basis conversion factors in Box 4.

A more common asset swap is from non-dollar fixed-interest bonds into floating-rate dollars. An example of such a *synthetic dollar FRN* is illustrated in Diagram 35. At the start, the investor pays a principal amount of dollars through the swap in exchange for Deutsche marks, which are used to buy the Deutsche mark bonds. The periodic Deutsche mark interest received on the bond is then converted by the swap into dollar interest. At maturity, the principal amount of Deutsche marks received when the bond is redeemed is exchanged through the swap for dollars. The exchange rate used for the re-exchange is the one agreed at the start of the swap for the original exchange of principal amounts, thus avoiding any currency risk.

Diagram 35: Arbitrage with assets — using a cross-currency coupon swap to create a synthetic dollar FRN

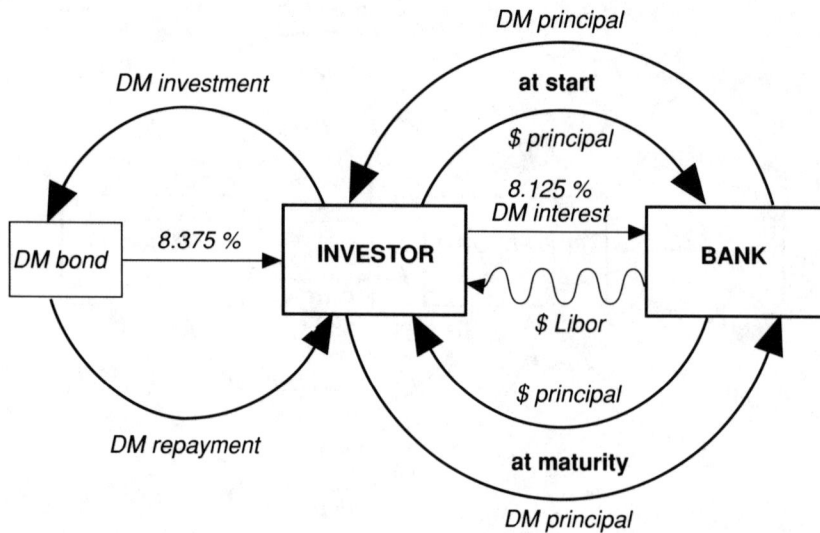

Receipts	fixed Deutsche mark interest on asset	8.375%
	floating dollar interest through swap	Libor
Payments	fixed Deutsche mark interest through swap	8.125%
Net receipts	floating dollar interest	Libor + 25bp*

* Arbitrage gain is converted using basis conversion factors in Box 4[1].

Asset swaps are described in greater detail in the *IFR Self-Study Workbook* on *Financial Engineering with Swaps*.

Arbitrage opportunities

The pricing discrepancies which provide cross-currency arbitrage opportunities occur for a variety of reasons, but all have the same effect in encouraging the *segmentation* of the international capital market into distinct currency sectors. As a result of this segmentation, the relative pricing of the same two issuers may differ between currency sectors, allowing arbitrage through currency swaps.

■ Segmentation limits the *lending capacity* of particular sectors and means that the supply of new issues by large and frequent borrowers can easily saturate demand. A classic example is provided by World Bank issuance in the Swiss franc bond market. Capacity constraints may encourage large issuers to swap into particular currencies rather than issue directly, in order to reduce their cost of funds or achieve the desired size of funding.

■ The segmentation of the international capital market is also apparent in the differences in the *risk premia* demanded by different currency sectors for lending to one borrower compared to another. For example, the extra margin demanded in the Eurobond and domestic European bond markets for BBB-rated borrowers compared to AAA-rated borrowers has tended to be much less than in the US domestic market. This is the source of the comparative advantage which has provided the classic opportunity for new issue arbitrage. The narrower range of risk premia demanded in some markets reflects a number of factors, including less discriminating credit analysis (which means that some lesser credits get lumped together with better credits), higher savings rates (which produce more abundant and cheaper capital) and lower absolute yield levels (the width of margins is in proportion to overall yields). Traditionally, narrower ranges of risk premia have been associated with the practice of *name recognition*, which is the subjective preference given to issuers with household names. Name recognition for many years allowed well-known companies like McDonalds to issue cheaper Eurobonds than minor sovereigns like Spain.

■ The segmentation of the international capital markets is most obvious where it is imposed in the form of *investment restrictions* such as exchange controls and prudential limits on investment portfolios.

■ The international capital market is also segmented by a range of subtle *market preferences*, such as an inclination to avoid the inconvenience of settlement or tax procedures in foreign markets, suspicion towards foreign borrowers and aversion to the currency risk in foreign bonds.

■ Price discrepancies are often generated by *tax* distortions. Where bonds issued in a domestic market are subject to withholding tax on the interest paid, investors may find it difficult or inconvenient to reclaim tax. Such bonds therefore tend to have to offer higher yields to investors in order to offset tax. This type of situation drove the new issue arbitrage which was common between fixed-interest Ecu and floating-interest dollars and is illustrated in Diagram 36. This arbitrage is between Certificati di Credito del Tesoro in Ecu (CTE) issued by the Republic of Italy and AAA-rated Ecu Eurobond issues. CTEs are subject to withholding tax and pay a higher extra yield to compensate, at times as much as 100bp over good-quality Ecu Eurobonds. Intermediary banks have been able to use this differential to offer Ecu Eurobond issuers a swap into cheap floating-interest dollars and investors an asset swap from CTEs into high-yielding dollar FRNs.

Diagram 36: Ecu/dollar new issue arbitrage

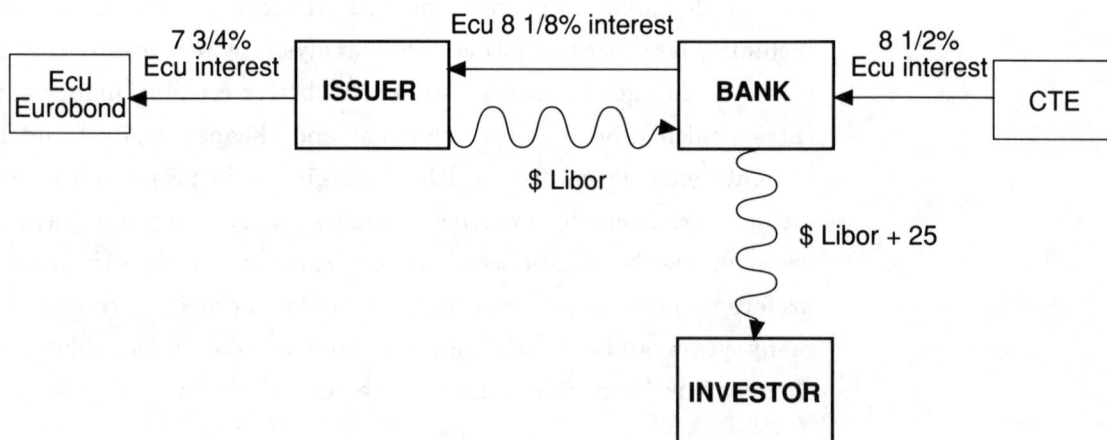

Return management with swaps: arbitrage with LTFX

In *Part One*, it was explained that currency swaps are functionally the same as long-term forward foreign exchange instruments (LTFX), in that they both create currency risk. This similarity means that one instrument can be used in arbitrage against the other.

In practice, because the exchange of principal amounts which is usually involved in currency swaps entails too much credit risk and also limits the liquidity of the instrument, currency swaps are not originated for the purpose of arbitrage against LTFX. Rather, such arbitrage tends to be in response to opportunities identified during the hedging by swap intermediaries of currency swaps which have been originated in order to swap assets or liabilities. For example, an intermediary may transact a currency swap with a customer as part of a new issue arbitrage. It could hedge that swap with a matching swap, or within a swap portfolio, or it may hedge it with a LTFX transaction. The intermediary may well decide to use LTFX as a hedge, where the two instruments are not quite exact offsets of each other and the price discrepancy offers an arbitrage profit.

If the currency swap being hedged is a zero-coupon currency swap (fixed-against-fixed), only a single LTFX transaction is necessary and the structure of the arbitrage is quite simple. As explained in *Part One*, this type of swap is structurally the same as LTFX, in that both instruments make only a single exchange of principal amounts at maturity. However, in practice, the most common type of currency swap is the cross-currency coupon swap (fixed-against-floating) involving dollar Libor. In this case, arbitrage would require:

■   the currency swap to be converted from fixed-against-floating to fixed-against-fixed[2]: this would be done by combining it with a dollar coupon swap;

■   a series of LTFX transactions, one against each exchange of interest through the currency swap.

An example

An intermediary has transacted a five-year $/DM cross-currency coupon swap with a notional principal amount of $100m, in which it pays 6.00% per annum in Deutsche mark fixed interest and receives six-month dollar Libor. In order to hedge this swap, the intermediary could undertake the following transactions:

■ a fixed-against-fixed $/DM swap would be constructed from the cross-currency coupon swap by transacting a five-year dollar coupon swap in which the intermediary receives fixed interest and pays Libor. If the coupon swap pays 6.00% against Libor, the combination is effectively a five-year fixed-against-fixed currency swap between Deutsche marks at 6.00% and dollars at 6.00%. The two Libor streams cancel out.

■ assuming an annual exchange of interest through the swap, the LTFX side of the arbitrage would consist of five outright forward transactions. Each outright forward would sell dollars received through the coupon swap for the Deutsche marks to be paid out through the currency swap. Any surplus dollars would be arbitrage profits.

The structure of the arbitrage is illustrated in Diagram 37 and the calculations are set out in Table 13.

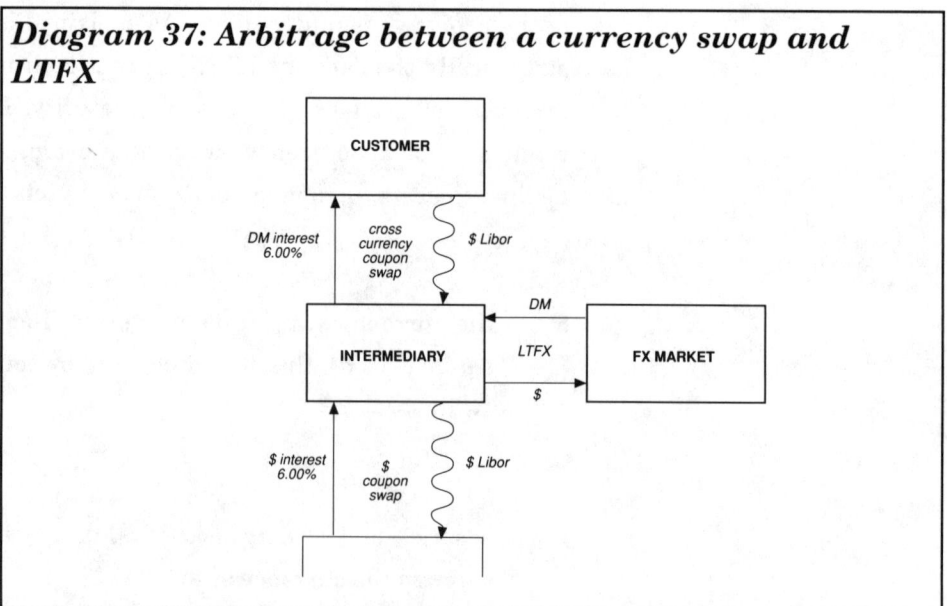

Diagram 37: Arbitrage between a currency swap and LTFX

Table 13: Cash flows in arbitrage between a currency swap and LTFX

year	currency swap		LTFX		
	$ cash flows	DM cash flows	$/DM rates	$ cash flows	net $ receipts
1	+ 6.00	− 9.00	1.5545	− 5.79	+ 0.21
2	+ 6.00	− 9.00	1.5827	− 5.69	+ 0.31
3	+ 6.00	− 9.00	1.5758	− 5.71	+ 0.29
4	+ 6.00	− 9.00	1.5420	− 5.84	+ 0.16
5	+ 6.00	− 9.00	1.5146	− 5.94	+ 0.06
	+ 100.00	− 150.00	1.5146	− 99.04	+ 0.96

The cross-currency coupon swap and dollar coupon swap used in the arbitrage in the above example constitute a *circus swap*, which is of course a type of *cocktail swap* (see *Part One*).

Notes

1. Assume that all interest rates are quoted on the same basis in terms of day count, annual basis and compounding conventions.

2. As explained in *Part One*, a zero-coupon swap has to be fixed-against-fixed because of the way it is priced. The single payments exchanged at maturity in a zero-coupon swap are calculated by compounding to maturity the interest payments which would have been exchanged through the comparable conventional swap. This is not possible, unless the size of the future interest payments are known in advance, which means both interest rates must be fixed.

Self Study Exercises: <u>Questions</u>   Part 2

Assume in all questions that all interest rates are quoted on the same basis in terms of day count, annual basis and compounding conventions.

Question 2.1:   A UK company with largely sterling revenues has issued a US dollar bond which has some years remaining to maturity. It now expects sterling to depreciate against the dollar and UK interest rates to fall over the period to maturity.

> ■   Design a swap transaction to take advantage of these expectations.

Question 2.2:   A US company with largely dollar revenues has issued a Swiss franc bond which has some years remaining to maturity. It now expects the Swiss franc to appreciate and US interest rates to rise over the period to maturity.

> ■   Design a swap transaction to take advantage of these expectations.

Question 2.3:   A Japanese investment institution holds US dollar bonds which have some years remaining to maturity. It now expects the dollar to depreciate against the yen and the yen to depreciate against the Deutsche mark over the period to maturity. In view of these expectations, the investor decides to shift its currency exposure from dollars into Deutsche mark. However, German interest rates are expected to rise sharply over the period to maturity.

> ■   Design a swap transaction to take advantage of these expectations.

Question 2.4:   A French company has issued a US dollar Eurobond which has some years remaining to maturity. It now expects the dollar to depreciate against the French franc and US interest rates to fall over the period to maturity.

> ■   Design a swap transaction to take advantage of these expectations.

Question 2.5: A UK company issues a US dollar bond to fund an investment in the US. It intends to service the debt from dollar earnings.

- If the £/$ exchange rate is expected to be very volatile over the life of the investment, what special type of currency risk will the UK company face?

- What instrument would be best suited to hedge this risk and why?

Question 2.6: A German company DemAG plans a programme of investment in the US. It wishes to borrow seven-year fixed-interest dollars to fund its investment, but has no established access to the US dollar bond market. On the other hand, it could probably borrow seven-year Deutsche mark at 8% per annum. Seven-year dollar/Deutsche mark currency swaps are quoted at 5.50–5.625% for fixed-interest dollars and 8.15–8.25% for fixed-interest Deutsche marks.

- Design a swap transaction to provide fixed-interest dollars to DemAG.

- What would be DemAG's net cost of dollars through the swap?

A seven-year basis conversion factor table is provided at the end of this section.

Question 2.7: Five-year Deutsche mark bonds are yielding 8.5% per annum and five-year dollar/Deutsche mark cross-currency coupon swaps are quoted at 8.125–8.25% for fixed-interest Deutsche marks against dollar Libor.

- What would be the net return on synthetic dollar floating-rate notes (FRN)?

A five-year basis conversion factor table is provided at the end of this section.

Question 2.8: A Swiss company, Chef, requires 10-year fixed-interest dollars, while a US company, AmInc, requires 10-year fixed-interest Swiss francs. They can borrow in the Swiss franc and US dollar bond markets at the costs set out in the table.

	Swiss franc bonds	US dollar bonds
Chef	6 3/8%	4 3/8%
AmInc	7 1/8%	4 1/2%

A currency swap is suggested. In order to undertake the swap:
— Chef wants to end up with dollars at 4 1/8% per annum;
— AmInc wants to end up with Swiss francs at 7% per annum;
— the intermediary bank wants to make a turn of 12.5 basis points per annum in dollars.

A 10-year basis conversion factor table is provided at the end of this section.

■ Can these targets be achieved with a swap?

■ If they can, describe the necessary swap.

■ What would be the swap rates, if the intermediary bank was to absorb any residual currency risk to which the counterparties might be left exposed by the swap?

Question 2.9: A UK company, BritCo, requires five-year floating-interest US dollars, while a US company, USInc, requires five-year fixed-interest sterling. They can borrow in the Eurosterling bond market and Eurodollar FRN market at the costs set out in the table.

	sterling bonds	US dollar FRN
BritCo	8 1/2%	Libor + 5/8%
USInc	9%pa	Libor + 1/8%

A currency swap is suggested. In order to undertake the swap:

— BritCo wants to end up with dollars at Libor + 1/8% per annum;

— USInc wants to end up with sterling at 8 3/4% per annum;

— the intermediary bank wants to make a turn of 10 basis points per annum in sterling.

A five-year basis conversion factor table is provided at the end of this section.

■ Can these targets be achieved with a swap?

■ If they can, describe the necessary swap.

■ What would be the swap rates, if the intermediary bank was to absorb any residual currency risk to which the counterparties might be left exposed by the swap?

Question 2.10: A US bank issued a seven-year Eurodollar bond two years ago. It now expects the dollar to appreciate against the Deutsche mark over the next five years and wishes to convert its liabilities from dollars to fixed-interest Deutsche marks. A German company, DemAG, requires five-year fixed-interest dollars, but has no access to the dollar bond market, although it can issue Deutsche mark bonds at fine rates.

■ Design a swap transaction to provide fixed-interest Deutsche mark to the US bank and fixed-interest dollars to DemAG. Assume there are no intermediaries in this transaction.

15/01/93 16–16 GMT LAST UPDATE   P20222
[FIVE YEAR BASIS CONVERSION FACTORS]

	STG	YEN	DM	SFR	C$	ECU	A$
US$	1.102	0.971	1.007	1.086	1.066	1.059	1.109
	STG	0.850	0.922	0.855	0.933	0.927	0.971
		YEN	1.084	1.006	1.098	1.090	1.142
			DM	0.928	1.013	1.006	1.053
				SFR	1.091	1.084	1.135
					C$	0.994	1.040
						ECU	1.047
							A$

15/01/93 16–16 GMT LAST UPDATE   P20223
[SEVEN YEAR BASIS CONVERSION FACTORS]

	STG	YEN	DM	SFR	C$	ECU	A$
US$	1.185	0.958	1.096	0.957	1.082	1.064	1.123
	STG	0.809	0.876	0.808	0.913	0.898	0.948
		YEN	1.083	0.999	1.129	1.110	1.172
			DM	0.922	1.042	1.025	1.082
				SFR	1.130	1.111	1.173
					C$	0.983	1.038
						ECU	1.056
							A$

5/03/93 17–31 GMT LAST UPDATE   P20224
[TEN YEAR BASIS CONVERSION FACTORS]

	STG	YEN	DM	SFR	C$	ECU	A$
US$	1.238	0.926	1.015	1.101	1.106	1.061	1.126
	STG	0.748	0.820	0.756	0.893	0.857	0.910
		YEN	1.095	1.010	1.194	1.145	1.216
			DM	0.922	1.090	1.045	1.110
				SFR	1.182	1.134	1.204
					C$	0.959	1.018
						ECU	1.062
							A$

Self Study Exercises: Answers   Part 2

Answer 2.1:   The UK company should transact a sterling/dollar *cross-currency coupon swap* (fixed-to-floating) in which:

- during the life of the swap, it pays sterling floating interest and receives dollar fixed interest;

- at maturity, it pays a principal amount of sterling in exchange for a principal amount of dollars: this will be at an exchange rate agreed at the start of the swap (probably, but not necessarily, the prevailing spot rate at the start of the swap).

The swap is illustrated in the diagram below:

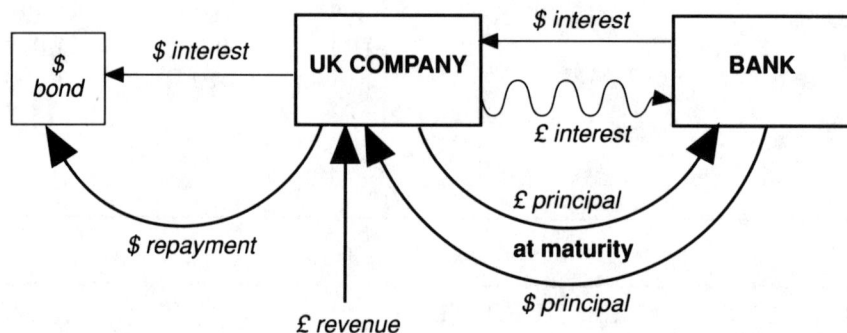

It can be seen from the diagram that after the swap:

- if UK interest rates fall as expected, the company will pay decreasing amounts of sterling interest through the swap;

- if sterling depreciates against the dollar as expected, the company will be protected against the consequent increase in the sterling cost of its dollar bond, because the exchange of principal amounts through the swap at maturity will provide it with the dollars needed to repay the bond at an exchange rate against sterling fixed at the start of the swap.

As the company has already disposed of the proceeds of its dollar bond, there is no initial exchange of principal amounts. The sterling principal exchanged for dollars at the maturity of the swap will be funded from accumulated sterling revenues.

Answer 2.2

The US company should transact a dollar/Swiss franc *currency swap* (fixed-to-fixed) in which:

■ during the life of the swap, it pays dollar fixed interest and receives Swiss franc fixed interest;

■ at maturity, it pays a principal amount of dollars in exchange for a principal amount of Swiss franc: this will be at an exchange rate agreed at the start of the swap (probably, but not necessarily, the prevailing spot rate at the start of the swap).

The swap is illustrated in the diagram below:

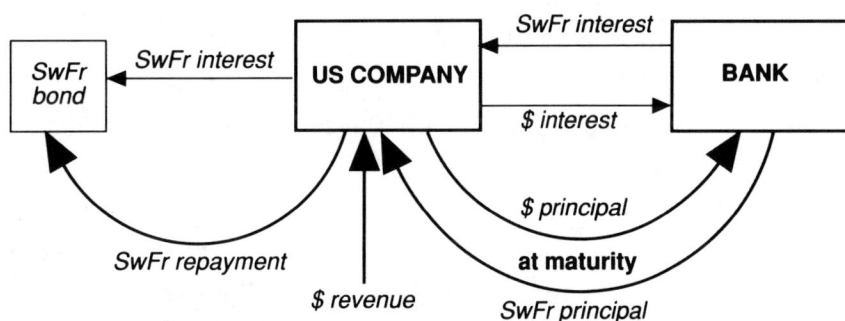

It can be seen from the diagram that:

■ if US interest rates rise as expected, the company will be protected, as its dollar interest payments through the swap are at a fixed interest rate;

■ if the Swiss franc appreciates against the dollar as expected, the company will be protected against the consequent increase in the dollar cost of its Swiss franc bond, because the exchange of principal amounts through the swap at maturity will provide it with the Swiss franc needed to repay the bond at an exchange rate against dollars fixed at the start of the swap.

As the company has already disposed of the proceeds of its Swiss franc bond, there is no initial exchange of principal amounts. The dollar principal exchanged for Swiss francs at the maturity of the swap will be funded from accumulated dollar revenues.

Answer 2.3   The Japanese investor should transact a dollar/Deutsche mark *cross-currency coupon swap* (fixed-to-floating) in which:

■ during the life of the swap, it receives Deutsche mark floating interest and pays dollar fixed interest;

■ at maturity, it receives a principal amount of Deutsche mark in exchange for a principal amount of dollars: this will be at an exchange rate agreed at the start of the swap (probably, but not necessarily, the prevailing spot rate at the start of the swap).

The swap is illustrated in the diagram below:

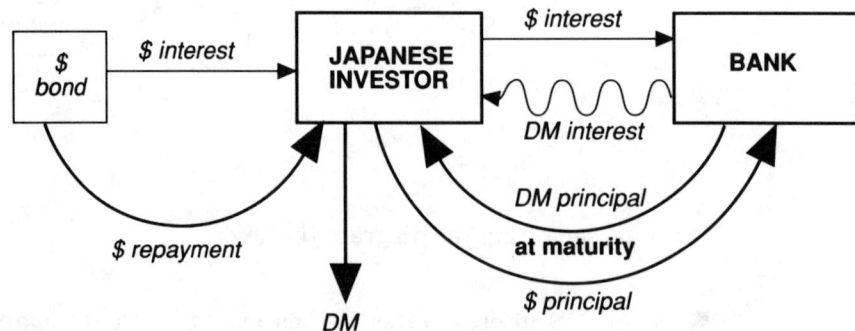

It can be seen from the diagram that:

■ if German interest rates rise as expected, the investor will receive increasing Deutsche mark interest;

■ if the dollar depreciates against the yen and the yen depreciates against the Deutsche mark as expected, the investor will be protected against the consequent decrease in the yen value of its dollar bond, because the exchange through the swap of principal amounts at maturity will provide it with a Deutsche mark repayment at an exchange rate fixed at the start of the swap.

As the investor has already disposed of its investment funds, there is no initial exchange of principal amounts. The dollar principal exchanged through the swap for Deutsche marks at maturity will be funded from the repayment of the maturing dollar bond. The Deutsche mark principal received in exchange might be sold for yen or re-invested in new Deutsche mark instruments.

Answer 2.4: The French company should transact a dollar *coupon swap* (fixed-to-floating) in which it pays dollar floating interest and receives dollar fixed interest. It should not transact a currency swap, as the expected depreciation of the dollar against the French franc will reduce the franc cost of repaying the dollar bond.

Answer 2.5: ■ As the accounts of the UK company are in sterling, its dollar liabilities have to be translated into sterling terms for reporting purposes. Fluctuations in the sterling/dollar exchange rate therefore produce unexpected changes in the balance sheet and profit and loss account of the company, despite the fact that there will be no exchange of principal until maturity. These changes are purely the result of exchange rate fluctuations on the translation of dollar amount of the bond into sterling terms. This uncertainty is therefore called **translation exposure.**

Currency swaps

■ Conventional instruments such as LTFX lack the liquidity to efficiently hedge longer-term foreign currency liabilities and have irregular cash flow structures which complicate the hedging of capital market instruments. In contrast, currency swaps:

— are available for the necessary longer-term periods;
— involve continuous streams of interest, which makes them particularly convenient for hedging the translation exposure on a bond.

Answer 2.6: ■ In the circumstances, DemAG could:

— issue a seven-year Deutsche mark bond at 8% per annum;
— transact dollar/Deutsche mark *currency swap* (fixed-for-fixed) in which:

  - at the start of the swap, the proceeds of the Deutsche mark bond issue are exchanged for dollars at an agreed exchange rate (probably, but not necessarily, the prevailing spot rate at the start of the swap);
  - during the life of the swap, it pays dollar fixed interest and receives Deutsche mark fixed interest;
  - at maturity, it pays a principal amount of dollars in exchange for a principal amount of Deutsche mark: this will be at an exchange rate agreed at the start of the swap;
  - the Deutsche mark principal received at maturity through the swap are used to repay the Deutsche mark bond.

DemAG will pay 5.625% per annum in dollar interest through the swap and receive 8.15% per annum in Deutsche marks. Remember the quote of 5.5–5.625% in dollars and 8.15–8.25% in Deutsche marks means the quoting intermediary expects either:

— to pay 5.5% in dollars and receive 8.25% in Deutsche marks;
— to receive 5.625% in dollars and pay 8.15% in Deutsche marks.

This principle is illustrated in the diagram below, which sets out the transaction:

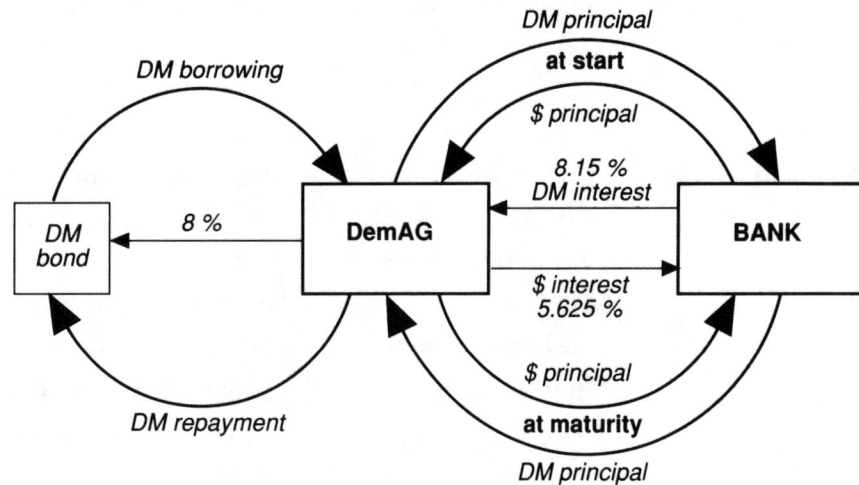

- The net cost of swapped funds to DemAG will be 5.625% per annum in dollars less 15bp arbitrage gain in Deutsche marks. Using the table of basis conversion factors for seven-year funds, it can be seen that 15bp per annum in Deutsche marks is equal to 14bp per annum in dollars (= 15/1.096). The net cost of swapped funds is therefore 5.49% per annum in dollars (= 5.625 – 14).

Answer 2.7: A synthetic dollar FRN produced from a fixed-interest Deutsche mark bond yielding 8.5% per annum and a dollar/Deutsche mark cross-currency coupon swap quoted at 8.15–8.25% for fixed-interest Deutsche marks against dollar Libor is illustrated in the diagram.

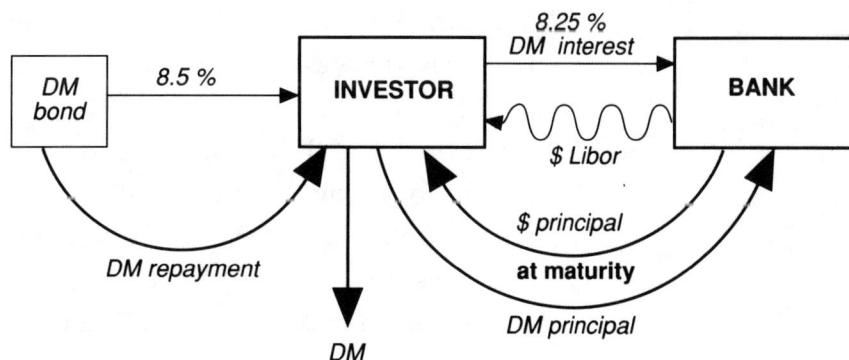

The net return on the synthetic FRN will be dollar Libor plus 25 basis points in Deutsche marks. Using the table of conversion factors for five-year funds, it can be seen that 25 basis points per annum in Deutsche marks is equal to 23 basis points per annum in dollars (= 25/1.007). The net return is therefore Libor plus 23 basis points per annum in dollars.

Answer 2.8:

■ What is noticeable about the relative funding costs of the two borrowers is that Chef can fund itself more cheaply than AmInc by 75 basis points in 10-year Swiss francs, but by only 12.5 basis points in 10-year dollars. Chef therefore has a comparative advantage in Swiss francs and AmInc in dollars which creates an overall arbitrage opportunity of about 62.5 basis points (the figure is not exact, as the basis points are in different currencies together). The arbitrage opportunity is just enough to satisfy the demands of the various parties to the swap: Chef wants to reduce its cost of dollars by 25 basis points (from 4 3/8% to 4 1/8%), AmInc wants to reduce its cost of Swiss francs by at least 12.5 basis points (from 7 1/8% to 7%) and the intermediary wants a turn of 12.5 basis points in dollars. Therefore, the swap is probably feasible.

■ To realise this arbitrage, the following steps are required:

Step 1 Chef borrows fixed-rate Swiss francs by issuing a 10-year bond at 6 3/8% per annum and AmInc borrows fixed-rate dollars by issuing a 10-year bond at 4 1/2% per annum.

Step 2 Chef and AmInc then swap for 10 years the principal amounts they have borrowed at a negotiated exchange rate (probably, but not necessarily, the prevailing spot exchange rate).

Step 3 During the life of the swap, Chef and AmInc swap interest with each other (through the intermediary). Chef would receive Swiss franc interest from USInc which it would use to service the interest obligations on its Swiss franc bond. In exchange, AmInc would receive dollar interest from Chef which it would use to service the interest obligations on its dollar bond. The swap would leave Chef paying fixed dollar interest to AmInc and AmInc paying fixed Swiss franc interest to Chef.

Step 4   At maturity, Chef and AmInc would reverse the initial **exchange of** principal amounts. This re-exchange would be at the **exchange rate** agreed for the original exchange of principal. Thus, Chef would **repay** dollars to AmInc and AmInc would repay Swiss francs to Chef (through the intermediary). The two counterparties would use these amounts to repay their bonds.

Step 5   The dollar and Swiss franc interest rates exchanged through the currency swap are negotiated between Chef and AmInc. Given the targets for the cost of funds, the interest rates paid through the swap would probably be 6 3/8% per annum for Swiss francs and for dollars, 4 1/8% to and 4% from the intermediary (giving the intermediary a turn of 1/8%). The transaction is illustrated in the diagram.

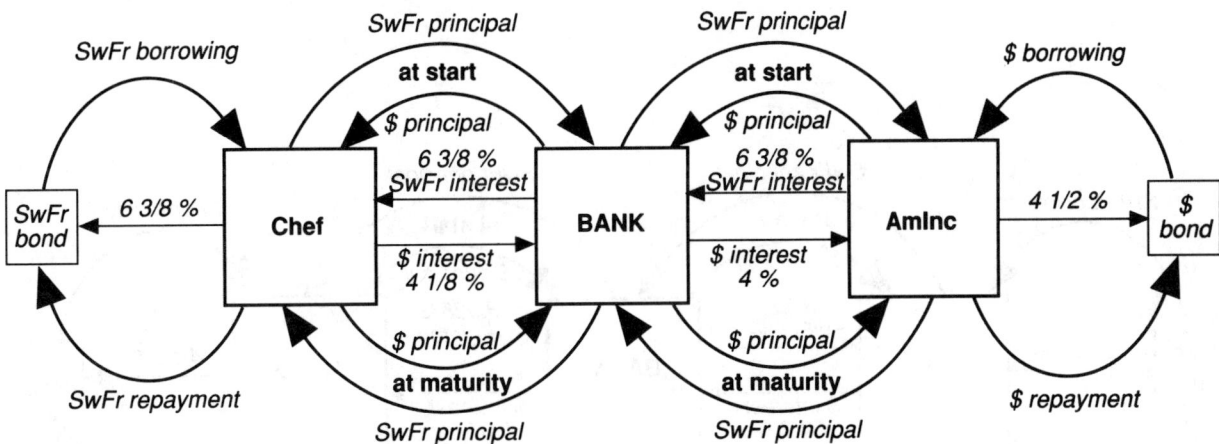

It can be seen that:

— Chef breaks even in Swiss francs, as it receives 6 3/8% per annum through the swap and pays 6 3/8% per annum on its bond, and so ends up paying a net cost of funds of 4 1/8% per annum in dollars through the swap.

— AmInc loses 50 basis points in dollars between the 4% received through the swap and 4 1/2% paid on its bond, and so ends up paying a net cost of funds of 6 3/8% per annum in Swiss francs through the swap plus 50 basis points in dollars. The net cost of funds to AmInc is not simply the sum of the 6 3/8% and 50 basis points. From the table of conversion factors, it can be seen that 50 basis points in dollars is equal to 55 basis points in Swiss francs (= 50 x 1.101). AmInc therefore ends up paying 6.925% in Swiss francs (= 6 3/8% + 55), which is within target.

■ From the diagram, it can be seen that, despite the swap, AmInc is exposed to residual currency risk in the form of the 50 basis points in dollars it loses between the 4% received through the swap and 4 1/2% paid on its bond. This dollar shortfall must be funded in Swiss francs (as AmInc wants to swap into Swiss francs) and so creates currency risk for AmInc. The intermediary bank could absorb the risk for USInc by restructuring the swap in the following way:

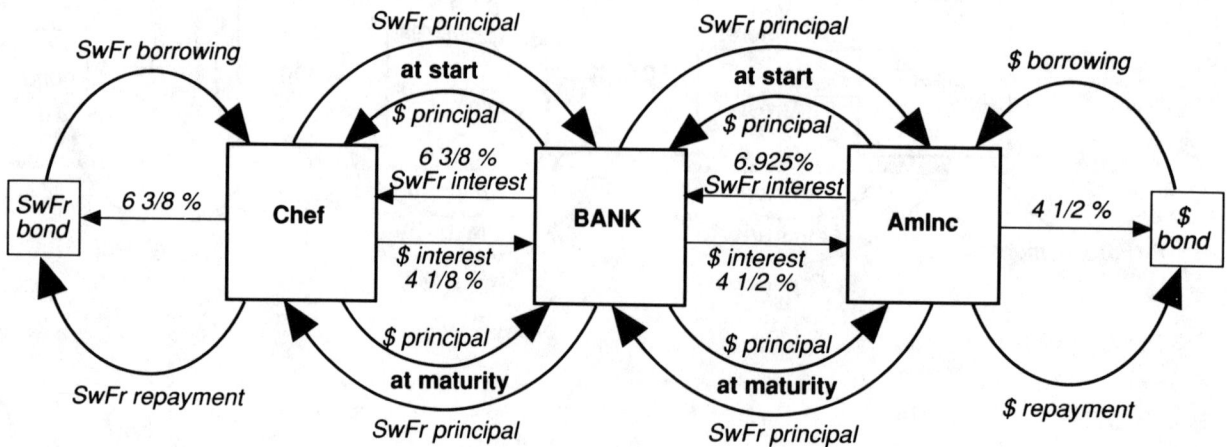

Answer 2.9: ■ What is noticeable about the relative funding costs of the two borrowers is that BritCo can fund itself more cheaply than USInc by 50 basis points in five-year sterling, but USInc can fund itself more cheaply than BritCo by the same amount in five-year dollars. Both borrowers have an absolute advantage in borrowing, although in different currencies. This indicates an overall arbitrage opportunity of about 100 basis points (the figure is not exact, as the basis points is in different currencies together). The arbitrage opportunity is just about enough to satisfy the demands of the various parties to the swap: BritCo wants to reduce its cost of dollars by 50 basis points (from Libor + 5/8% to Libor + 1/8%), USInc wants to reduce its cost of sterling by 25 basis points (from 9% to 8 3/4%) and the intermediary wants a turn of 10 basis points in sterling. Therefore, the swap is probably feasible.

■ To realise this arbitrage, the following steps are required:

Step 1 BritCo borrows fixed-rate sterling by issuing a five-year bond at 8 1/2% per annum and USInc borrows floating-interest dollars at Libor + 1/8% per annum.

Step 2 BritCo and USInc then swap for 5 years the principal amounts they have borrowed at a negotiated exchange rate (probably, but not necessarily, the prevailing spot exchange rate).

Step 3 During the life of the swap, BritCo and USInc swap interest with each other (through the intermediary). BritCo would receive sterling interest from USInc which it would use to service the interest obligations on its sterling bond. In exchange, USInc would receive dollar interest from BritCo which it would use to service the interest obligations on its dollar borrowing. The swap would leave USInc paying fixed sterling interest to BritCo and BritCo paying floating dollar interest to USInc.

Step 4 At maturity, BritCo and USInc would reverse the initial exchange of principal amounts. This re-exchange would be at the exchange rate agreed for the original exchange of principal. Thus, BritCo would repay dollars to USInc and USInc would repay sterling to BritCo (through the intermediary). The two counterparties would use these amounts to repay their borrowings.

Step 5 In a cross-currency coupon swap against floating-interest dollars, the market convention is to use dollar Libor. The sterling interest rate exchanged through the currency swap is negotiated between BritCo and USInc. Given the targets for the cost of funds, the interest rates paid through the swap would probably be 8.60% per annum for sterling to the intermediary and 8 1/2% from the intermediary (giving the intermediary a turn of 10 basis points). The transaction is illustrated in the diagram.

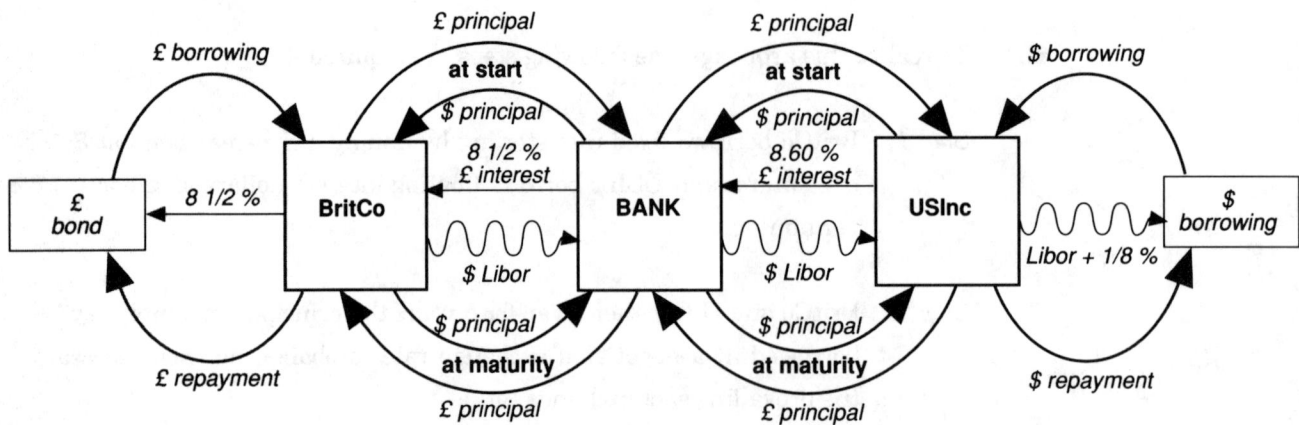

It can be seen that:

— BritCo breaks even in sterling, as it receives 8 1/2% per annum through the swap and pays 8 1/2% per annum on its bond, and so ends up paying a net cost of funds of dollar Libor through the swap.

— USInc loses 12.5 basis points in dollars between the Libor received through the swap and Libor + 1/8% paid on its borrowing, and so ends up paying a net cost of funds of 8.60% per annum in sterling through the swap plus 12.5 basis points in dollars. The net cost of funds to USInc is not simply the sum of 8.60% and 12.5 basis points. From the table of conversion factors, it can be seen that 12.5 basis points in dollars is equal to 14 basis points in sterling (= 12.5 x 1.102). USInc therefore ends up paying 8.74% in dollars (= 8.60% + 0.14%), just within its target.

■ From the diagram, it can be seen that, despite the swap, USInc is exposed to residual currency risk in the form of the 12.5 basis points in dollars it loses between the Libor received through the swap and Libor + 1/8% paid on its borrowing. This dollar shortfall must be funded in sterling (as USInc wants to swap into sterling) and so creates currency risk for USInc. The intermediary bank could absorb the risk for USInc by restructuring the swap in the following way:

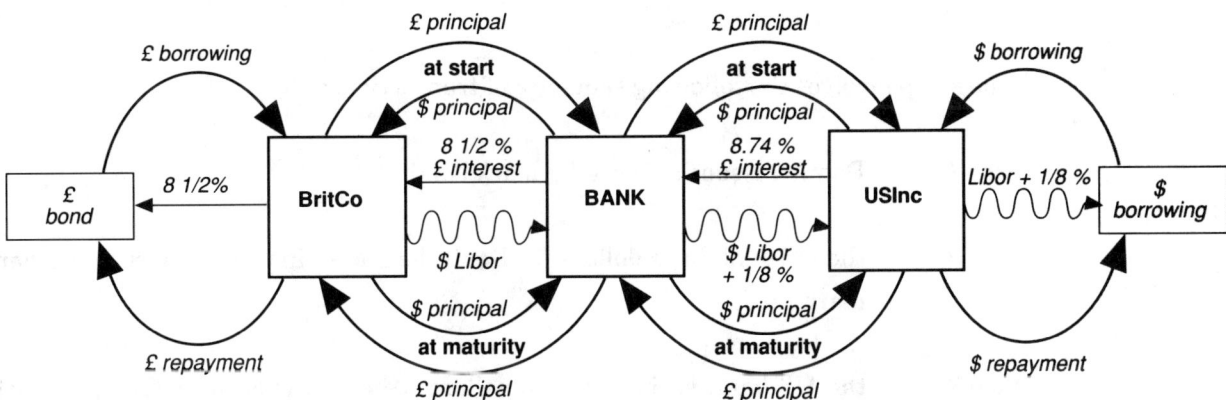

Answer 2.10: The US bank does not need to acquire Deutsche marks through the currency swap, which means that there does not have to be an initial exchange of principal amounts. But DemAG does need to acquire dollars, which means there should be an initial exchange of principal amounts. This problem is resolved by means of the swap structure illustrated in the diagram:

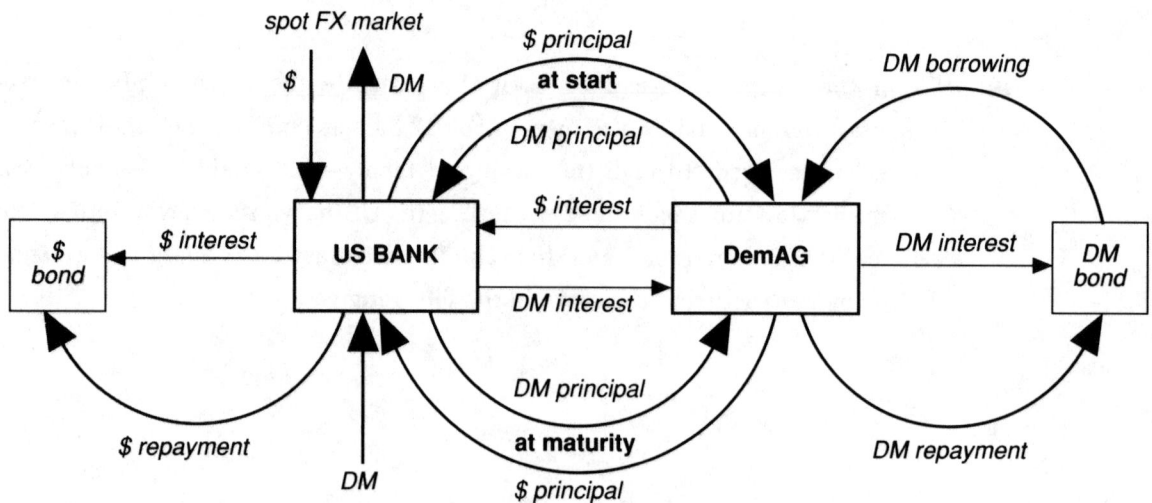

The swap involves the following sequence of transactions:

Step 1   DemAG issues a Deutsche mark bond;

Step 2   the US bank buys dollars for Deutsche marks in the spot foreign exchange market;

Step 3   the US bank exchanges the dollars it has purchased in the spot market through the swap with DemAG for Deutsche marks at the spot exchange rate: the US bank uses the Deutsche marks received through the swap to fund the spot purchase of dollars;

Step 4   DemAG uses the Deutsche mark proceeds of its bond issue to fund the exchange of principal amounts through the swap;

Step 5   during the life of the swap, the US bank pays Deutsche mark fixed interest to DemAG and receives dollar fixed interest in exchange: these payments are used by the counterparties to service the interest obligations on their bond issues;

Step 6   at maturity, the US bank pays a principal amount of Deutsche marks to DemAG through the swap in exchange for a principal amount of dollars: the exchange will be at the spot exchange rate prevailing at the start of the swap, while the Deutsche mark exchanged by the US bank will be produced from the assets purchased with the proceeds of the dollar bond, or Deutsche mark earnings, or dollar earnings converted into Deutsche marks;

Step 7   the US bank will use the principal amount of dollars it receives through the swap at maturity to repay its dollar bond and DemAG will use the principal amount of Deutsche marks it receives through the swap at maturity to repay its bond.

3 Trading currency swaps

Dealing procedures

Dealing technology

The market in currency swaps, like that in interest rate swaps, is an *over-the-counter (OTC)* market. Trading is conducted principally by telephone. Price information is disseminated over screen-based telecommunication networks operated by companies such as *Reuters* and *Telerate*. As for interest rate swaps, the displayed prices for currency swaps are purely indicative. However, screens for currency swaps are much less common, reflecting the relative illiquidity of that market. Financial information companies such as *IFR* and *Thomson Financial Services* contribute data and analysis to screen-based telecommunications networks. Brokers provide price, other market information and transactions advice directly to their customers.

Deal details

In negotiating a swap, key financial details are agreed verbally between dealers. The list of these details is quite long and becomes even longer for non-generic currency swaps. After a deal has been agreed verbally, key details are confirmed by an exchange of telexes or faxes, usually within 24 hours. Full contract documentation is agreed, signed and exchanged subsequently: thus, swaps are sometimes said to be dealt on an **as of** basis. However, in the UK, a contract is generally assumed to exist on the basis of the initial verbal agreement between dealers, rather than the telex or fax confirmations, or the contract documentation (this assumption may have legal weaknesses and may not be applicable at all outside the UK).

Swap documentation

Coverage of swap documentation

A contract is *evidence* of the agreement of the counterparties to a specific transaction and provides a detailed *definition* of the transaction itself in respect of:

■ *financial* terms and conditions of the transaction, meaning the rights which can be exercised and the obligations which must be performed by the counterparties: in other words, the details of the deal;

■ *legal* framework for the contract, meaning rights in law of *enforcement* of the agreed financial terms and conditions, in the event of problems such as default by a counterparty: this covers matters such as the definition of an *event of default*, methods of computing damages, governing law and so forth.

Moves to standardise documentation

Early swap trading was hampered by the complexity of documentation, which reflected the novelty of the instrument and the consequent need to provide adequate financial and legal definitions. One major issue was whether swaps were gaming contracts, as the latter are legally unenforceable or void. The need to establish **swaps** as genuine instruments of commerce was particularly important in the early days of swaps, when there was a lack of legal precedent, and little custom and usage which the markets could offer to the courts as evidence. Contracts therefore contained extensive legal opinion in support of the commercial nature of swaps. As a result, even on fairly straightforward transactions, contracts could extend to 60 pages and take over three months to finalise. They were therefore expensive. Serious backlogs in documentation developed in the swaps market by 1984. Other resulting problems were that:

■ the *liquidity* of the market was constrained;

■ documentation added to *transactions costs*, which could not be sustained with dealing spreads under competitive pressure;

■ swaps usually commence before they are documented, so that subsequent failures to agree documentation mean *unexpected loss of protection* or of *profit,* as hedges, risk positions or arbitrage positions which are assumed to be in place suddenly collapse;

■ lack of uniformity between contracts obstructed the *netting* of payments due through different swaps, preventing swap intermediaries from making more efficient use of their credit lines;

■ lack of uniformity between contracts, and the consequent lack of transparency, obscured the overall *risk exposure* of swap counterparties and made it difficult to manage swaps within portfolios;

■ lack of uniformity between contracts, and the consequent lack of transparency, obstructed attempts to trade existing swaps and develop a *secondary market.*

In order to overcome these problems, active swap counterparties have tried to standardise documentation: initially, on a *bilateral* basis with other active counterparties; and then, through *multilateral* efforts sponsored by market associations.

Bilateral documentation   Intermediaries in the swap market gradually installed **master contracts** with other active counterparties which permitted negotiations for most swaps to be limited to key details, with other terms and conditions agreed simply by reference to the master contract. Most master contracts covered interest rate swaps, but a few covered currency swaps. Contracts were often differentiated by type of counterparty, for example, into bank-bank and bank-corporate categories, as well as in terms of whether the counterparty was domestic or foreign.

Multilateral documentation

Bilateral master contracts helped but did not solve the delays in swap documentation, prompting various efforts to produce a market-wide standard for documentation which could be used by a wide range of counterparties for a wide range of swaps. The two principal initiatives originated from:

■ British Bankers' Association (BBA);

■ International Swap Dealers' Association (ISDA).

BBA documentation

In August 1985, the British Bankers' Association (BBA) promulgated its *Recommended Terms and Conditions for London Interbank Interest Rate Swaps (BBAIRS Terms)*. These allowed the negotiation of swaps to be limited to agreement on key details, with reference to BBAIRS Terms covering other terms and conditions. BBAIRS Terms were intended to apply to swaps of less than two years' maturity, traded interbank in London and involving US dollars, sterling, Deutsche marks, Swiss francs or yen in:

■ single-currency coupon swaps;

■ currency swaps (fixed-against-fixed);

■ cross-currency coupon swaps (fixed-against-floating);

■ cross-currency basis swaps (floating-against-floating).

The Terms provide definitions of financial terms and conditions, sample confirmations and provisions setting out rights of enforcement in the event of a default. A sample BBAIRS confirmation for a currency swap is reproduced in *Box 5*. In addition to documentation, BBAIRS Terms also provide conventions for conducting deal negotiations. The aim was to establish 'normal market practice' for London and the convention was that, from 2 September 1985, unless otherwise stated, short-term swaps dealt in London were to be assumed to be subject to BBAIRS Terms.

Box 5: BBAIRS Term — example of a confirmation between currency swap counterparties

CURRENCY A PAYER BANK PLC

Main Street

LONDON EC2

To: Currency B Payer Bank Inc   Date: 12th October 1984
        London Branch   Ref: XYZ002
        Moorgate
        LONDON EC2

CONFIRMATION OF A CROSS-CURRENCY INTEREST RATE SWAP AGREEMENT

We hereby confirm particulars in respect of the following Cross Currency Interest Rate Swap Agreement entered into between us subject to the British Bankers' Association's Recommended Terms and Conditions ("BBAIRS terms") dated August 1985.

Contract Date:	12th October 1984
Currency A:	Dollars
Currency B:	Swiss Francs
Currency A Payer:	Currency A Payer Bank Plc
Currency B Payer:	Currency B Payer Bank Inc
Direct/Broker:	Broker
Commencement Date:	18th October 1984
Maturity Date:	18th October 1986
Currency A Amount:	US$9,797,775.00
Currency B Amount:	SwFr25,000,000.00
Foreign Exchange Rate Reference:	N/A
Initial Exchange:	Yes
Currency A Rate:	6 months BBAIRS Settlement Rate
Currency A Payment:	N/A
Currency A Payment Dates	18/4/85 — 18/10/85 — 18/4/86 — 18/10/86
Currency B Rate:	N/A
Currency B Payment:	Equal annual amounts of SwFr1,475,000.00
Currency B Payment Dates:	18/10/85. 18/10/86
Variation to BBAIRS Terms:	None
Currency A Payer's Account:	A/c 000123 with X Bank, Zurich
Currency B Payer's Account:	A/c 000456 with Y Bank, New York

PLEASE TELEPHONE OR CABLE US IMMEDIATELY SHOULD THE PARTICULARS OF THIS CONFIRMATION NOT BE IN ACCORDANCE WITH YOUR UNDERSTANDING

For   _____
        _____

        (title)

Source: BBA

BBAIRS Interest Settlement Rate

A practical step taken in the BBAIRS Terms was to define the Libor index to be used for periodically fixing the floating interest rate in swaps. To support this definition, the BBA arranged for *Telerate* to calculate and publish daily a list of these *BBAIRS Interest Settlement Rates* for each monthly maturity between one and 12 months, for each of the 11 selected currencies: these are published on *Telerate* screen pages 3740–50. A copy of a page is reproduced in Diagram 38.

Diagram 38: BBAIRS Interest Settlement Rates

[BRITISH BANKERS ASSOC   INTEREST SETTLEMENT RATES]   PG 3750

[PG 3745] FOR INDEX OF REFERENCE BANKS,RECAP & BBA DEFINITIONS
RATES AT 11:00 LONDON TIME 02/NOV/92   [OTHER LIBORS–3740]

	[FIXED]	[FIXED]	[FIXED]	[FIXED]	[FIXED]	[FIXED]
CCY	USD	GBP	DEM	CHF	JPY	ECU
1MO	3.25000	8.18750	9.12500	6.39063	3.93750	10.56250
2MO	3.62500	7.87500	9.06250	6.50000	3.87500	10.50000
3MO	3.62500	7.62500	9.00000	6.43750	3.79688	10.37500
4MO	3.62500	7.39063	8.85938	6.37500	3.37500	10.12500
5MO	3.62500	7.23438	8.72656	6.32813	3.75000	9.97656
6MO	3.62500	7.06250	8.62500	6.32813	3.75000	9.83594
7MO	3.65625	7.01563	8.50000	6.25000	3.75000	9.69531

BBAIRS Terms proved a reasonably successful initiative. Their relative simplicity appealed to dealers and they performed well within the cohesive London market. The Terms were widely adopted as a model in other centres, for example, providing the basis for the AIRS Terms in Australia[1], and were also adapted by some counterparties for swaps beyond two years' maturity. However, the BBAIRS Terms solved only part of the documentation problem and have now largely been superseded by the more comprehensive attempt at standardisation undertaken by ISDA.

ISDA documentation

In June 1985, the International Swap Dealers' Association (ISDA)[2] published a *Code of Standard Wording, Assumptions and Provisions for Swaps* (the *ISDA Swaps Code*). This is a menu from which counterparties can draw when drafting a contract for US dollar swaps. The Code deals mainly with financial terms and conditions such as calculation of interest and termination payments. The Code was revised and expanded in 1986, to address rights of enforcement and credit provisions.

In 1987, ISDA published two master contracts for:

■ US dollar interest rate swaps — the *Interest Rate Swap Agreement* (*Rate Swap Master* agreement);

■ interest rate and currency swaps in or between a variety of currencies[3] — the *Interest Rate and Currency Exchange Agreement* (*Rate and Currency Swap Master* agreement).

The dollar contract was based on the ISDA Swap Code and the non-dollar contract on a supplement to the Code, the *1987 Interest Rate and Currency Exchange Definitions*. The former is limited to State of New York law, but the latter is also available under English law.

ISDA master contracts are divided into two parts:

■ Basic terms and conditions.

■ A *Schedule* on which to complete, supplement or modify the basic terms and conditions. The Schedule includes a residual *Other Provisions* category to which credit provisions can be added (eg, special cross-default clauses, covenants and credit enhancements such as guarantees and collateral). ISDA issued a *User's Guide* to assist the customisation of the Schedule.

An ISDA master contract, once in place between two counterparties, absorbs all subsequent swaps between them (called **netting by novation** in the US). All deals are covered by a single integrated contract. The details of new swaps are added to the master contract as appendices. The fact all swaps are subsumed within a single contract significantly facilitates netting and portfolio management of swaps. Of course, use of a master contract only makes sense between active counterparties and therefore tends to be limited to interbank relationships.

The primary market: banks

Arrangers

Early intermediaries tried to avoid taking risk in the swap market by acting as **arrangers** of swap deals between end-users. Rather than participate as principals in the transactions, arrangers act as *agents*, introducing matching counterparties to each other and then stepping aside. They accordingly charge *fees,* rather than taking dealing spreads. Arrangers in the early swaps market were typically merchant and investment banks, reflecting the balance sheet constraints on this type of institution and the importance of new issue arbitrage, which is a corporate finance function and therefore a natural line of business for merchant and investment banks.

Arrangement continues to be a feature of the swaps market, especially for currency swaps. Currency swaps involve greater credit risk and often have more complex structures, which can make the participation of a principal intermediary uneconomic.

Matched-book dealers

As more diverse end-users entered the market, it became necessary for intermediaries to act as *principals* in swaps. There were a number of reasons, including the requirement of some end-users for anonymity. However, the principal reason is credit risk. Many end-users lack their own credit analysis capability and have therefore proved reluctant to accept credit risk on non-banks, particularly in view of the degree of credit risk in a currency swap. The exposure to credit risk involved in acting as a principal intermediary encouraged *commercial banks* to enter the swap market. Commercial banks tend to be ready to deal with a wider variety of counterparties than other financial institutions, as they typically have the capability to analyse credit risk and the balance sheet to accommodate it. Notwithstanding their own credit problems, commercial banks are generally preferred to non-bank names, which may not be acceptable at all to other non-banks[4]. In return, commercial banks have been attracted by the role which swaps could play in supporting the securities businesses which they have been establishing by providing new opportunities for new issue arbitrage. The off-balance sheet nature of swaps has also been an attractive source of profits for banks with balance sheets impaired by sovereign and other debt problems.

Principal intermediaries initially limited themselves to running **matched books**, meaning they only transacted a swap if there was a more or less equal and opposite swap immediately available as a hedge. Finding such matching or **reverse swaps** could take weeks or months. To cover their credit risk exposure to end-users, intermediaries charge risk-related dealing spreads in the form of differences between the fixed interest rate paid to one end-user and that received from the other (making a net percentage return per annum rather than the one-off percentage represented by a fee). Arrangement fees were also charged by early dealers, but are now found only for complex swaps.

Market-makers

While currency swaps, like interest rate swaps, originated for the purpose of new issue arbitrage, they have gradually become a tool of asset and liability management as well. The more active and continuous nature of this function has required greater liquidity. Some has been provided through the emergence of intermediaries willing to make markets, which means continuously quoting two-way prices at which they stand ready to deal in 'reasonable' amounts in most trading conditions and without matching swaps being immediately available. However, the extent of market-making in currency swaps is very much less than in interest rate swaps, being limited to a handful of the most active swap intermediaries which make markets in interest rate swaps in several currencies and is focussed largely on generic cross-currency coupon swaps involving US dollar Libor. Market-makers still aim to run broadly matched books (or hedged portfolios), but will accommodate temporary exposure to risk on unmatched swap positions. This willingness reflects the development of techniques for:

- temporarily hedging individual swaps before matching swaps become available — so-called **warehousing**;

- **portfolio management** of the aggregate risk on swap books, rather than on individual swaps;

- offsetting risk by combining individual swaps in **cocktail swaps**;

- amalgamating the management of currency swaps with that of **LTFX**.

Assignment broking

Competition in the swap market has so narrowed dealing spreads that many market-makers, particularly institutions with relatively small balance sheets and limited risk capital, have tried to avoid building up large swap books and exposures to credit risk by selling or **assigning** swaps from their own swap books. Such assignment broking is not broking in the strict sense of acting like an agent, as assigned swaps cross the balance sheet. Assignment broking has been facilitated by the standardisation of swap documentation and the wider inclusion of assignment clauses in swap contracts. However, it tends to be a technique associated much more with interest rate swaps than currency swaps.

Table 14: Types of swap intermediation

Intermediary role	Type of intermediary	Return	Risk
arranger	merchant bank investment bank	arrangement fee	no risks
matched-book dealer	commercial bank	arrangement fee and dealing spread	permanent credit risk but no market risk
market-maker	commercial bank	dealing spread	permanent credit risk and temporary market risk
assignment broker	merchant bank investment bank	dealing spread	temporary credit risk and temporary market risk

Warehousing currency swaps

It was explained in *Part One*, that currency swaps create both:

■ interest rate risk;

■ currency risk.

Currency swaps are therefore inherently more complicated to hedge than interest rate swaps. The hedging of currency swaps is complicated further, where the intermediary absorbs the cash flow surpluses and deficits in different currencies which typically arise in a matched currency swap. This problem was described in *Part Two* and is illustrated in Diagrams 39 and 40.

Diagram 39: Currency exposure in new issue arbitrage with currency swaps
(SwFr net interest deficit for counterparty R versus $ gross interest)

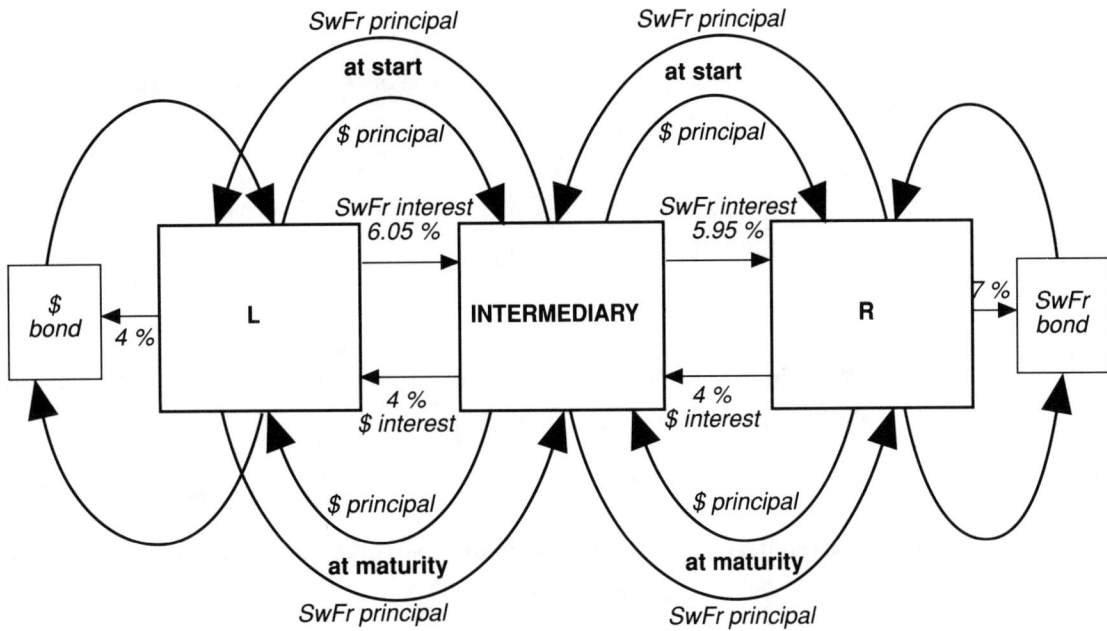

Diagram 40: Currency exposure in new issue arbitrage with cross-currency coupon swaps
($ net interest deficit for counterparty L against SwFr gross interest)

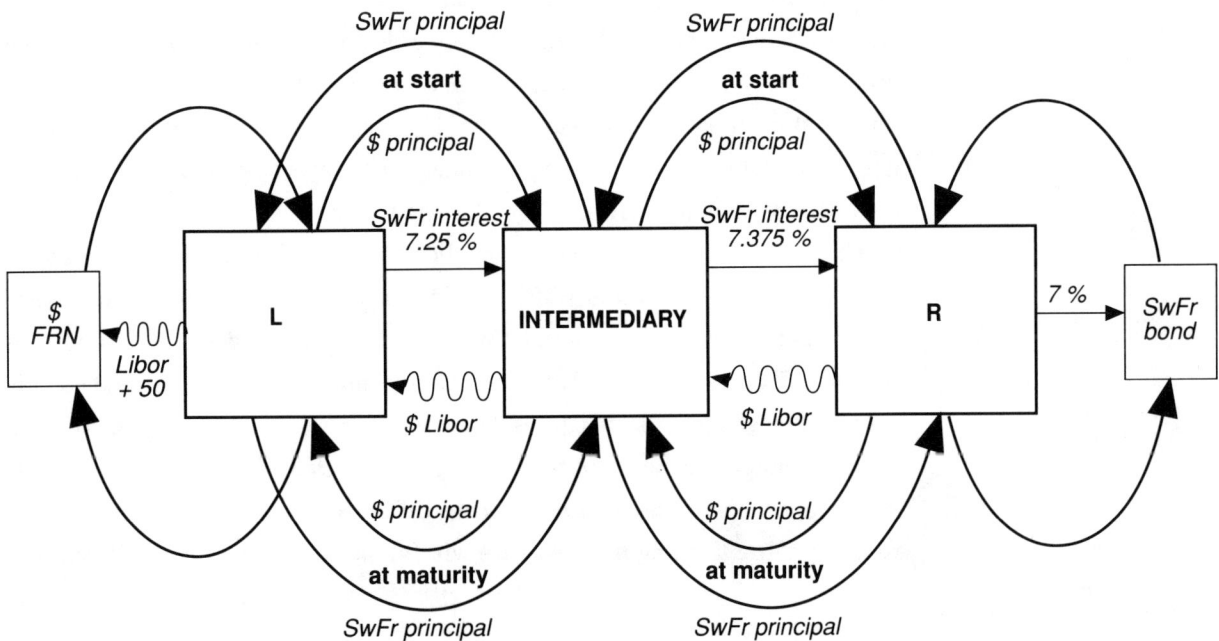

Typically, the cash flow surpluses and deficits illustrated above would be dealt with by:

■ borrowing the net present value of the surplus currency;

■ selling the borrowed amount of surplus currency for deficit currency in the spot foreign exchange market;

■ investing the purchased deficit currency to yield a cash flow which will cover the deficit on the swap.

Alternatively, the future stream of surplus currency could be converted into a stream of deficit currency using LTFX.

Hedging with cash instruments

It was also explained in *Part One* that currency swaps were the off-balance sheet equivalent of interest rate and currency positions opened up on the balance sheet using cash instruments. Appropriate cash securities in the relevant currencies should therefore be able to provide a combined interest rate and currency hedge. The hedging instruments should be liquid enough to be put on and taken off easily and cheaply, and be free of credit risk, so that they are dependable. The only cash bonds which are sufficiently liquid and also default-free are government bonds. However, even where there are liquid markets in the relevant government bonds, the hedging of interest rate risk in currency swaps remains difficult in practice. Currency swap rates and government bond yields are not closely correlated, as swap rates tend to reflect special arbitrage opportunities which do not affect government bonds (eg, oversupply of bond issues by a borrower). It is therefore not uncommon for market-makers to hedge only the currency risk (which is more serious) and accept open positions on interest rate differentials, or at most hedge the next refixing of the floating interest rate with short-term interest rate futures.

An example

Consider the example of an intermediary seeking to warehouse a five-year dollar/Deutsche mark cross-currency coupon swap, with an initial exchange of principal, in which it is a payer of Deutsche mark fixed interest and receiver of six-month dollar Libor.

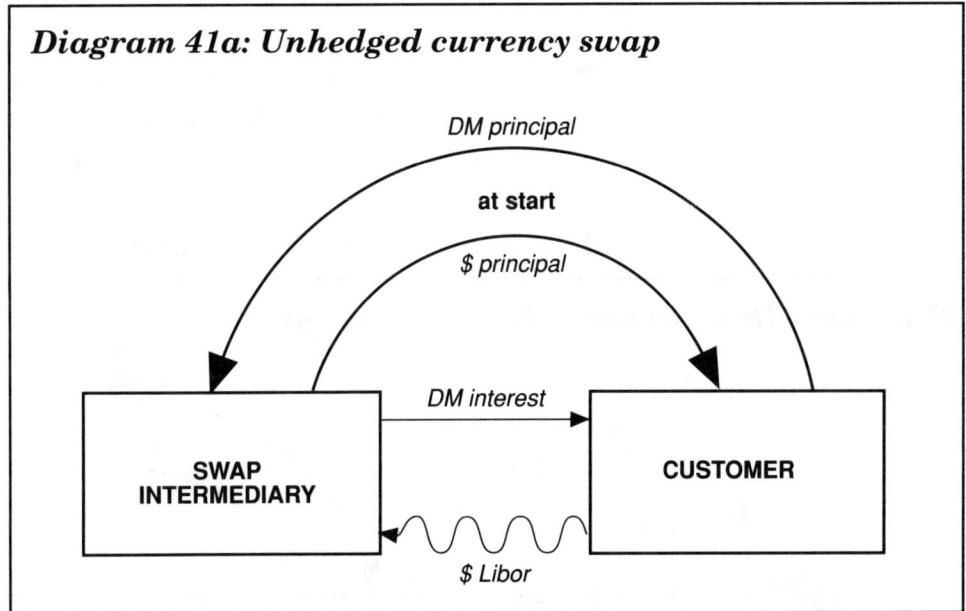

Diagram 41a: Unhedged currency swap

The intermediary is exposed to the risk that, before a matching swap can be agreed, there would be:

■ a fall in five-year German interest rates, which would mean that the matching swap would pay less in fixed interest than is being paid out by the intermediary on the existing swap;

■ a rise in dollar Libor, which would mean that until the next Libor refixing date more interest would be paid out on the floating interest side of the matching swap than is being received on the existing swap; if Libor for the matching swap is set out of phase with the setting of Libor for the existing swap — because the matching swap is transacted later — this will be a permanent **mismatch risk**;

■ a fall in the exchange rate of the dollar against the Deutsche mark, which would mean that a smaller principal amount of Deutsche marks would be received through a matching swap at maturity than would have to be paid out on the existing swap (for the same amount of dollars).

To put a cash hedge on this swap, it is necessary to:

■ buy five-year German government bonds or other appropriate Deutsche mark securities: these are purchased with the principal amount of Deutsche marks received in the initial exchange through the swap;

■ borrow dollars to fund the payment of the principal amount of dollars in the initial exchange through the swap: as the hedge is temporary and for an unknown period, it is usual to fund it with overnight money.

This hedge is illustrated in the diagram below.

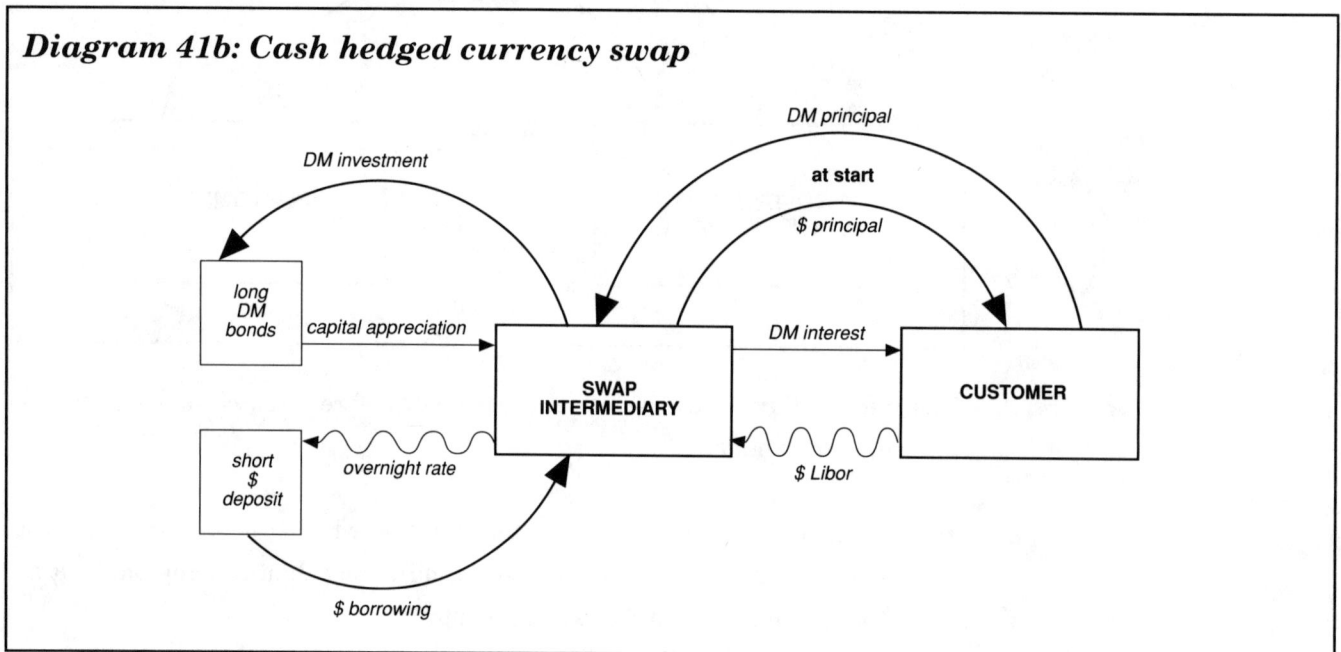

Diagram 41b: Cash hedged currency swap

Any subsequent fall in German interest rates will increase the price of the Deutsche mark bond hedge. If the swap and the bond have the same maturity, the capital gain on the bonds, if invested, should more or less equal the income loss on the eventual matching swap[5]. There may be a problem in this hedge of the basis risk between the overnight rate paid for the borrowed dollars and the six-month Libor received through the swap, due to the difference in the frequency of refixing the two rates. In the event of a stable inverted yield curve, there would be an increasing interest loss. A fall in the $/DM exchange rate will be hedged by an increase in the dollar value of the Deutsche mark bonds.

If the swap to be warehoused involved the intermediary receiving Deutsche mark fixed interest and paying dollar Libor (which would also mean that it paid a principal amount of Deutsche marks in the initial exchange against a receipt of dollars), it could hedge by:

■ borrowing the appropriate Deutsche mark bonds and then selling them to establish a short position: the proceeds from this sale would be used to fund the payment of Deutsche marks in the initial exchange of principal;

■ invest the dollars received in the initial exchange of principal: as the hedge is temporary and for an unknown period, it is usual to invest overnight.

This hedge is illustrated in the diagram below.

Diagram 42: Cash hedged currency swap

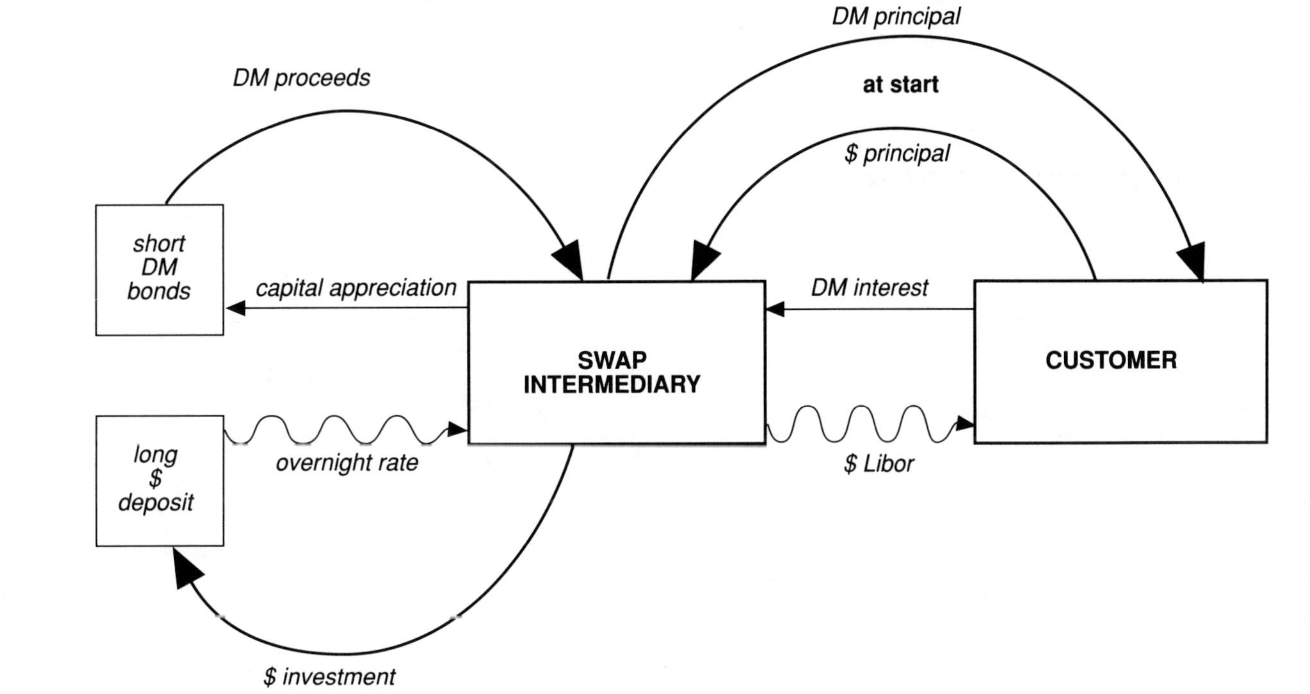

DM principal

at start

DM proceeds

$ principal

short DM bonds

capital appreciation

DM interest

CUSTOMER

SWAP INTERMEDIARY

long $ deposit

overnight rate

$ Libor

$ investment

Hedging with LTFX

The alternative to the cash hedging of currency swaps is to use LTFX. It was explained in *Part One* that LTFX is structurally equivalent to a zero-coupon fixed-against-fixed currency swap and that currency swaps could be approximately replicated with a series of LTFX. The principle of hedging a currency swap with LTFX was demonstrated in *Part Two* in the explanation of arbitrage between the two instruments. Because of these similarities, currency swap and LTFX activities have increasingly been combined, encouraging cross-hedging.

Hedging with cocktail swaps

The most traditional way of hedging currency swaps has been to combine several different currency swaps, each of which offsets only part of the risk on the other swaps, but which together form a fully hedged structure. These *cocktail swaps* often include interest rate swaps and LTFX. An example of a cocktail swap was illustrated in Diagram 9 in *Part One*. It was explained that the most common link between the components of a cocktail swap is dollar Libor. A very common cocktail swap consists of two cross-currency coupon swaps (fixed-against-fixed), both involving dollar Libor, combined so as to cancel out the dollar Libor cash flows in order to hedge a currency swap (fixed-against-fixed). This is illustrated in Diagram 43.

Diagram 43: Hedging with a cocktail swap

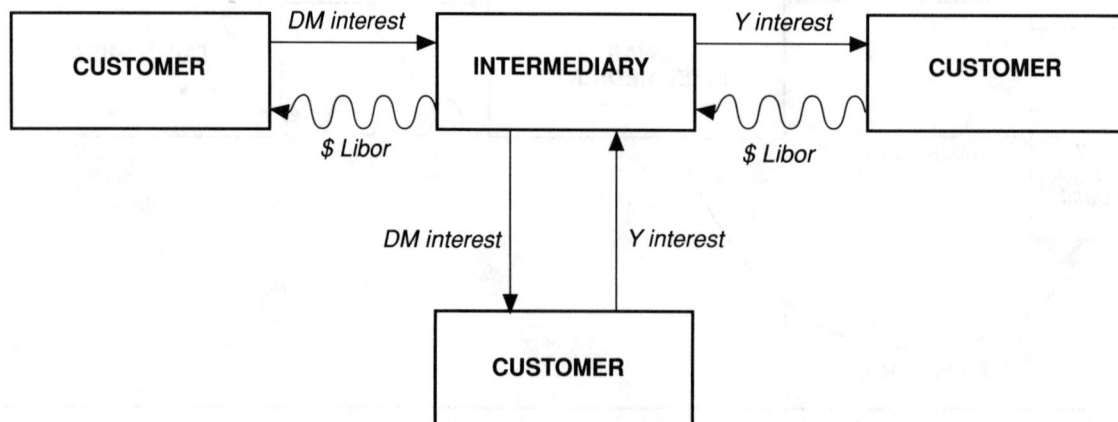

Another common cocktail swap is a combination of a cross-currency coupon swap involving dollar Libor and a dollar coupon swap, again involving dollar Libor, then with the dollar Libor cash flows cancelling out, leaving a currency swap (fixed-against-fixed) between non-dollar currencies. This cocktail swap is known specifically as a *circus swap* and was illustrated in Diagram 11 in *Part One*.

Cocktail swaps are often used to produce cross-currency basis swaps (floating-against-floating) using LTFX to cancel out the fixed-interest sides of the swaps in the cocktail. This structure is illustrated in Diagram 44.

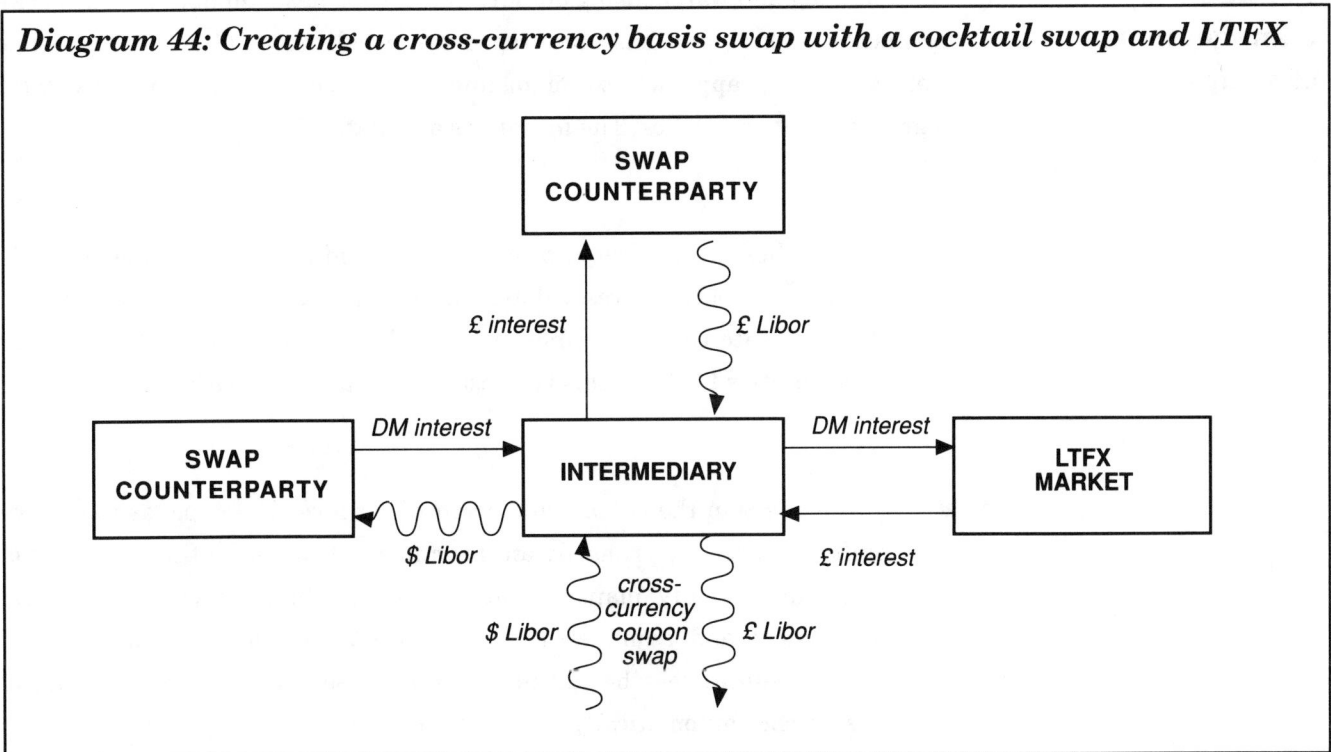

Diagram 44: Creating a cross-currency basis swap with a cocktail swap and LTFX

Risk tolerance

While cocktail swaps, the overlap with LTFX and the development of warehousing techniques have been responsible for enabling market-making in swaps, this has also reflected the fact that swap intermediaries have become more familiar with the risks associated with swaps and more confident of their ability to manage risk positions. Swap risks have been recognised as being equivalent to those generated by conventional cash instruments and LTFX. Greater confidence about swap risks means that market-makers sometimes do not warehouse their currency swaps completely and, as noted already, frequently absorb the interest rate risk. In part, this willingness to absorb hedging mismatches reflects the attraction of the wider dealing spreads received in return for taking the risk. Ultimately, however, such flexibility is a practical requirement of market-making. Market-makers need to accept mismatching, if they are going to be able to transact any volume of swaps.

Portfolio management of swaps

The matching and warehousing of individual swaps has a number of drawbacks for market-makers and has encouraged the development of a *pooling* rather than a *pairing* approach to managing swap books which involves their aggregation into portfolios. The incentives are that:

■ mismatches are not easy to hedge by individual matching (particularly mismatches between reset dates on floating interest rates and between floating interest rate indexes), while pooling can offer greater opportunities to offset: this is classic *diversification* of risk[6];

■ the increase in the *volume* and *speed* of turnover in swaps, as they have shifted from being primarily an instrument of corporate finance to one of asset and liability management, has made their individual matching impractical and administratively too costly: portfolio management of swaps requires less hedging activity because the internal offsetting of mismatches automatically reduces total risk;

■ recognition that the risks generated by swaps are analagous to those on conventional cash instruments and LTFX has encouraged the *integration* of swap book management with general asset and liability management and with market-making activities in LTFX, using the risk or arbitrage positions taken through the balance sheet and on LTFX books to hedge currency swaps, and vice versa;

■ it is difficult to match *complex swaps* individually: within a portfolio, however, there is more opportunity to hedge the various features of a complex structure.

Building a portfolio

The integration of currency swaps into a portfolio depends on the **unbundling** or breaking up of each swap into individual cash flows which are simple enough to be compared and offset against each other and against the cash flows from other swaps (as well as other types of instrument).

Before individual cash flows are offset against each other, they are adjusted for the time value of money by discounting to *present value*. Discount rates are taken from the yield curves of relevant interest rate (usually ignoring the bid-offer spread). By netting out the present value of matching individual cash flows, *residual risk exposures* are left, which should be much smaller than the exposure on a swap book in which transactions are individually warehoused and matched. Any hedging in a portfolio is limited to this residual exposure.

The primary market: brokers

The role of brokers

Dealers can trade currency swaps through **brokers,** who act as agents, arranging deals by matching swap counterparties, but not actually participating in transactions themselves. Unlike dealers, who seek to earn a dealing spread, but similar to arrangers, brokers are paid flat fees or **brokerage** which are related to the size of a deal (in terms of its notional principal amount) and its maturity, rather than its price. This form of remuneration is intended to ensure that brokers are solely interested in arranging deals and therefore in securing mutually attractive prices for counterparties. Typical brokerage rates for swaps, before volume-related discounts, are a flat one basis point from each counterparty. Brokerage is paid upfront.

Broking

A broker continuously takes prices from customers, and then selects and broadcasts the cheapest selling price and the most generous buying price to have been quoted for each maturity of the swap. The series of two-way prices for a range of maturities which a broker broadcasts back to customers is called a **broker's run**. If a customer *hits* one of these prices, the broker passes the name of the customer who originated the price and vice versa. For this reason, swaps brokers are often called *name-passing brokers*.

Brokers' information screens

Brokers disseminate swap prices over information networks such as *Reuters* and *Telerate*. The prices posted on screens are *indicative* only, and a dealer would need to contact the broker directly in order to secure *firm* dealing prices. A typical broker's screen is reproduced in Diagram 45 below.

Diagram 45: Broker's currency swap screen

```
                                                              REUTER MONITOR      1132


0745   PREBON YAMANE (UK) LTD                                 071-638-0143      SWAQ
NEW YORK 212-952-2676            LUXEMBOURG 27671                         213-622-1141
       YAMANE TANSHI                PRODUCTS TOKYO 03-5640-0627
       US TREAS      USD/USD        YEN/YEN     YEN/USD         SHORT  TERM     IRS
       ACT/365       ACT/360        ACT/365     ACT/365         USD   M/M       YEN   M/M


2 YRS  T + 29–25     4.81–77        3.78–76     3.75–71         USD   J/J       YEN   J/J
3 YRS  T + 44–39     5.43–38        4.07–05     4.06–01
4 YRS  C + 44–40     5.91–86        4.44–43     4.42–38         USD/  S/S       YEN   S/S
5 YRS  T + 33–29     6.29–25        4.65–63     4.62–58
7 YRS  T + 38–34     6.77–73        4.97–94     4.95–90         USD   D/D       YEN   D/D
10YRS  T + 38–34     7.04–00        5.17–14     5.15–10

       X-PAGE UPDATING X
P
                                              NEWS ALERT AASS                   1132
```

Source: Prebon Yamane (UK) Ltd

Advisory services

Brokers do not just recycle swap prices and match customers. They also:

■ provide information on the state of the market, based on their unique perspective (this is a requirement for authorisation to operate as a broker in London);

■ broke transactions complementary to swaps being brokered, eg, where the counterparties to a brokered swap are both seeking to warehouse their sides of that swap, the broker can arrange for the payer of fixed interest through the swap to buy bonds from the seller of fixed interest, so that dealing spreads on the bonds are avoided;

■ offer technical assistance to customers, such as suggestions for structuring profitable transactions involving arbitrages (the more deals involved, the more brokerage).

The secondary market: assignment

What is assignment?

Instead of reversing or terminating swaps, it is possible to sell or **assign** them to new counterparties[7]. In other words, a buyer (the *assignee*) substitutes for one of the original counterparties (the *assignor*). For reasons of credit risk, assignment requires that the remaining counterparty approve the assignee. In recent years, assignment has been by **novation**, meaning that the swap contract to be assigned is in fact terminated and a new but identical contract created between the remaining counterparty and the assignee. The assigning of swaps could create a nascent *secondary market*, but assignment is very limited in currency swaps.

Assignment valuation

When a swap is assigned, it is valued and a cash payment made between the buyer and the seller to compensate whoever is expected to make a profit on the swap over the remainder of its life. Assignment (and termination) is therefore a way of immediately realising the value of a swap. The valuation of currency swaps is discussed in *Part Four* on *Pricing and Valuing Currency Swaps*.

Assignability in contracts

Assignment has been facilitated by the emergence of standardised swap documentation, which makes swaps more transparent and transferable. Newer swap documentation also tends to include, as a matter of course, an *assignment clause* which allows either counterparty to assign its participation. The rights of the remaining party to refuse assignment are sometimes circumscribed by a statement to the effect that agreement may not be reasonably withheld. In practice, however, such ambiguous rights have had little practical effect.

Notes

1. Australian Financial Markets Association's General Terms and Conditions for Australian Dollar Fixed and Floating Interest Rate Swaps.

2. ISDA was formed, in March 1985, around the informal group of bank representatives which was formed in New York in 1984 to work on the standardisation of swap documentation.

3. 14 currencies: Belgian francs, Canadian dollars, Deutsche marks, Dutch guilder, Ecu, French francs, Hong Kong dollars, Italian lire, Luxembourg francs, New Zealand dollars, sterling, Swiss francs, US dollars and yen.

4. In the UK, there are also tax reasons: interest payments through a swap are subject to withholding tax, unless one of the counterparties is a bank or a recognised swap trader.

5. It is necessary to take into account the transactions cost of putting on the hedge, in the form of the dealing spread paid on the bonds. Assuming the hedger takes rather than makes prices in Deutsche mark securities, the bonds are bought at the quoting dealer's *selling* price and sold at the quoting dealer's *buying* price, thereby losing the intervening dealing spread.

6. The sort of risk being diversified is known by investment managers as **unsystematic risk**: risk which is specific to particular investments and so varies between them, allowing some offsetting when diverse investments are combined within a portfolio.

7. Assignments are sometimes called **buy-outs** or **sales**.

Self-Study Exercises: Questions   Part 3

Question 3.1: In the sterling/dollar cross-currency coupon swap illustrated in the diagram below, what are the risks to the intermediary between transacting the swap and warehousing it?

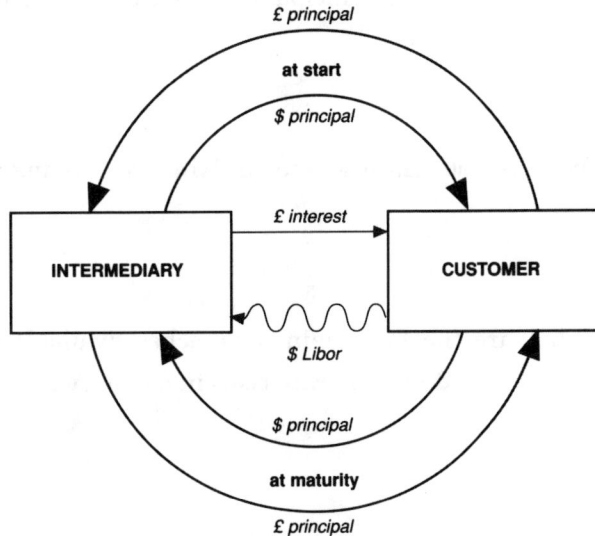

Question 3.2: How could the swap described in the previous question be warehoused using cash instruments?

Question 3.3: How could the intermediary manage the risks from the cash flow surplus and deficit arising in the cross-currency coupon swaps illustrated in the diagram below?

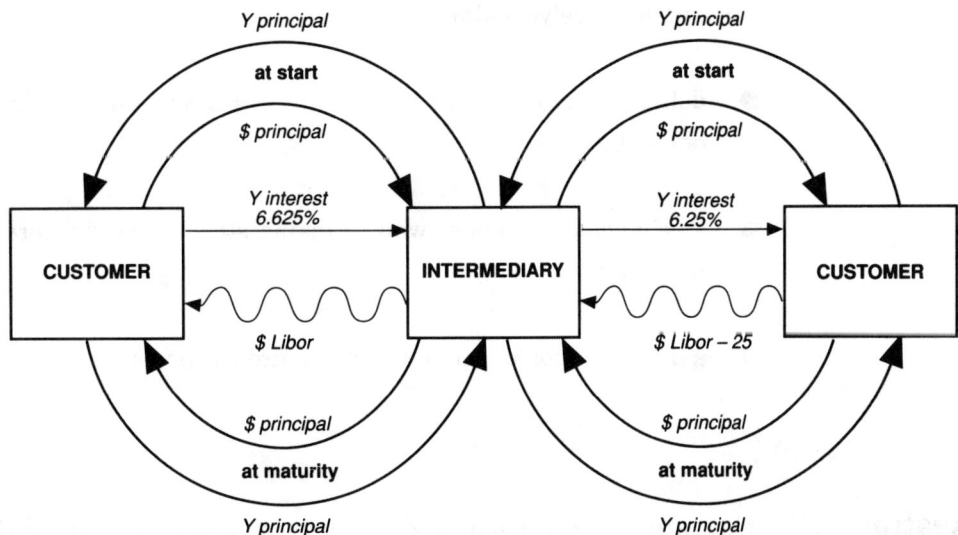

Question 3.4: Which two market associations produced the first widely-accepted standardised documentation for swaps?

Question 3.5: What are the two principal functions of documentation?

Question 3.6: What is a standard source for fixing the floating interest rate in swaps?

Question 3.7: What are the four main approaches available to market-makers for managing the currency and interest rate risks in currency swaps?

Question 3.8: How can LTFX be used to hedge the currency and interest rate risks in cross-currency coupon swaps?

Question 3.9: Construct a cocktail swap to hedge a sterling/dollar currency swap in which you pay sterling and receive dollars using:

- dollar/yen cross-currency coupon swap receiving yen fixed interest and paying dollar Libor;

- sterling/yen currency swap receiving sterling fixed interest and paying yen fixed interest;

- a dollar coupon swap in which you are the payer;

Question 3.10: What are the principal differences between reversals, terminations and assignments?

Self-Study Exercises: Answers   Part 3

Answer 3.1:   Other than the credit risk on the customer (which cannot be hedged by warehousing), the intermediary in the diagram below is exposed, before a matching swap can be agreed, to:

■ *interest rate risk* — a fall in sterling interest rates, which would mean that the eventual matching swap would pay less in fixed interest than is being paid out by the intermediary on the existing swap;

■ *interest rate risk* — a rise in dollar Libor, which would mean that until the next Libor refixing date more interest would be paid out on the floating interest side of the matching swap than is being received on the existing swap: if Libor for the matching swap is set out of phase with the setting of Libor for the existing swap — because the matching swap is transacted later — this will be a permanent **mismatch risk**;

■ *currency risk* — a rise in the £/$ exchange rate, which would mean that a larger principal amount of dollars would have to be paid by the intermediary through a matching swap at maturity than will have to be paid out on the existing swap (for the same amount of pounds).

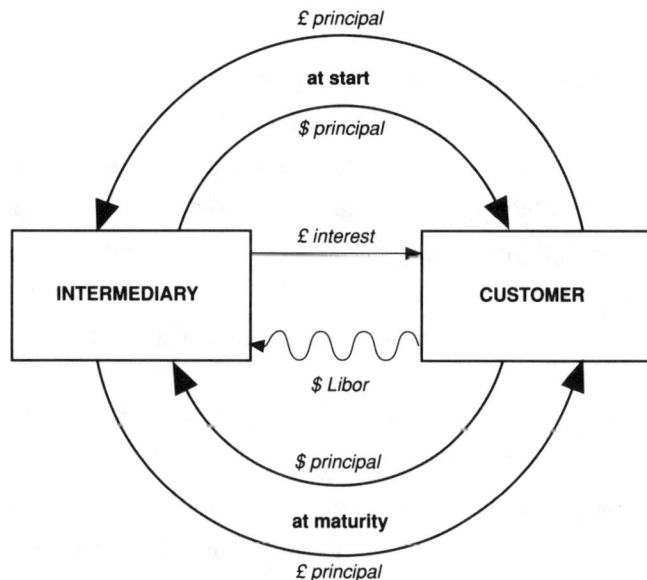

Answer 3.2: To hedge the swap in the previous question with cash instruments, it is necessary to:

- buy UK government bonds of the same maturity as the swap: these are purchased with the principal amount of sterling received in the initial exchange through the swap;

- borrow dollars to fund the payment of the principal amount of dollars in the initial exchange through the swap: as the hedge is temporary and for an unknown period, it is usual to fund it with overnight money.

This hedge is illustrated in the diagram below.

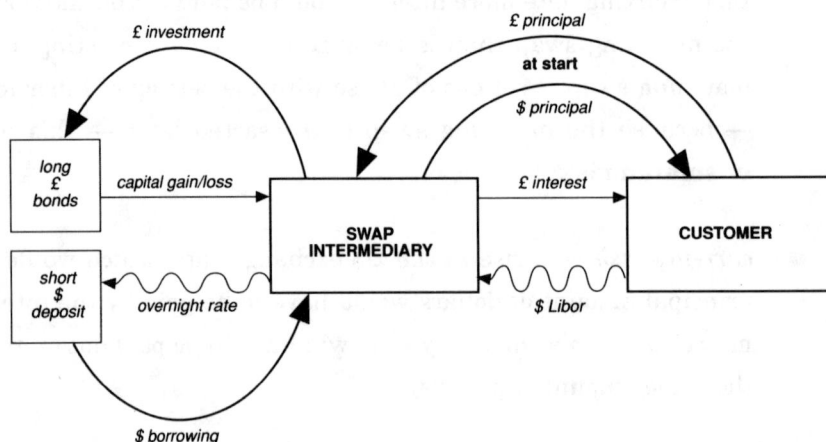

Any subsequent fall in sterling interest rates will increase the price of the UK government bond hedge. If the swap and the bond have the same maturity, the capital gain on the bonds, if invested, should more or less equal the income loss on the eventual matching swap. There may be a problem in this hedge of basis risk between the overnight rate paid for the borrowed dollars and the six-month Libor received through the swap, due to the difference in the frequency of refixing the two rates. In the event of a stable inverted yield curve, there would be an increasing interest loss.

Answer 3.3: In the matched swap illustrated in the diagram below, the intermediary will accumulate surplus yen (the difference between the 6.625%pa received through one swap and the 6.25%pa paid out on the other) and be short of dollars (the difference between the Libor paid out through one swap and the Libor minus 25bp received on the other). Typically, this problem would be dealt with by:

- borrowing the net present value of the surplus currency (yen);

- selling the borrowed amount of surplus currency for deficit currency (US dollars) in the spot foreign exchange market;

- investing the purchased deficit currency to yield a cash flow which will cover the deficit on the swap.

Alternatively, the future stream of surplus currency could be converted into a stream of deficit currency using LTFX.

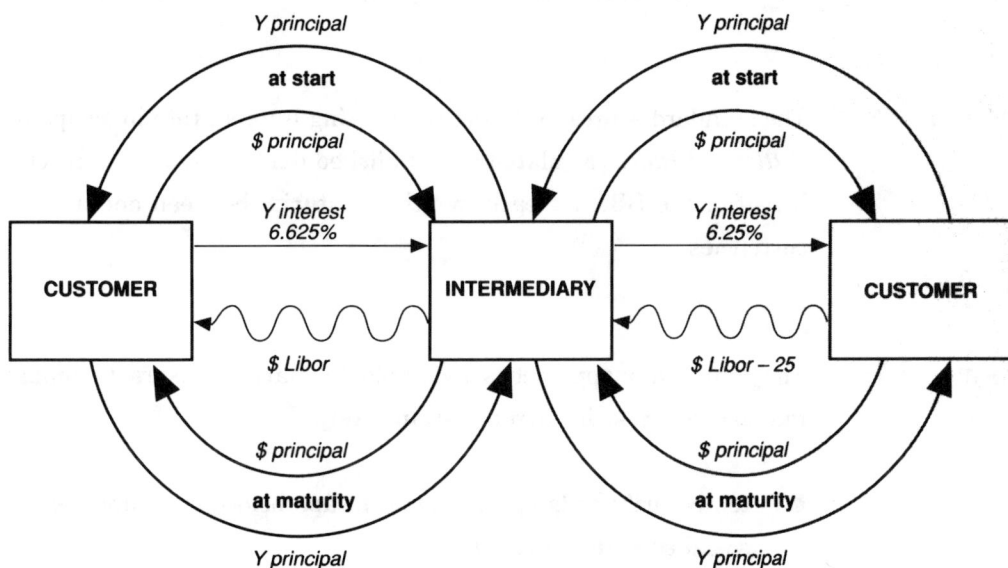

Answer 3.4: The two market associations which produced the first widely-accepted standardised documentation for swaps were:

- the British Bankers' Association (BBA);

- the International Swap Dealers' Association (ISDA).

Answer 3.5: Documentation provides *evidence* of the agreement of the counterparties to a specific transaction and provides a detailed *definition* of the transaction itself in respect of:

- *financial* terms and conditions of the transaction, meaning the rights which can be exercised and the obligations which must be performed by the counterparties: in other words, the details of the deal;

- *legal* framework for the contract, meaning rights in law of *enforcement* of the agreed financial terms and conditions, in the event of problems such as default by a counterparty: this covers matters such as the definition of an event of default, methods of computing damages, governing law and so forth.

Answer 3.6: The standard source for fixing the floating interest rate in swaps is the *BBAIRS Interest Settlement Rates* calculated and published daily by *Telerate* (on screen pages 3740–50) on behalf of the BBA for each monthly maturity between one and 12 months for selected currencies.

Answer 3.7: The four main approaches available to market-makers to manage the currency and interest rate risks in currency swaps are:

- temporarily hedging individual swaps before matching swaps become available — so-called **warehousing**;

- **portfolio management** of the aggregate risk on swap books, rather than on individual swaps;

- offsetting risk by combining individual swaps into **cocktail swaps**;

- amalgamating the management of currency swaps with that of **LTFX**.

Answer 3.8: To hedge a cross-currency coupon swap (fixed-against-floating) with LTFX, it is usual to:

- convert the cross-currency coupon swap from fixed-against-floating to fixed-against-fixed by combining it with a coupon swap, thereby cancelling out the floating interest cash flows (the combination is called a circus swap);

■ then fix the exchange rates between the two cash flows which incorporate fixed interest payments with a series of LTFX transactions, one against each exchange of payments through the circus swap.

This hedge is illustrated in the diagram below.

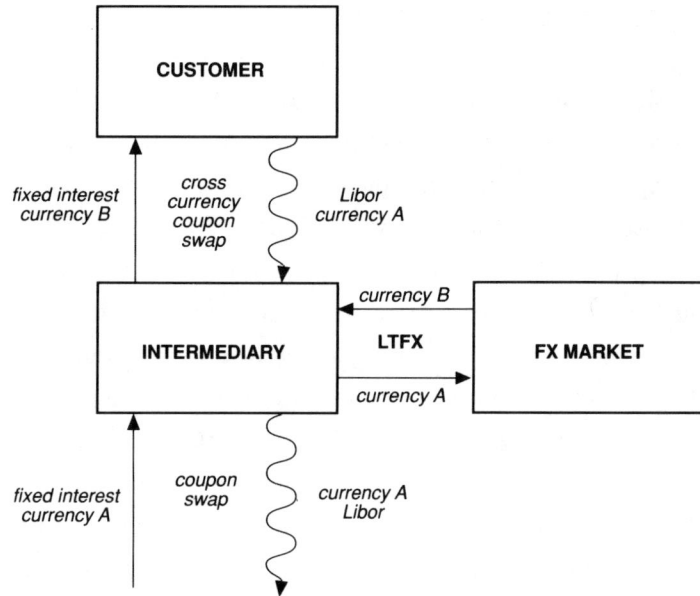

Answer 3.9: The appropriate cocktail swap is illustrated in the diagram below (no exchanges of principal are illustrated).

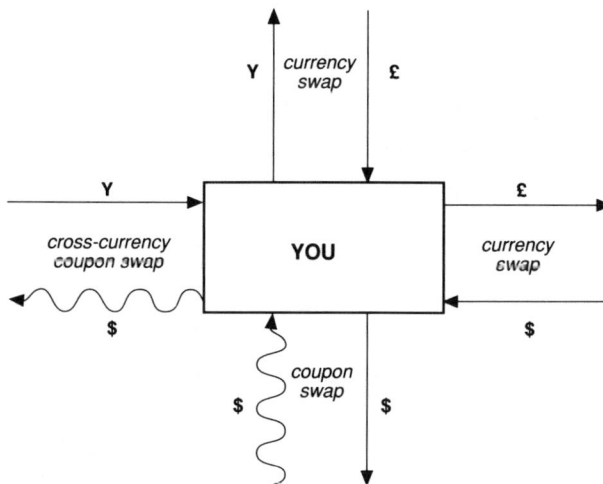

Answer 3.10: **Reversal** is to hedge an existing swap with a matching or **reverse** swap (ie, an equal and opposite swap).

Termination is the cancellation of a swap contract by mutual agreement of both counterparties. When a swap is terminated, it is valued and a payment made between the buyer and the seller to compensate whoever is expected to make a profit on the swap over the remainder of its life.

Assignment is the sale of a participation in a swap to a new counterparty. In other words, a buyer (the *assignee*) substitutes for one of the original counterparties (the *assignor*). For reasons of credit risk, assignment requires that the remaining counterparty approve the assignee. In recent years, assignment has been by **novation**, meaning that the swap contract to be assigned is in fact terminated and a new but identical contract created between the remaining counterparty and the assignee. When a swap is assigned, it is valued and a cash payment made between the buyer and the seller to compensate whoever is expected to make a profit on the swap over the remainder of its life. The key differences are:

- a reversal can be undertaken by a swap counterparty *unilaterally,* whereas termination and assignment require the consent of the other counterparty.

- termination and assignment eliminate the swap, whereas a reversal is a hedge and actually doubles up on the number of swaps.

- unrealised profits and losses in a swap can be realised by reversal, termination and assignment.

4 Pricing and valuing currency swaps

Pricing and valuation

Price

The price of a currency swap consists of:

- the *interest rates* which determine the interest payments exchanged through the swap;

- the *exchange rate* which determines the relative size of the principal payments exchanged at maturity.

The interest rates which are *quoted* in the price of a swap depend on which type of currency swap it is:

- *currency swaps* (fixed-against-fixed) are quoted in terms of both fixed interest rates;

- *cross-currency coupon swaps* (fixed-against-floating) are quoted in terms of their fixed interest rates only;

- *cross-currency basis swaps* (floating-against-floating) are quoted in terms of both floating-rate indexes.

Value

The value of a currency swap is the difference between the value of the future cash flow to be paid through the swap and the value of the future cash flow to be received in exchange, where the value of the future cash flow in one currency is translated into the other currency. The value of each future cash flow is measured in terms of the *net present value* (NPV) of the future interest and principal payments which form the cash flow: what it is worth paying now to receive that stream of future payments. The value of the whole swap is therefore the difference between the NPVs of the two future cash flows being swapped translated into the same currency.

$$\text{value of currency swap} = \text{NPV}_{\text{currency A cash flow}} - \frac{\text{NPV}_{\text{currency B cash flow}}}{\text{exchange rate}_{\text{A/B}}}$$

Par swaps

The value of a generic swap (a swap with no special risk features) priced at current market rates — a so-called **par swap** — should be *zero*. In other words, there should be no difference between the NPV of the future cash flow to be paid in one currency and the NPV of the future cash flow to be received in another currency (where the NPVs of the future cash flows are translated into the same currency).

If a swap is not a par swap and its value is therefore not zero, the counterparty due to pay the future cash flow with the lower NPV and receive the future cash flow with the higher NPV should not transact, unless it receives compensation from the other counterparty for the difference in NPVs. This compensation usually takes the form of a special cash payment made at the start of the swap.

A generic swap which is priced at par at the time it is negotiated should start with zero value. The initial NPV of each of the future cash flows (which should be the same) is calculated by *discounting* at the interest rates prevailing at the start of the swap. One NPV is then netted against the other by *translating* into the same currency, at the exchange rate fixed at the start of the swap. Subsequent changes in the interest rates and the exchange rate which prevail in the markets will change the NPVs of the two future cash flows, which are therefore likely to diverge from each other. This means a swap will tend to acquire a non-zero value after it is transacted.

Where a swap has a non-zero value, this represents an expected *profit* to one counterparty (the one for whom the difference between the NPVs of the future cash flows to be swapped is positive) and an expected *loss* to the other counterparty (the one for whom the difference between the NPVs of the future cash flows to be swapped is negative). The profit and loss are only *expected,* because the NPVs are expectations of *future* cash flows.

Non-par swaps

Swaps can have non-zero values for a variety of reasons. They might be:

■ *non-generic* swaps, which incorporate special risk features such as options that modify the value of the swap;

■ deliberately priced at *off-market* rates in order to generate cash flows with profiles which match those on underlying instruments such as bonds (see below);

■ par swaps when they are negotiated, but have become non-par swaps because the interest rates and exchange rate which constitute their prices have become increasingly *out-dated* and off-market as market rates change.

Cash flow adjustment with off-market swaps

Off-market swaps are commonly used for **cash flow adjustment** purposes. The upfront cash payment which is usually made between the counterparties of an off-market swap is used to change the cash flow profile of payments due between them: a stream of future payments can be converted into a single upfront payment, or vice versa. Of course, cash flow adjustment through a currency swap also involves a change in the currency of cash flows.

Valuing swaps for assignment and termination

Valuation is necessary when swaps are terminated or assigned (see *Part Three* on *Trading Swaps*). As noted already, par swaps tend to become off-market, as their exchange rates and interest rates become outdated. They therefore tend to accrue a non-zero value, which represents an expected interest rate and/or exchange rate gain to one of the counterparties. As assignment or termination will deprive this counterparty of its expected gain, agreement to assignment or termination should depend on it receiving compensation in the form of a cash payment. Valuation establishes the size of the cash payment.

Valuing generic currency swaps

The rest of this chapter focuses on the valuation of generic currency swaps. The valuation of non-generic swaps is covered in the Workbook in this series on *Financial Engineering with Swaps*.

As noted already, the value of a currency swap is the difference between the NPVs of the two future cash flows to be swapped:

$$\text{value of currency swap} = \text{NPV}_{\text{currency A cash flow}} - \frac{\text{NPV}_{\text{currency B cash flow}}}{\text{exchange rate}_{\text{A/B}}}$$

Each cash flow through a generic currency swap consists of:

■   a stream of regular payments of *interest*;

■   a payment of *principal* at maturity;

and is therefore a function of:

■   the absolute *principal* amounts of currencies to be exchanged at maturity;

■   the *exchange rate* which is part of the price of the swap and determines the relative size of the agreed principal amounts of currencies to be exchanged at maturity;

■   the *interest rates* which are also part of the price of the swap and are applied to the agreed principal amounts of currencies in order to determine the interest payments to be exchanged through the swap.

The *NPV* of each future cash flow is a function of the above factors plus:

■ *current market interest rates*, which are used to *discount* future cash flows back to NPV;

■ *current market exchange rate*, which is used to *translate* NPVs into the same currency in order to net the NPVs and determine the value of the swap as a whole.

Valuing future fixed-interest cash flows

Calculating the NPV of future cash flows which include a stream of *fixed* interest payments is straightforward as these future payments are known in advance. Such a cash flow is similar to that generated by a bond and its NPV can therefore be calculated using the formula for the price of a bond:

$$NPV_{\text{fixed interest + principal}} = \sum_{n=1}^{n} \frac{C_n}{V^n} + \frac{P}{V^n}$$

where

$$V^n = \left[1 + \frac{i \times \text{day count}}{100 \times \text{annual basis}}\right]^n$$

and

C_n	= fixed interest cash flow
P	= principal cash flow
i	= prevailing market interest rate
n	= number of years to maturity

The examples of NPV calculations in this Workbook are performed on a bond calculator and accordingly use the standard notation:

n   = number of years remaining to maturity
i   = prevailing market interest rate
PV = net present value
PMT = swap (fixed) interest rate
FV = principal exchanged at maturity

An example

Consider the following dollar/Deutsche mark currency swap (fixed-against-fixed):

life	= 3 years
dollar fixed interest rate	= 4%pa
Deutsche mark fixed interest rate	= 10%pa
dollar principal	= $100m
Deutsche mark principal	= DM150m
$/DM exchange rate	= 1.5000

Current rates prevailing in the market are:

3-year Deutsche mark interest rate	= 9%pa
3-year dollar interest rate	= 5%pa
current $/DM exchange rate	= 1.4500

To calculate the NPV of the *Deutsche mark* cash flow, the following data are input into the bond calculator:

n	= 3 years
i	= 9%pa
PMT	= 10%pa
FV	= 100 (= DM150m)

which gives an NPV of:

PV   = 102.53 (= DM153,796,942)

To calculate the NPV of the *dollar* cash flow, the following data are input into the bond calculator:

n   = 3 years
i   = 5%pa
PMT = 4%pa
FV   = 100 (= $100m)

which gives an NPV of:

PV   = 97.28 (= $97,276,752)

The value of the swap is the difference between the NPVs of the Deutsche mark and dollar cash flows. To calculate the difference, the Deutsche mark cash flow must be translated into dollars. This is done at the current $/DM exchange rate of 1.4500, to give:

DM153,796,942/1.4500 = $106,066,857

The value of the swap is therefore:

$106,066,857 − $97,276,752 = $8,790,105

Valuing future floating-interest cash flows

The calculation of the NPV of cash flows through currency swaps which include a stream of *floating interest* payments is problematic, as the size of each future floating interest cash flow cannot be known until the start of the particular interest period to which it applies (which is when the floating index is reset for that period). Note that the NPV of the principal payment, which is known in advance, can be calculated separately. There are two solutions adopted by the swap market to the valuation of floating interest cash flows. These involve calculating the NPV of the interest stream using either:

■ *forward-forward interest rates*;

■ *matching coupon swaps*.

Valuing future floating-interest cash flows using forward-forward interest rates

Forward-forward interest rates apply to future (forward-forward) interest periods. They are calculated from overlapping cash interest rates:

$$\left[\frac{1+\left[\dfrac{\text{cash interest rate}_{\text{far date}} \times \text{day count}_{\text{far date}}}{100 \times \text{annual basis}}\right]}{1+\left[\dfrac{\text{cash interest rate}_{\text{near date}} \times \text{day count}_{\text{near date}}}{100 \times \text{annual basis}}\right]}-1\right] \times \left[\frac{100 \times \text{annual basis}}{\text{day count}_{\text{near-far date}}}\right]$$

Forward-forward interest rates are not explicit forecasts of future rates and may not accurately presage the cash interest rates that actually come to prevail when the relevant forward-forward periods become cash periods. However, because they are implied from cash rates prevailing in the open market, forward-forward interest rates are often adopted as a neutral solution to the problem of valuing future floating interest.

In practice, forward-forward interest rates are factored into the valuation of swaps, not directly as interest cash flows, but *indirectly* in terms of the notional principal amounts (NPAs) which generate those interest cash flows.

For each cash flow, it is assumed that the NPA of the swap is borrowed at the start of the relevant interest period by the counterparty paying floating interest through the swap and lent by the counterparty receiving floating interest. It is also assumed that exactly the same NPA is repaid at the end of the interest period. The payer of floating interest through the swap is thus represented as paying interest on the notional borrowing, until it is cancelled by the notional repayment; and vice versa for the receiver of floating interest. This approach recalls the fact that a swap replicates the cash flows which are produced by a combination of a cash asset and a cash liability (see *Part One*). The approach is illustrated in Diagram 46 below.

Diagram 46: *Representing future floating interest cash flows (for the payer of floating interest)*

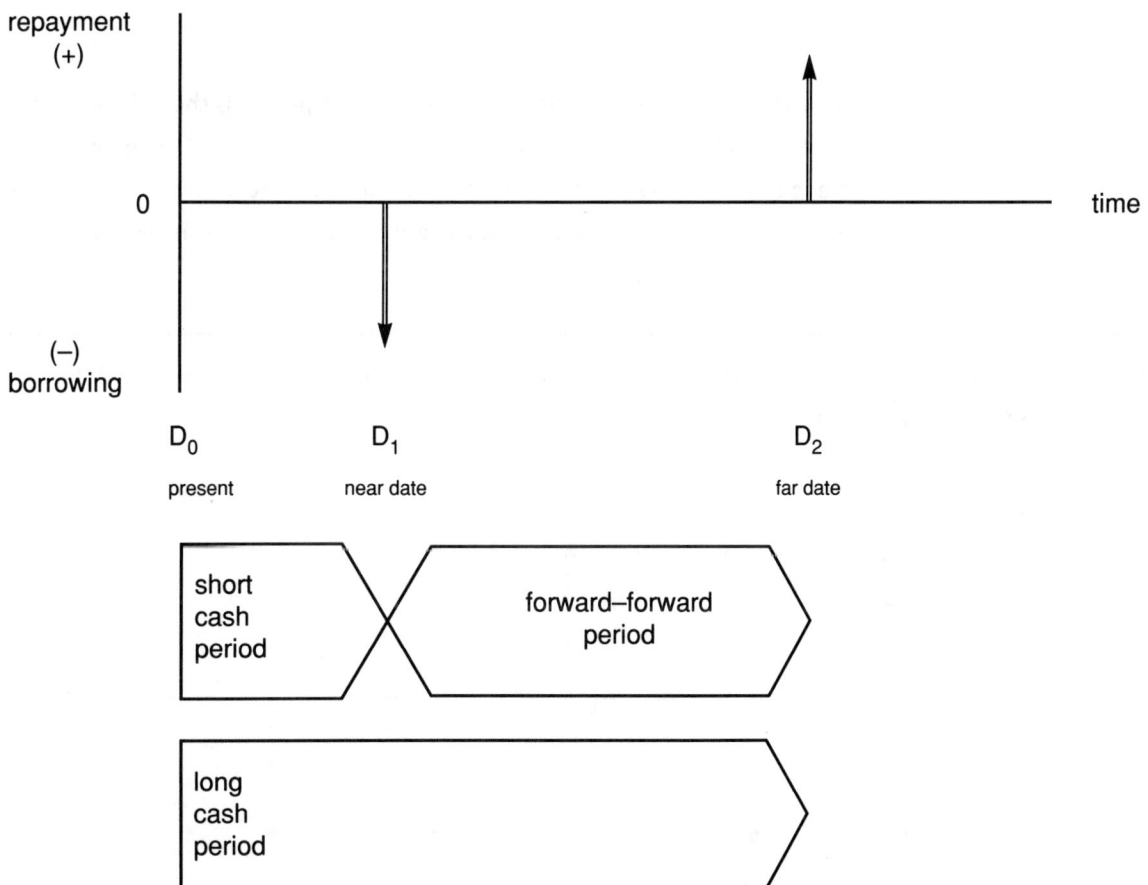

When the notional borrowing (at D_1 in the diagram above) and its repayment (at D_2) are each discounted back to present values (at D_0), being of different signs, they largely cancel out. The residual difference between the present values of the notional borrowing and repayment is in fact equal to the present value of the interest paid on the notional borrowing for the forward-forward interest period (D_{1-2}). This fact is more obvious if it is remembered that the difference represents the amount by which the repayment is reduced when it is discounted from D_2 back to D_1; it is therefore equivalent to the interest due on borrowing between D_1 and D_2. Thus, in calculating the NPV of interest cash flows through a swap, the use of NPAs at the start and end of each future interest period has the same net cash flow impact as direct inclusion of interest cash flows. The relevant forward-forward interest rates are implicit in the discounting of the NPAs. The arithmetic behind this equation may be summarised as:

$$\text{PV (borrowing at } D_1) + \text{PV (repayment at } D_2) = \text{NPV (interest for } D_{1-2})$$

In the case of a swap with several interest periods, the NPAs at the start and end of each interest period largely offset each other. For example, take a two-year cash flow calculated using a six-month floating interest rate. The floating interest payments would be represented as illustrated in Diagram 47 below.

Diagram 47: Representing the value of future floating interest cash flows (for the receiver of floating interest)

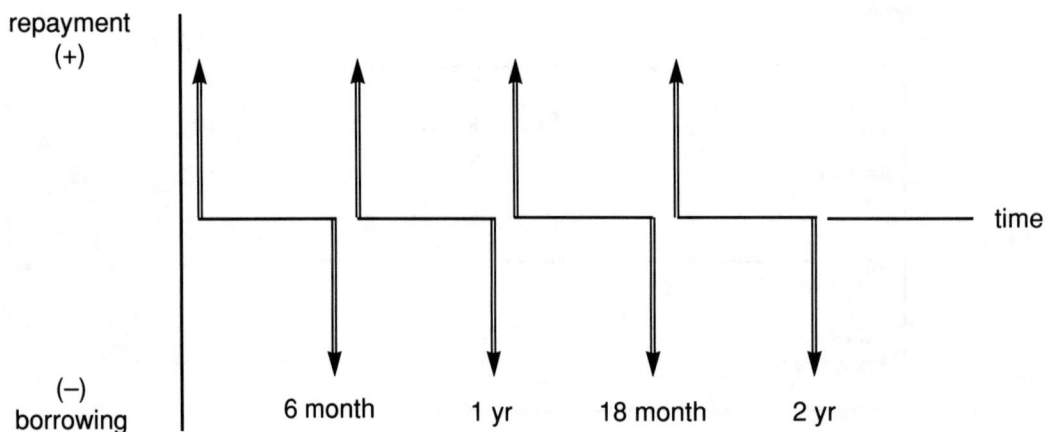

It can be seen that all NPAs cancel out except for the very first and very last, as illustrated in Diagram 48.

Diagram 48: *Representing the value of future floating interest cash flows (for the receiver of floating interest)*

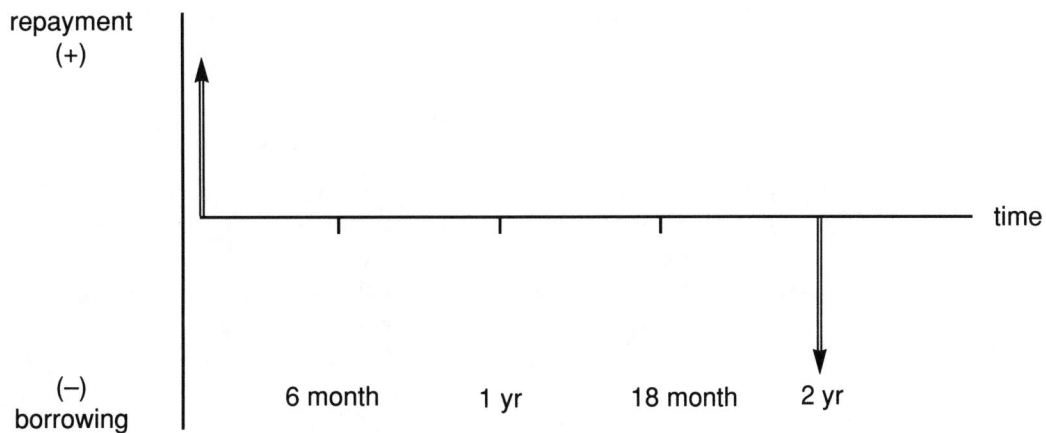

The value of the floating interest cash flows for an entire swap is therefore very conveniently represented by the NPA now and the same amount (but with a different sign) at the end of the swap. For generic swaps, the present value of the NPA now (for which the day count is zero) is:

$$PV\,(NPA) = \frac{NPA}{1 + \left[\dfrac{\text{market interest rate x day count}}{100 \text{ x annual basis}}\right]} = NPA$$

Consequently, for a generic swap, the present value of the whole floating interest cash flow is given simply by:

$$PV_{(swap)} = NPA + PV(NPA)$$

An example

Consider the following sterling/dollar cross-currency coupon swap:

life	= 1 year
sterling fixed interest rate	= 9%pa
dollar interest rate	= 6-month Libor
sterling principal	= £100m
dollar principal	= $160m
$/DM exchange rate	= 1.6000
1-year day count	= 365 days

Current rates prevailing in the market are:

3-year sterling interest rate	= 7%pa
6-month dollar Libor	= 3.25%pa
12-month dollar Libor	= 3%pa
current $/DM exchange rate	= 1.8000
6-month day count	= 181 days

To calculate the NPV of the *sterling* cash flow, the following data are input into the bond calculator:

n	= 1 year
i	= 7%pa
PMT	= 9%pa
FV	= 100 (= £100m)

which gives an NPV of:

PV = 101.87 (= £101,869,159)

As regards the valuation of the *dollar* cash flow, the NPV of the *principal* amount of $160m is:

n	= 1 year
i	= 3%pa
PMT	= 0
FV	= 100 (= $160m)

which gives an NPV of:

PV = 97.09 (= $155,339,806)

To calculate the NPV of the dollar floating *interest* cash flow, the two alternative approaches which use forward-forward interest rates are:

■   *using forward-forward interest rates* directly —

Libor for this future period is taken to be the forward-forward interest rate for the period. The forward-forward rate is:

$$\left[\frac{1+\left[\dfrac{\text{cash interest rate}_{\text{far date}} \times \text{day count}_{\text{far date}}}{100 \times \text{annual basis}}\right]}{1+\left[\dfrac{\text{cash interest rate}_{\text{near date}} \times \text{day count}_{\text{near date}}}{100 \times \text{annual basis}}\right]} - 1\right] \times \left[\frac{100 \times \text{annual basis}}{\text{day count}_{\text{near-far date}}}\right]$$

$$\left[\frac{1+\left[\dfrac{3 \times 365}{100 \times 360}\right]}{1+\left[\dfrac{3.25 \times 181}{100 \times 360}\right]} - 1\right] \times \left[\frac{100 \times 360}{184}\right] = 2.7098\%\,\text{pa}$$

The floating interest expected to be due in six months is:

$$\$160,000,000 \times \frac{3.25 \times 181}{100 \times 360} = \$2,614,444$$

The floating interest expected to be due in 12 months is:

$$\$160,000,000 \times \frac{2.7098 \times 184}{100 \times 360} = \$2,216,014$$

The present values of these amounts (discounted at the prevailing 6 and 12-month cash rates of 3.25% and 3% per annum, respectively) are:

$$\frac{\$2{,}614{,}444}{1+\left[\dfrac{3.25 \times 181}{100 \times 360}\right]} = \$2{,}572{,}410$$

$$\frac{\$2{,}216{,}014}{1+\left[\dfrac{3 \times 365}{100 \times 360}\right]} = \$2{,}150{,}599$$

The NPV of the floating interest cash flow is therefore:

$2,572,410 + $2,150,599 = $4,723,009

■   *using notional principal amounts —*

to replicate the value of future floating interest cash flows, NPAs of $160m are recorded at the start and end of the swap and then discounted. The first amount does not need to be discounted (because it is multiplied by a day count of 0). Discounting the last amount (using the prevailing 12-month cash rate of 3% per annum) produces a present value of $155,276,992. The NPV is therefore:

$160,000,000 − $155,276,992 = $4,723,009

This result is the same as that achieved through the forward-forward interest rates. The calculation is illustrated in the table below.

	0 months	12 months
notional principal amounts	+160,000,000	−160,000,000
cash rates	n/a	3%
present values	+160,000,000	−155,276,992
net present value		−4,723,009

Valuing future floating-interest cash flows using matching coupon swaps

The simplest method of valuing the floating interest cash flow through a currency swap is to determine the price (fixed interest rate) of a new single-currency coupon swap in the same currency as the floating interest side of the currency swap. If the single-currency coupon swap is a par swap, the NPVs of its future cash flows should net to zero, which means that fixed interest rate in that swap has the equivalent value to the floating interest rate. This equivalent fixed interest rate can then be substituted for the floating interest rate in the currency swap and used to calculate its NPV using bond calculations.

In effect, this method of valuation involves the construction of a notional *circus swap*, in other words, a fixed-against-fixed currency swap formed from a cross-currency coupon swap and a single-currency coupon swap which share a common floating interest rate index (typically, US dollar Libor). This method of valuation, while simple, is limited to cross-currency coupon swaps which involve floating interest in a currency with a liquid market in interest rate swaps.

Valuing the whole swap

Having seen how the value of the future fixed and floating interest cash flows through a swap are calculated, it is possible to value an entire currency swap.

An example

Consider the sterling/dollar cross-currency swap in the earlier example. As explained already, the value of a currency swap is the difference between the NPVs of the two future cash flows to be swapped:

$$NPV_{\text{currency A cash flow}} - \frac{NPV_{\text{currency B cash flow}}}{\text{exchange rate}_{A/B}}$$

For the sterling/dollar cross-currency swap, the value is either:

$$NPV_{sterling\ cash\ flow} - \frac{NPV_{dollar\ cash\ flow}}{£/\$\ exchange\ rate}$$

or

$$(NPV_{sterling\ cash\ flow} \times £/\$\ exchange\ rate) - NPV_{dollar\ cash\ flow}$$

The NPV of the *sterling* cash flow was calculated as £101,869,159 (see the previous example). At the current £/$ exchange rate of 1.8000, this is equivalent to:

£101,869,159 x 1.8000 = $183,364,486

The NPV of the *dollar* cash flow was calculated in two parts (see the previous example): the principal payment and the floating interest cash flow. The total NPV is:

$155,339,806 + $4,723,009 = $160,062,815

The overall value of the swap is therefore:

$183,364,486 – $160,062,815 = $23,301,671

Given that the NPV of the sterling cash flow is greater that the NPV of the dollar cash flow, this figure represents an expected profit to the payer of dollars and receiver of sterling. The expected profit to the payer of dollars reflects:

■ a fall in sterling interest rates since the transaction of the swap: this increases the NPV of the sterling cash flow (by reducing the impact of discounting), thereby benefiting the counterparty receiving the sterling cash flow;

■ an appreciation of sterling against the dollar: this means the counterparty receiving the sterling principal at maturity avoids a foreign exchange loss by having fixed the amount of dollars to be exchanged at 1.6000, while a current exchange would cost 1.8000.

In other words, both the sterling interest rate and £/$ exchange rate have moved in favour of the payer of dollars and receiver of sterling. However, interest rates and exchange rates could have moved in opposite directions. Thus, for example, if the £/$ exchange rate had instead depreciated to 1.5713, the exchange rate change would have almost exactly offset the interest rate change. At a rate of 1.5713, the NPV of the sterling cash flow would be equivalent to:

£101,869,159 x 1.5713 = £160,067,010

which would produce an overall value for the swap close to zero:

$160,067,010 – $160,062,815 = $4,195

Discounting to net present value

The next issue in valuation is what interest rates to use to discount the swap cash flows back to NPV. Yields-to-maturity (YTM) are average interest rates applying to series of future cash flows. YTM is appropriate therefore for valuing cash flows involving fixed interest, but not for single future payments (unless the yield curve is flat and each individual cash flow is therefore equal to the average represented by the YTM). The appropriate rates to use for discounting are zero-coupon interest rates. The need to use zero-coupon rates has been avoided in this Workbook by limiting the remaining life of the cross-currency coupon swaps used in examples to periods of one year: one-year Libor is effectively a zero-coupon interest rate, since it applies to a single payment of interest at maturity, whereas interest rates for periods above a year apply to a series of two or more interest payments (at least once a year) and are therefore yields-to-maturity.

Discount factors

Discount rates are normally presented in the form of fractions called **discount factors,** meaning:

$$\frac{1}{\left[1 + \dfrac{\text{discount rate x day count}}{100 \text{ x annual basis}}\right]^{n}}$$

where n = number of years remaining to maturity

A discount factor represents the present value of one unit of money due at a given future date: what it is worth paying now to receive that unit at the future date. Discount factors are a convenience: they allow discounting to be performed by multiplication by a single factor. Thus, to calculate the present value of any future cash flow, it is simply multipied by the discount factor for the relevant maturity. In the example above, the discount factor applying to the one-year period of the swap is:

$$\frac{1}{\left[1 + \dfrac{3 \text{ x } 365}{100 \text{ x } 360}\right]^{1}} = \frac{1}{1.030417} = 0.9704812$$

In other words, \$1 in one year's time is currently worth \$0.9704812. Multiplying this by the notional principal amount of \$160m produces a present value of \$155,276,992.

Valuing a swap structure

In *Part Two* of this Workbook, the general principles were explained of how to use currency swaps to manage risk and return. Among other things, it was shown how hedging with currency swaps can be used to avoid currency risk and lock in currency gains on foreign currency borrowing and how arbitrage with currency swaps can be used to reduce the cost of borrowing. *Part Four* has explained the techniques which are required to value currency swaps. This section brings together the general principles of using currency swaps (as explained in *Part Two*) and the techniques of valuing currency swaps (as explained in *Part Four*) to explain the valuation of the swap structures used in new issue arbitrages.

In order to simplify the explanation, a number of assumptions have been made about the swap structure being discussed:

■ the arbitrage involves a new issue by one counterparty only, with the other counterparty swapping existing debt, which means that the issuer of the new debt is not able to swap the proceeds with the other swap counterparty, as that counterparty has no new funds to exchange at the start of the swap: instead, it sells the proceeds of its new issue in the foreign exchange market.

■ the swap is fixed-against-fixed (in other words, it is the proceeds of bonds which are being swapped).

The swap is illustrated in the following diagram.

Diagram 49: New issue arbitrage swap structure

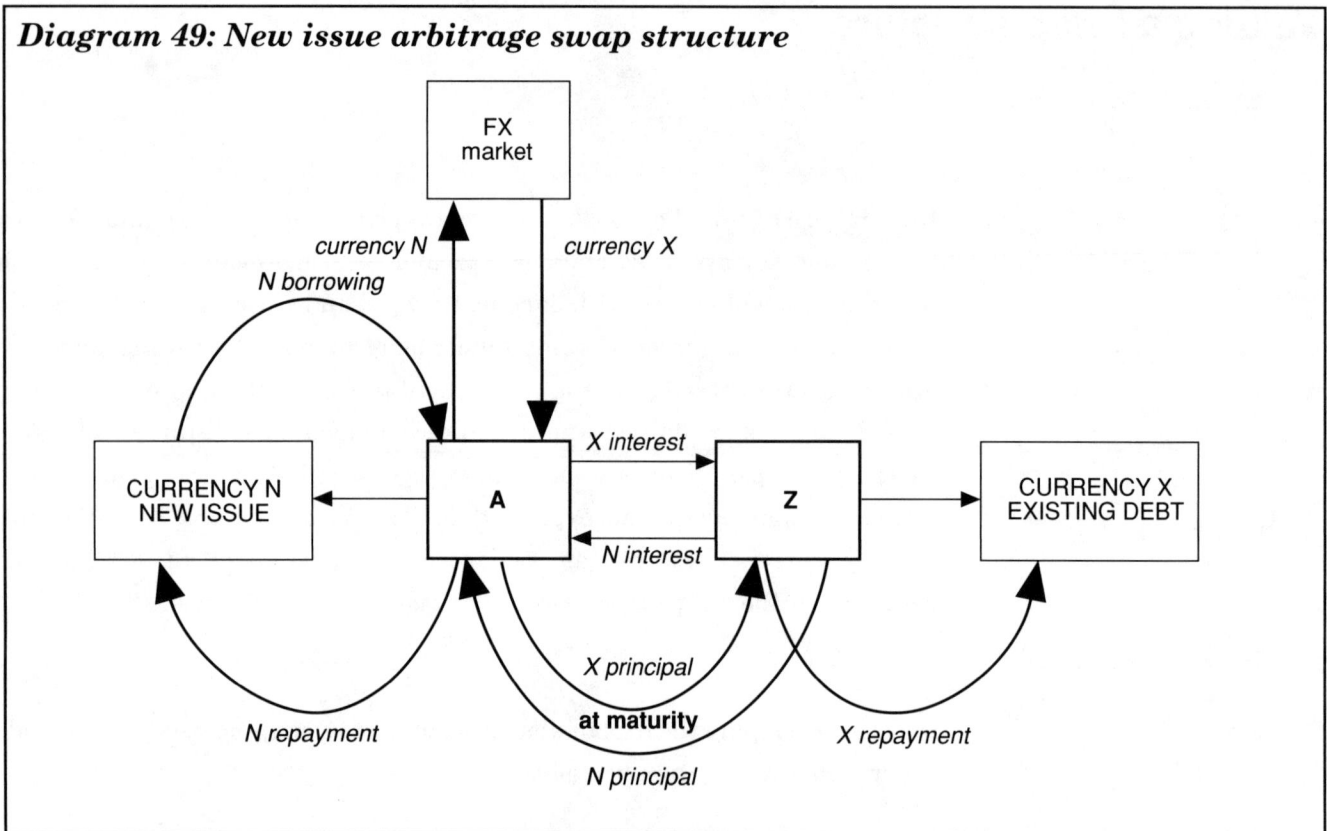

The usual sequence of steps in valuing a new issue swap structure of the type illustrated above is:

- to determine the size of the swap, by deciding the *principal* amount to be exchanged at maturity of one of the two currencies being swapped: it is assumed here that a decision is first made about how much to swap of the currency of the existing debt — in the diagram, currency X issued by counterparty Z — but it is possible to make the decision the other way round and fix the size of the new issue first;

- for each counterparty to decide the *target cost of funds* through the swap which it will seek before agreeing to participate in the transaction;

■ negotiate the *exchange rate* at which the exchange of principal is to be made at maturity: this is usually (but not necessarily) the spot exchange rate prevailing at the start of the swap;

■ determine the *principal* amount to be exchanged at maturity of the other currency being swapped — currency N issued by counterparty A: this amount is the net present value of the principal amount of currency (X) which was fixed in the first step, discounted at the rate of interest which represents the target cost of funds fixed in the second step for the counterparty paying that currency through the swap (counterparty Z) and converted at the exchange rate agreed between the counterparties in the previous step;

■ determine the face value of the *new issue*: this is equal to the principal amount (of currency N) determined in the previous step plus issuing fees;

■ at this stage, it is possible to determine the *cost of funds* (in currency N) to the second counterparty (Z): this is the market interest rate (i in terms of the notation used in bond calculators).

This sequence of valuation is illustrated in the *Case Study* which follows.

Case Study: Valuing a new issue swap structure

The transaction which is the subject of this case study is the seminal deal between the World Bank and IBM in 1981/82 which helped establish the general credibility of the currency swap. The background to the deal was as follows:

- **IBM** had issued bonds in the late 1970s in Deutsche marks (DM) and Swiss francs (SwFr), and sold the proceeds for dollars in the spot foreign exchange market. The DM bonds had a coupon of 10% and the SwFr bonds a coupon of 6.1875%; both were due to mature on 30 March 1986. Subsequent to issuance, the dollar had appreciated sharply against the Deutsche mark and the Swiss franc. This reduced the dollar cost to IBM of its foreign currency borrowing. IBM was keen to lock in this exchange rate gain by hedging its bonds.

- the **World Bank** adopted a policy of borrowing in low-yielding currencies such as the Deutsche mark and the Swiss franc, but the size and frequency of its issuance had saturated demand in these markets. On the other hand, the World Bank was still perceived to be a desirable name in the larger US dollar market. However, it was not keen to borrow high-yielding dollars.

The solution to both problems was proposed by Salomon Brothers in the form of currency swaps (fixed-against-fixed). The transaction involved the following sequence of steps:

- the World Bank issued a double-tranche $210m Eurobond with a coupon of 16%, paying assumed fees of 2.15% and maturing on 30 March 1986 (at the same time as the IBM bonds). The bond was issued on 11 August 1981 and settled on 25 August 1981.

- the dollar proceeds of the World Bank issue — assumed to be $205,485,000 (equivalent to 97.85% of the face value after deduction of the assumed fees of 2.15%) — were sold in the foreign exchange market for DM and SwFr. In fact, the proceeds were sold forward on 11 August 1981 for value on 25 August 1981. Assuming outright forward rates of about 2.56 ($/DM) and 2.18 ($/SwFr), it is assumed the World Bank received SwFr191,367,479 and DM301,316,488.

- the World Bank hedged its $/DM and $/SwFr risk, and IBM locked in current $/DM and $/SwFr exchange rates, by transacting currency swaps (fixed-against-fixed) with each other:

  — during the life of the swap, the World Bank paid DM fixed interest at 10% per annum and SwFr fixed interest at 6.1875% per annum and, in exchange, received dollar fixed interest at 16% per annum from IBM: the World Bank used the dollar interest to service the interest obligations on its new Eurobond and IBM used the DM and SwFr interest to service the interest obligations on its existing issues

  — at maturity, the World Bank paid DM300m and SwFr200m to IBM in exchange for $210m: the World Bank used the dollar principal amount to redeem its Eurobond and IBM used the DM and SwFr to redeem its issues.

The swaps were transacted with effect from 30 March 1982. This was 215 days after the bond issue, a delay required to align the start of the swaps with the next coupon date on the IBM bonds. The whole World Bank-IBM deal is illustrated in the diagram.

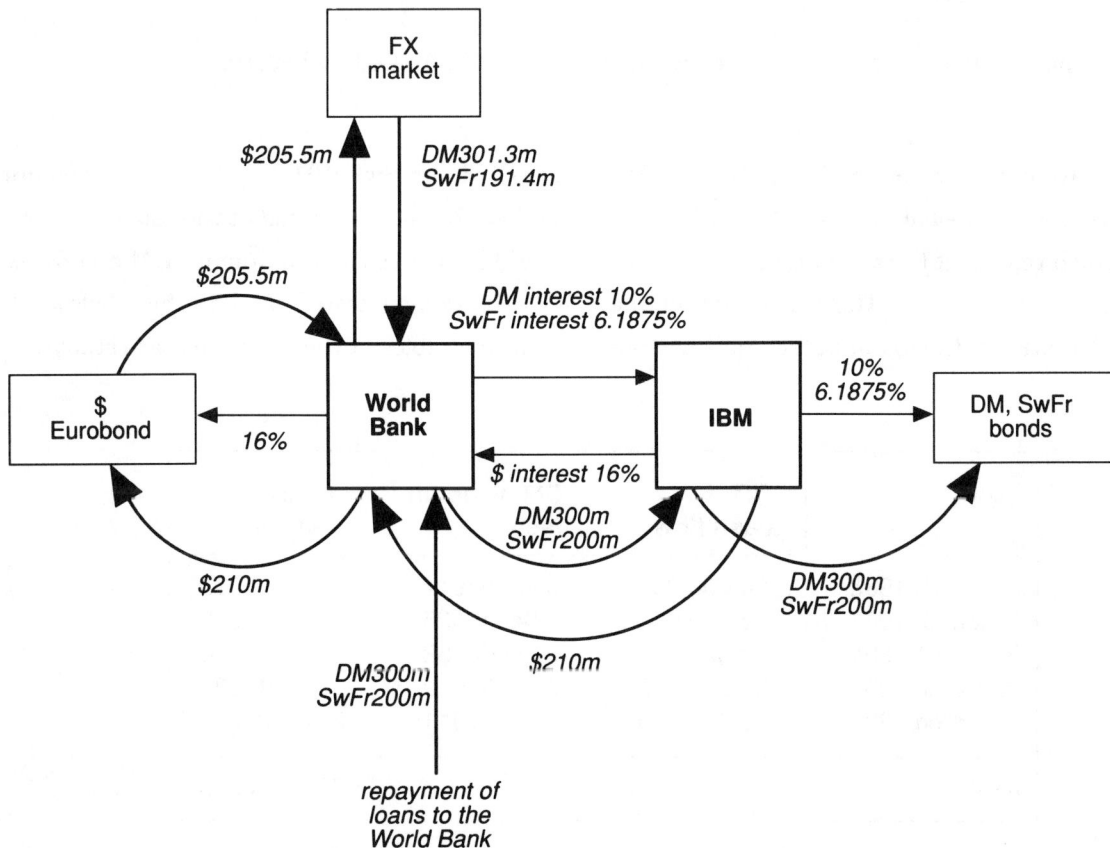

The valuation of the World Bank-IBM deal required the following sequence of steps:

- the counterparties agreed swaps with an exchange at maturity of principal amounts of DM300m and SwFr200m against dollars;

- the World Bank negotiated target costs of funds of 11% per annum for DM and 8% per annum for SwFr;

- given these target costs of funds, the following cash flows consisting of:

  — annual payments during the life of the swap of DM interest at 10% per annum (on DM300m);

  — annual payments during the life of the swap of SwFr interest at 6.1875% per annum (on SwFr200m);

  — payments at maturity of principal amounts of DM300m and SwFr200m;

imply borrowings by the World Bank of DM301,315,273 and SwFr191,367,478. These amounts are the net present values (NPV) of DM300m and SwFr200m, discounted at the rates of interest which represent the target cost of funds for the World Bank (11% per annum for DM and 8% per annum for SwFr). The calculation of these NPVs is demonstrated in the tables below (the calculation of the discount factors is demonstrated in the tables at the end of the case study).

	DM cash flow	DM discount factor	present values
30 March 1982	30,000,000	0.93957644	28,187,293
30 March 1983	30,000,000	0.84646526	25,393,958
30 March 1984	30,000,000	0.76258132	22,877,440
30 March 1985	30,000,000	0.68701020	20,610,306
30 March 1986	330,000,000	0.61892811	204,246,276
NPV			301,315,273

	SwFr cash flow	SwFr discount factor	present values
30 March 1982	12,375,000	0.95507746	11,819,084
30 March 1983	12,375,000	0.88433099	10,943,596
30 March 1984	12,375,000	0.81882499	10,132,959
30 March 1985	12,375,000	0.75817128	9,382,270
30 March 1986	212,375,000	0.70201045	149,089,469
NPV			191,367,478

■ as the World Bank is actually borrowing dollars and buying the DM and SwFr in the forward foreign exchange market, the proceeds of its Eurobond issue must be the dollar equivalent, at the forward rates of 2.56 ($/DM) and 2.18 ($/SwFr), of DM301,316,488 and SwFr191,367,479:

$$\text{SwFr191,367,479/2.18} = \$87,783,247$$
$$\text{DM301,316,488/2.56} = \underline{\$117,701,753}$$
$$\$205,485,000$$

■ given required proceeds (after fees) of $205,485,000 and assuming fees of 2.15%, the face value of the World Bank Eurobond issue had to be $210,000,000 ($205,485,000 is 97.85% of $210,000,000, in other words, $210,000,000 less fees of 2.15%).

■ the cost to IBM of dollar funds through the swap can now be calculated: the calculation is set out in the following table.

PMT	30 March 1982	$20,066,667*
	30 March 1983	$33,600,000
	30 March 1984	$33,600,000
	30 March 1985	$33,600,000
	30 March 1986	$243,600,000
n		4.597222 years
PV		98.75 (= $205,485,000)
FV		100.00 (= $210,000,000)
i		*16.6%*

* From 25 August 1981 to 30 March 1982 is 215 days, so this coupon payment is less than the others, which are for a year.

		Calculation of discount factors		
	period up to coupon date	discount factor exponent*	DM discount factor $i = 11\%$	SwFr discount factor $i = 8\%$
30 March 1982	215 days	215/360 = 0.597222	0.93957644	0.95507746
30 March 1983	360 days	575/360 = 1.597222	0.84646526	0.88433099
30 March 1984	360 days	935/360 = 2.597222	0.76258132	0.81882499
30 March 1985	360 days	1.295/360 = 3.597222	0.68701020	0.75817128
30 March 1986	360 days	1.655/360 = 4.597222	0.61892811	0.70201045

* The discount factor exponent is n in the formula: $\dfrac{1}{(1 + \frac{i}{100})^n}$

Self-Study Exercises: <u>Questions</u>   Part 4

Assume in all questions that all interest rates are quoted on the same basis in terms of day count, annual basis and compounding conventions.

Question 4.1:   For what reasons can swaps have non-zero values?

Question 4.2:   For what function are off-market swaps used?

Question 4.3:   Why is it necessary to value swaps which are being terminated or assigned?

Question 4.4:   What is the value of the following dollar/Deutsche mark currency swap:

life	= 6 years
dollar fixed interest rate	= 7%pa
Deutsche mark fixed interest rate	= 6%pa
dollar principal	= $40m
Deutsche mark principal	= DM56m
$/DM exchange rate	= 1.4000

where current rates prevailing in the market are:

6-year dollar interest rate	= 4%pa
6-year Deutsche mark interest rate	= 8%pa
current $/DM exchange rate	= 1.2700

Question 4.5:   Which counterparty to the swap in the question above would receive an upfront cash payment, if the swap was terminated?

Question 4.6: What methods are commonly used to value floating interest streams in cash flows through swaps?

Question 4.7: What is the value of the following dollar/Deutsche mark cross-currency coupon swap:

life	= 1 year
Deutsche mark fixed interest rate	= 8%pa
dollar interest rate	= 6-month Libor
Deutsche mark principal	= DM145m
dollar principal	= $100m
$/DM exchange rate	= 1.4500
1-year day count	= 365 days

Current rates prevailing in the market are:

1-year Deutsche mark interest rate	= 7%pa
6-month dollar Libor	= 3.5%pa
12-month dollar Libor	= 4%pa
current $/DM exchange rate	= 1.4000
6-month day count	= 182 days

Question 4.8: What is the value of the following dollar/Swiss franc cross-currency coupon swap:

life	= 1 year
Swiss franc fixed interest rate	= 7%pa
dollar interest rate	= 6-month Libor
Swiss franc principal	= SwFr65m
dollar principal	= $50m
$/SwFr exchange rate	= 1.3000
1-year day count	= 365 days

Current rates prevailing in the market are:

1-year Swiss franc interest rate	= 6%pa
12-month dollar Libor	= 3.5%pa
current $/SwFr exchange rate	= 1.3750

One-year dollar coupon swaps (semi-annual payment of fixed interest) are currently quoted at 4% per annum.

Self-Study Exercises: <u>Answers</u>   Part 4

Answer 4.1:   Swaps can have non-zero values for a variety of reasons. They might be:

■   *non-generic swaps*, which incorporate special risk features such as options that modify the value of the swap;

■   deliberately priced at *off-market* rates in order to generate cash flows with profiles which match those on underlying instruments such as bonds;

■   par swaps when they are negotiated, but have become non-par swaps because the interest rates and exchange rate which constitute their prices have become increasingly *out-dated* and off-market as market rates change.

Answer 4.2:   Off-market swaps are commonly used for **cash flow adjustment** purposes. The upfront cash payment which must be made between the counterparties of an off-market swap is used to change the cash flow profile of payments due between them: a stream of future payments can be converted into a single upfront payment, or vice versa. Cash flow adjustment through a currency swap also involves a change in the currency of cash flows.

Answer 4.3:   Valuation is necessary when swaps are terminated or assigned because assignment or termination might deprive one of the counterparties of its expected profit from the swap. This expected profit would be equal to the difference between the net present value of the future cash flow expected to be received through the swap and the net present value of the future cash flow expected to be paid out. The counterparty expecting to receive this difference should only agree to assignment or termination of the swap if it is offered compensation in the form of an upfront cash payment. Valuation establishes the size of the appropriate cash payment.

Answer 4.4:   To calculate the NPV of the Deutsche mark cash flow, the following data are input into a bond calculator:

n   = 6 years
i   = 8%pa
PMT = 6%pa
FV   = 100 (= DM56m)

which gives an NPV of:

PV   = 90.75 (= DM50,822,375)

To calculate the NPV of the dollar cash flow, the following data are input into the bond calculator:

n   = 6 years
i   = 4%pa
PMT = 7%pa
FV   = 100 (= $40m)

which gives an NPV of:

PV   = 115.73 (= $46,290,564)

The value of the swap is the difference between the NPVs of the Deutsche mark and dollar cash flows. To calculate the difference, the Deutsche mark cash flow must be translated into dollars. This is done at the current $/DM exchange rate of 1.2700, to give:

DM50,822,375/1.2700 = $40,017,618

The value of the swap is therefore:

$46,290,564 − $40,017,618 = $6,272,946

Answer 4.5:   Given that the NPV of the dollar cash flow is greater that the NPV of the Deutsche mark cash flow, the receiver of dollars and payer of Deutsche marks would expect to profit from the swap and should therefore require an upfront cash payment before agreeing to a termination.

Answer 4.6:   There are two methods commonly used by the swap market to the value floating interest streams in cash flows through swaps. These involve the calculation of the NPV of the floating interest stream using either:

■ *forward-forward interest rates* to value future interest cash flows;

■ *matching coupon swaps* to convert the floating interest rate through a cross-currency coupon swap into an equivalent fixed interest rate by determining the price (fixed interest rate) of a new single-currency coupon swap in the same currency as the floating interest side of the currency swap.

Answer 4.7:   To calculate the NPV of the Deutsche mark cash flow, the following data are input into the bond calculator:

```
n    = 1 year
i    = 7%pa
PMT  = 8%pa
FV   = 100 (= DM145m)
```

which gives an NPV of:

```
PV   = 100.93 (= DM146,355,140)
```

As regards the valuation of the dollar cash flow, the NPV of the *principal* amount of $100m is:

n   = 1 year
i   = 4%pa
PMT = 0
FV = 100 (= $100m)

which gives an NPV of:

PV   = 96.15 (= $96,153,846)

To calculate the NPV of the dollar floating interest cash flow, two alternative approaches are available:

■   *using forward-forward interest rates* directly —

Libor for this future period is taken to be the forward-forward interest rate for the period. The forward-forward rate is:

$$\left[\frac{1+\left[\dfrac{\text{cash interest rate}_{\text{far date}} \times \text{day count}_{\text{far date}}}{100 \times \text{annual basis}}\right]}{1+\left[\dfrac{\text{cash interest rate}_{\text{near date}} \times \text{day count}_{\text{near date}}}{100 \times \text{annual basis}}\right]}-1\right] \times \left[\frac{100 \times \text{annual basis}}{\text{day count}_{\text{near-far date}}}\right]$$

$$\left[\frac{1+\left[\dfrac{4 \times 365}{100 \times 360}\right]}{1+\left[\dfrac{3.5 \times 182}{100 \times 360}\right]}-1\right] \times \left[\frac{100 \times 360}{183}\right] = 4.4192\%\text{pa}$$

The floating interest expected to be due in six months is:

$$\$100,000,000 \times \left(\frac{3.5 \times 182}{100 \times 360} \right) = \$1,769,444$$

The floating interest expected to be due in 12months is:

$$\$100,000,000 \times \left(\frac{4.4192 \times 183}{100 \times 360} \right) = \$2,246,427$$

The present values of these amounts (discounted at 6 and 12-month cash rates of 3.5% and 4% per annum, respectively) are:

$$\frac{\$1,769,444}{1 + \left(\frac{3.5 \times 182}{100 \times 360} \right)} = \$1,738,679$$

$$\frac{\$2,246,427}{1 + \left(\frac{4 \times 365}{100 \times 360} \right)} = \$2,158,873$$

The NPV of the floating interest cash flow is therefore:

$$\$2,158,873 + \$1,738,679 = \$3,897,552$$

- *using notional principal amounts.*

To replicate the value of future floating interest cash flows, NPAs of $100m are recorded at the start and end of the swap and then discounted. The first amount does not need to be discounted (because it has a day count of 0). Discounting the last amount (using the prevailing 12-month cash rate of 4% per annum) produces a present value of $96,102,509. The NPV is therefore:

$100,000,000 − $96,102,509 = $3,897,491

This result is the same as that achieved through the forward-forward interest rates. The calculation is illustrated in the table below.

	0 months	12 months
notional principal amounts	+100,000,000	−100,000,000
cash rates	n/a	4%
present values	+100,000,000	−96,102,509
net present value		−3,897,491

The NPV of the Deutsche mark cash flow was calculated as DM146,355,140. At the current $/DM exchange rate of 1.4000, this is equivalent to:

DM146,355,140/1.4000 = $104,539,386

The NPV of the dollar cash flow was calculated in two parts: the principal payment and the floating interest cash flow. The total NPV is:

$96,153,846 + $3,897,491 = $100,051,337

The overall value of the swap is therefore:

$104,539,386 − $100,051,337 = $4,488,049

Answer 4.8: To calculate the NPV of the Swiss franc cash flow, the following data are input into the bond calculator:

```
n    = 1 year
i    = 6%pa
PMT  = 7%pa
FV   = 100 (= SwFr65m)
```

which gives an NPV of:

```
PV   = 100.94 (= SwFr65,613,208)
```

As regards the valuation of the dollar cash flow, the price (fixed interest rate) of one-year dollar coupon swaps demonstrates that six-month Libor is currently equivalent to a fixed interest rate of 4% per annum. This allows the NPV of the floating interest side of the currency swap to be calculated on the bond calculator:

```
n    = 1 year
i    = 3.5%pa
PMT  = 4%pa
FV   = 100 (= $50m)
```

which gives an NPV of:

```
PV   = 100.48 (= $50,241,546)
```

The NPV of the Swiss franc cash flow was calculated as SwFr65,613,208. At the current $/DM exchange rate of 1.3750, this is equivalent to:

SwFr65,613,208/1.3750 = $47,718,697

The NPV of the swap as a whole is therefore:

$50,241,546 − $47,718,697 = $2,522,849

5 Currency swap risk and regulation

Credit risk in currency swaps

Types of risk in currency swaps

Previous chapters of this Workbook have examined the exposure which currency swaps open up to *interest rate and currency risks* (including the *basis risk* and other *mismatch risks* found in trying to hedge exposures in swaps). If the currency and interest rate risks taken through a swap turn out to be profitable, there is still the **credit risk** on the payments which have to be made through the swap before profits can be realised. This chapter examines the credit risk in currency swaps.

The impact of credit risk on currency swaps

The impact of credit risk on currency swaps compared to interest rate swaps differs in two key respects:

- whereas derivatives like interest rate swaps involve exchanges of interest only, *non-derivative* off-balance sheet instruments like currency swaps involve exchanges of both interest and principal. This means that the risk that one counterparty to a currency swap might make a payment before detecting a default by the other on the counterpayment (often called **delivery risk**) is much more serious than for interest rate swaps.

- as noted already, currency swaps create an exposure to both *interest rate and currency risks*, whereas interest rate swaps create an exposure to interest rate risk only. The magnitude of the risk of a default by a counterparty to a currency swap therefore depends on how adversely interest rates *and* the exchange rate have moved since the swap was transacted.

The material consequences of the impact of credit risk on both currency swaps and interest rate swaps depend on whether a swap is being used to:

- *hedge* — the default of one counterparty will leave the other exposed to the interest rate and currency risk which was being hedged: this will be an *actual* cost, if any of those risks are realised;

- *take risk* on interest rates (currency swaps are not used to take currency risk) — the default of one counterparty will deprive the other of the opportunity for making a profit on future interest rate movements, which is an *opportunity* rather than an actual cost (in theory, a default by one counterparty could relieve the other of a loss-making swap: in practice, the trustee or administrator of the defaulting counterparty would maintain such a swap, as it would be profitable for the defaulter);

- *arbitrage* — the default of one counterparty will deprive the other of the opportunity for making a profit on interest and/or exchange rate anomalies, which is an *opportunity* cost: however, the remaining side of the arbitrage may be in loss, in which case, the default of the swap would be an *actual* cost (arbitrage involves the buying and selling of the same commodity at different prices in order to produce a profit, which depends on the difference between prices, not on their absolute levels: if the purchase transaction moves into loss, the sale transaction will move into profit, or vice versa, depending on how prices move).

Measuring the impact of credit risk on currency swaps

The *impact* of credit risk on off-balance sheet instruments like currency swaps is often expressed in terms of the concept of **default risk**, where:

default risk = credit risk x market risk

Credit risk is the probability of a default occurring. Market risk is the loss which is incurred in the event of a default: in the case of currency swaps, market risk consists of interest rate and currency risk.

Measuring credit risk

The measurement of the credit risk component in the above equation involves the application of the standard techniques of credit analysis developed for use across the financial sector. However, credit risk analysis is not within the scope of this Workbook and readers should consult specialist texts[1].

Measuring market risk

In analysing the market risk component of the default risk on swaps, it is usual to distinguish between:

■ *current market risk*: the interest and currency loss which would be suffered in the event of an *immediate* default;

■ *future market risk*: the additional interest and currency loss which would be suffered in the event of a *future* default (between now and the maturity of the swap).

Current risk can be quantified with certainty, as it is a function of past interest and exchange rate movements. Future risk, however, can only be estimated, as it depends on expectations about future interest and exchange rate movements, as well as the timing of default.

Measuring current market risk

The immediate loss which would be suffered at the time of a default is usually measured in terms of the **replacement cost** of the defaulted swap. This is the upfront cash fee which must be paid by the **affected counterparty** in order to induce a new counterparty to transact a replacement swap which is an exact replica of the defaulted currency swap and which restores the status quo before default. As interest and exchange rates will have moved since the defaulted swap was originally transacted, the replacement swap will be priced at what are now historic (off-market) rates. If the replacement counterparty has to pay above current interest through the replacement swap or receive below current interest, or has to pay a higher exchange rate at maturity, it will require compensation for the difference between the original and current rates before it will transact the replacement swap. Note that the replacement cost will cover the immediate loss due to both interest and exchange rate changes over the life of the defaulted swap, in other words, *current market risk*.

The replacement cost of a currency swap should be equal to the value of a replacement swap priced at the original interest and exchange rates. It was explained in *Part Four* that the value of a new generic swap priced at current market rates (a so-called par swap) should be zero: this is because no counterparties will transact if they expect to pay more through the swap than they expect to receive. A replacement swap is, however, priced at historic rates and is therefore likely to have a non-zero value. The counterparty which accrues this value through the replacement swap will have to compensate the other counterparty in order to induce it to transact at historic rates. This compensation is the replacement cost.

It was also explained in *Part Four* that the value of a swap is calculated as the difference between the net present value (NPV) of the cash flow stream being received and the NPV of the cash flow stream being paid. In a currency swap, one NPV must also be translated into the same currency as the other in order to calculate the difference in the values of the two cash flow streams. Note that the streams of currencies being exchanged through a currency swap include, not only the interest cash flows being exchanged, but also the principal amounts which are exchanged at maturity. The replacement cost of a currency swap is therefore equal to the total NPV of the interest *and principal* cash flows of the replacement swap. However, if the interest component is floating, it is ignored when measuring credit exposure and the NPV of the cash flow is simply the present value of the principal amount. An alternative method of valuation is to convert the floating interest rate index (typically Libor) into the equivalent fixed interest rate. This is done by determining the current price (fixed interest rate) of a coupon swap in the same currency as the floating interest and of the same maturity. In effect, cross-currency coupon swaps are converted into currency swaps. For example, take the dollar floating interest stream of a dollar/yen cross-currency coupon swap with two years remaining to maturity. The equivalent fixed interest rate is given by the price of a current two-year dollar coupon swap using the same floating interest rate index (typically six-month dollar Libor). The coupon swap converts the dollar/yen cross-currency coupon swap (fixed-against-floating) into a dollar/yen currency swap (fixed-against-fixed). Both (fixed) interest streams (plus principal amounts) are then valued in order to calculate the replacement cost of the original cross-currency coupon swap.

The direction in which a replacement cost must be paid depends on interest and exchange rate movements since a currency swap was transacted. For *cross-currency coupon swaps* (fixed-against-floating):

■ if interest rates have *risen* between the transaction of a swap and default, a replacement swap at the original fixed interest rates will pay what is now a below-market rate: the replacement cost is paid to the *receiver* of the (below-market) fixed interest through the replacement swap;

■ if interest rates have *fallen*, a replacement swap at the original fixed interest rates will pay what is now an above-market rate: the replacement cost is paid to the *payer* of the (above-market) fixed interest through the replacement swap.

Note that only changes in *fixed interest* cash flows have been taken into account. The reason for this is that floating interest rates are reset periodically and frequently (at least every six months). It is therefore often assumed that replacement swaps will not represent much of a disturbance to the floating interest cash flow (although the mismatching of reset dates which might result when a swap is replaced can create serious basis risk).

For *currency swaps* (fixed-against-fixed), cash payments depend on the relative movement of the two fixed interest rates:

■ if the interest rates on the currency being paid through the swap have *risen* between the transaction of the swap and default, and interest rates on the currency being received have *fallen* over the same period, a replacement swap at the original fixed interest rates will pay what is now a below-market rate and will earn an above-market rate: the replacement cost is paid to the *receiver* of the below-market fixed interest, which is also the payer of the above-market fixed interest;

- if the interest rates on the currency being paid through the swap have *fallen* between the transaction of the swap and default, and interest rates on the currency being received have *risen* over the same period, a replacement swap at the original fixed interest rates will pay what is now an above-market rate and will earn a below-market rate: the replacement cost is paid to the *payer* of the below-market fixed interest, which is also the receiver of the above-market fixed interest;

- if the interest rates on the currency being paid through the swap and the interest rates on the currency being received have both *fallen* or have both *risen*, the direction in which the replacement cost is paid depends on their relative changes: for example, if the sterling interest rates on a sterling/dollar currency swap have risen between the transaction of the swap and default, and dollar interest rates on the currency being received have also risen over the same period, but not by as much, a replacement swap at the original interest rates will exchange what is now a below-market sterling rate against an even more below-market dollar rate, which means the replacement cost is paid to the payer of the (below-market) sterling interest, which is also the receiver of the (even-more below-market) dollar interest.

The impact of interest rate changes on replacement cost will be attenuated or accentuated by the movement of the *exchange rate* between the currencies being swapped. For example, take the payer of fixed Deutsche mark interest through a dollar/ Deutsche mark currency swap. If German interest rates rise and US interest rates fall, a subsequent default by the counterparty to the swap would mean that a replacement swap — transacted at historic interest rates — would entail paying Deutsche mark interest below current market rates and receiving dollar interest above current market rates. An upfront payment would be required to compensate the counterparty to the replacement swap. However, if the dollar had depreciated against the Deutsche mark before the default, less Deutsche marks would have to be exchanged through a replacement swap for the same dollar principal at maturity. This gain on the exchange of principal might offset some or all of the interest loss.

Diagram 50: The impact of interest and exchange rate changes on currency swap replacement cost

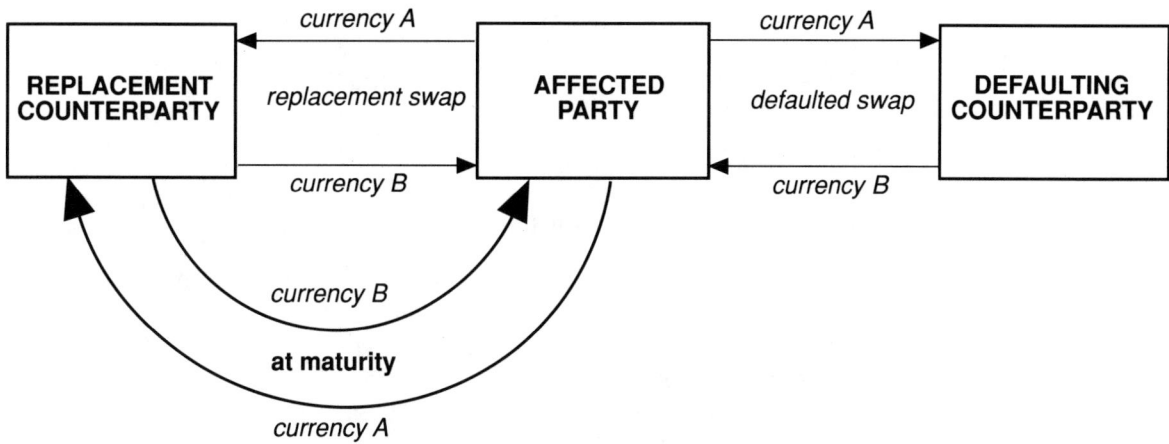

Change in rates between transaction and default		Action by affected counterparty
Interest rate	A interest rate RISES	PAYS replacement cost
	A interest rate FALLS	—
	B interest rate RISES	—
	B interest rate FALLS	PAYS replacement cost
Exchange rate	A APPRECIATES against B	—
	A DEPRECIATES against B	PAYS replacement cost

An example

Take the following dollar/yen *currency swap* (fixed-against-fixed):

life	= 5 years
dollar fixed interest rate	= 4%pa
yen fixed interest rate	= 6%pa
dollar principal	= $40m
yen principal	= Y5bn
$/Y exchange rate	= 125.00

Assume there is a default by the counterparty which pays dollars and receives yen, after exactly three years. The parameters of the swap are now:

life	= 2 years
dollar fixed interest rate	= 5%pa
yen fixed interest rate	= 9%pa
$/Y exchange rate	= 123.00

Assume a replacement swap is transacted with a new counterparty at the original interest and exchange rates. The value of the replacement swap — in other words, the replacement cost — is equal to the difference between the NPV of the dollar cash flow stream and the NPV of the yen cash flow stream, where the yen NPV is translated into dollars.

The NPV of the *dollar* cash flow through the replacement swap (which replicates the dollar cash flow through the defaulted swap) can be calculated, using a bond calculator, from the following data:

n	= 2 years
i	= 5%pa
PMT	= 4%pa
FV	= 100 (= $40m)

which gives an NPV of:

PV = 98.14 (= $39,256,236)

The NPV of the *yen* cash flow through the replacement swap (which replicates the yen cash flow through the defaulted swap) can be calculated, using a bond calculator, from the following data:

```
n    = 2 years
i    = 9%pa
PMT  = 6%pa
FV   = 100  (= Y5bn)
```

which gives an NPV of:

PV = 94.72 (= Y4,736,133,322)

At the new $/Y *exchange rate* of Y123.00, the NPV of the yen cash flow translates into:

Y4,736,133,322 / 123.00 = $38,505,149

The value of the swap and its replacement cost is therefore:

$39,256,236 – $38,505,149 = $751,087

The process of calculating replacement cost — involving as it does the application of current market rates — is called **marking to market.**

Because the NPV of the dollar cash flows is greater than the NPV of the yen cash flows, the payer of dollars and receiver of yen — which is the replacement counterparty — needs to be compensated in order to induce it to transact the replacement swap at off-market rates. This compensation, in the form of a replacement cost of $751,087, is paid *by* the affected counterparty *to* the replacement counterparty.

Diagram 51: Calculating replacement cost

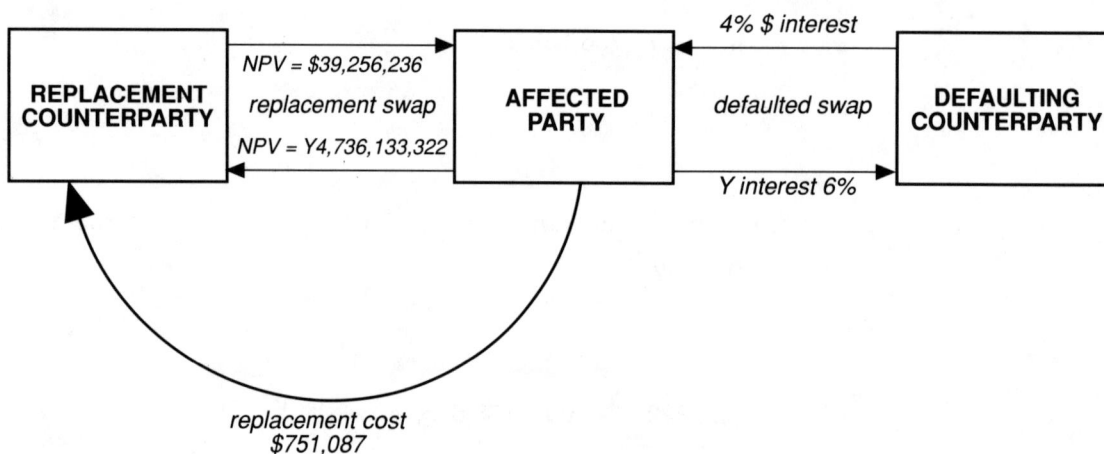

Diagram showing three boxes. REPLACEMENT COUNTERPARTY connected to AFFECTED PARTY with "replacement swap", NPV = $39,256,236 and NPV = Y4,736,133,322. AFFECTED PARTY connected to DEFAULTING COUNTERPARTY with "defaulted swap", 4% $ interest and Y interest 6%. A curved arrow from AFFECTED PARTY to REPLACEMENT COUNTERPARTY labeled replacement cost $751,087.

The direction of the payment of the replacement cost can be worked out another way. By the time of default, dollar interest rates had risen by only one percentage point, whereas yen interest rates had risen by three. Given that the replacement swap therefore pays a below-market dollar fixed interest rate and an even more below-market yen rate, the payer of dollars and receiver of yen — which is the replacement counterparty — can be seen to be the net loser on interest payments and requiring compensation. Account also has to be taken of the change in the $/Y exchange rate. This moved against the dollar, thereby reducing the principal amount of yen which must be exchanged at maturity for the original amount of dollars. However, the replacement swap is based on the historic exchange rate and is therefore to the advantage of the payer of dollars and receiver of yen — which is the replacement counterparty — and should reduce the replacement cost received in order to compensate for interest rate movements. As the relative change in the exchange rate is much smaller than the relative change in interest rates, the net replacement cost is due to the replacement counterparty. To see the effect of the exchange rate, consider the result, if the exchange rate had changed to about 120.65. The advantage to the replacement counterparty of the exchange rate paid in the replacement swap would more or less offset the interest rate disadvantage and the net replacement cost is therefore zero.

Another example

Take the following dollar/Deutsche mark *cross-currency coupon swap* (fixed-against-floating):

life	= 10 years
dollar interest rate	= Libor
Deutsche mark fixed interest rate	= 6%pa
dollar principal	= $40m
Deutsche mark principal	= DM60m
$/DM exchange rate	= 1.5000

Assume there is a default by the counterparty which receives dollars and pays Deutsche marks, after exactly five years. The parameters of the swap are now:

life	= 5 years
dollar fixed interest rate	= 3%pa
Deutsche mark fixed interest rate	= 4%pa
$/DM exchange rate	= 1.5500

Assume a replacement swap is transacted with a new counterparty at the original interest and exchange rates. The value of the replacement swap — in other words, the replacement cost — is equal to the difference between the NPV of the dollar cash flow stream and the NPV of the Deutsche mark cash flow stream, where the Deutsche mark NPV is translated into dollars. As the dollar interest rate is floating, only the dollar principal exchanged at maturity (and not the interest) is included in the value of the swap.

As explained at the start of this section, floating interest cash flows are ignored when measuring the credit exposure in swaps. The NPV of a cash flow composed of a stream of floating interest and a principal amount at maturity is, for the purpose of measuring credit exposure, taken to be the NPV of the principal amount only. Therefore, the NPV of the *dollar* cash flow through the replacement swap in this example is $40m discounted at 3% per annum, which is $34,504,351.

The NPV of the *Deutsche mark* cash flow through the replacement swap (which replicates the yen cash flow through the defaulted swap) can be calculated, using a bond calculator, from the following data:

```
n      = 5 years
i      = 4%pa
PMT  = 6%pa
FV    = 100  (= DM60m)
```

which give an NPV of:

PV = 108.90 (= DM65,342,187)

At the new $/DM *exchange rate* of 1.5500, the NPV of the Deutsche mark cash flow translates into:

DM65,342,187 / 1.5500 = $42,156,250

The value of the swap is therefore:

$42,156,250 – $40,000,000 = $2,156,250

However, as explained in *Part Four*, the value of a new generic swap priced at current market rates should be zero. The replacement swap has a non-zero value, because it is priced at off-market rates. Because the NPV of the Deutsche mark cash flows is greater than the NPV of the dollar cash flows, the payer of Deutsche marks and receiver of dollars — which is the replacement counterparty — needs to be compensated in order to induce it to transact the replacement swap at historic off-market rates. This compensation, in the form of a replacement cost of $2,156,250 is paid *by* the affected counterparty *to* the replacement counterparty.

Diagram 52: Calculating replacement cost

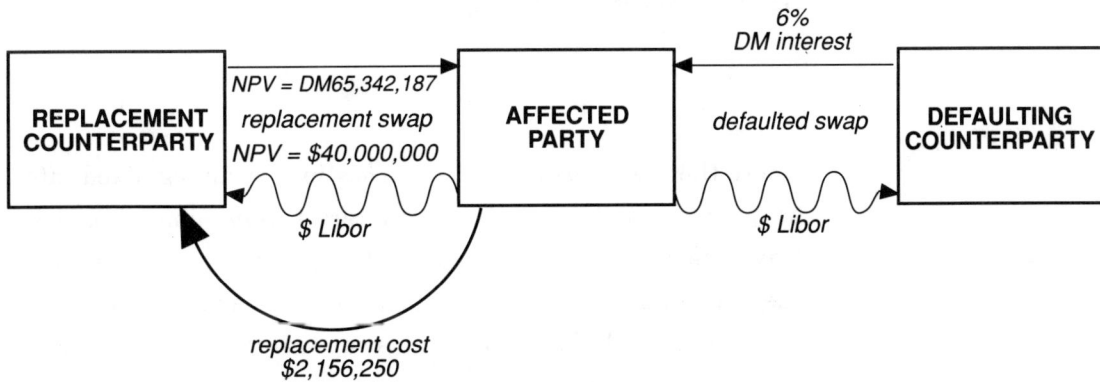

Change in the impact of credit risk over time

At the time a currency swap is negotiated its value is zero, implying that there is no current replacement cost, which means there is also no current interest rate and currency risk, and therefore no current default risk. As noted already, future replacement cost depends on the direction in which interest and exchange rates move in the future. This is stochastic and cannot be known with certainty. However, there are two tendencies which change the interest rate and currency risk on a swap in more deterministic ways as it moves to maturity:

■ as the life of a swap moves to maturity, the number of *interest payments* which are due through the swap declines: this automatically reduces the interest rate risk on the swap (ignoring any change in interest rate levels);

■ as the life of a swap moves to maturity, current swap rates become increasingly less likely to further diverge from or converge with the original price of the swap: this will tend to reduce further changes in the *replacement cost* of the swap;

■ where there are *payment mismatches* in a swap (eg, fixed interest may be paid annually and floating interest semi-annually), default may leave one counterparty having made a gross payment without receiving the entire amount of the offsetting counterpayment: the credit risk on the interest cash flows through a swap will therefore increase each time a mismatched payment is outstanding to a counterparty.

Risk capital requirements for swaps

Basle Agreement

In July 1988, the Committee on Banking Regulation and Supervisory Practices[2] of the Group of Ten industrialised countries (G-10)[3] — which meets regularly at the Bank for International Settlements (BIS) at Basle in Switzerland to co-ordinate the supervision of international banks — published its *Proposals for International Convergence of Capital Measurement and Capital Standards*. The objective was to ensure that, from the end of 1992 (from mid-1989 in the UK), standards of capital adequacy for international commercial banks *converged*. Every international commercial bank should have risk capital:

- of commonly-defined quality;

- including credit risk on and off the balance sheet, as measured according to common rules[4];

- covering at least 8% of credit risk (the so-called *Basle ratio*).

The *Basle Convergence Agreement* (more usually called the *Basle Agreement* or *Basle Accord*) currently only covers *default risk*: work is continuing to include what the authorities term *investment risk*, which is market risk and includes interest rate and exchange rate risks.

Calculating default risk for Basle

The method prescribed by the Basle Agreement for determining the minimum risk capital requirement for exchange rate instruments such as currency swaps follows the method described in the previous section and implicitly treats default risk as a function of:

- *credit risk* (probability of default);

- *market risk* (the loss due to default arising from interest rate and/or currency risk).

Calculating credit risk for Basle

Credit risk is classified under the Basle Agreement into five bands, largely defined by:

■ reference to whether a counterparty is an official or private entity;

■ whether it is based in a country within the OECD[5].

Each band has a **risk weight** measuring the probability of default for the purposes of calculating risk capital requirements. For the purposes of calculating the credit risk on interest rate and exchange rate instruments, including swaps, 100% risk weights have been reduced to 50%. This means that there are in fact only *four* bands for interest rate and exchange rate instruments. The normal five bands are listed in the table below.

Table 15: Basle risk weights

0%	cash
	bullion
	loans to OECD governments/central banks
	loans to non-OECD governments/central banks in own currency
10%	loans on the UK discount market
	short-term fixed-income debt on OECD central governments
	floating-rate debt on OECD central governments
	funded short-term debt of non-OECD central governments
20%	long-term fixed-income debt on OECD governments
	funded long-term debt on non-OECD central governments
	claims on multilateral development banks
	claims on OECD-incorporated banks
	funded short-term claims on non-OECD-incorporated banks
	claims on OECD non-commercial public sector organisations
50%	residential mortgages
100%	claims on non-bank private sector
	long-term claims on non-OECD banks
	unfunded and foreign currency claims on non-OECD governments
	claims on OECD public sector commercial companies
	claims on non-OECD public sector
	fixed assets
	property
	aggregate net short open foreign exchange positions

NB: Short-term means below 1 year and long-term means 1 year and longer; both refer to residual maturities. Funded means funded in the same currency. The 100% risk weight is only 50% for interest rate and exchange rate instruments, including swaps.

Calculating market risk for Basle

Market risk under the Basle Agreement is calculated using one of two alternative methods. National supervisors are free to select the method to be applied in their country:

■ **current exposure method** calculates market risk in terms of:
  — **current exposure**, which corresponds to current market risk and is the *replacement cost* of a currency swap, measured by *marking to market*: where a default on an instrument would benefit a counterparty and there is therefore no replacement cost, current exposure is zero;
  — **residual maturity** or **potential exposure**, which corresponds to future market risk, is measured by one of the following **residual maturity weights** (sometimes called *add-ons*), expressed as a flat percentage of the notional principal amount of a currency swap:

Residual maturity	Residual maturity weight
less than 1 year	1.0% flat
more than 1 year	5.0% flat

■ **original exposure method** does not distinguish between current and future market risk: market risk is calculated in terms of fixed weights, expressed as percentages (flat and annual) of principal amounts, related to the *original* maturity of the instrument:

Original maturity	Original maturity weight
less than1 year	2.0% flat
1–2 years	5.0% flat
more than 2 years	3.0%pa beyond 2 years

Market risk (calculated as either current or original exposure) is multiplied by credit risk (in the form of the Basle risk weights) to calculate the default risk on a swap or its **risk-adjusted balance**. The risk capital requirement is then 8% of this figure. The process of calculating the risk capital requirement for a currency swap under the Basle Agreement is illustrated in the diagram below.

The method for calculating risk capital requirements for currency swaps can be seen to be the same as for interest rate swaps. However, the weights for currency swaps are much heavier than for interest rate swaps because of the usual exchange of principal amounts and the increased delivery risk. It is thought that the imposition of the Basle Agreement has slowed down the growth of the currency swap market, although perhaps not by as much as was expected.

Diagram 53: Calculating risk capital requirements for exchange rate instruments

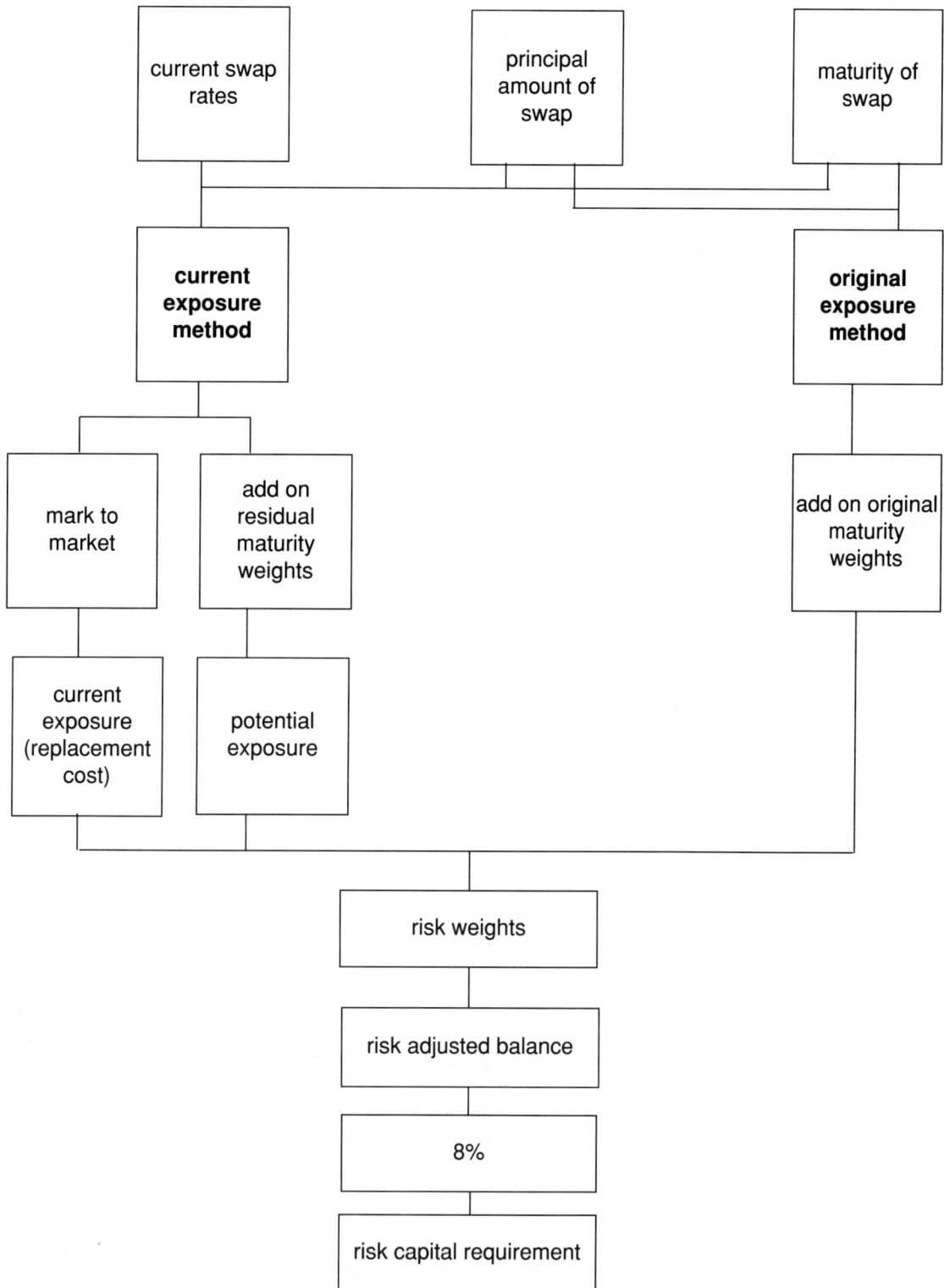

An example

A simplified illustration of the calculation of the risk capital requirements for a currency swaps book under the current exposure method of the Basle Agreement is given in the table below.

Table 16: Calculating Basle risk capital requirements

	transactions with 0% risk-weighted counterparties		transactions with 20% risk-weighted counterparties		transactions with 50% risk-weighted counterparties	
residual maturity	less than 1 year	more than 1 year	less than 1 year	more than 1 year	less than 1 year	more than 1 year
principal amount	645.5	505.7	458.7	350.3	250.9	106.4
current exposure (principal amounts) marked to market	6.567	6.123	3.367	4.693	1.923	0.887
residual maturity weights	1.0%	5.0%	1.0%	5.0%	1.0%	5.0%
potential exposure (weighted principal amounts)	6.455	25.285	4.587	17.515	2.509	5.320
total exposure	13.022	31.408	7.954	22.208	4.432	6.207
risk weights	0%	0%	20%	20%	50%	50%
risk adjusted balance	0	0	1.591	4.442	2.216	3.104
			= 6.033		= 5.320	
8% risk capital requirement	0	0	0.483		0.426	
			= £908,600 (rounded)			

EC Directives

The European Commission has been seeking to harmonise prudential supervision within the European Community (EC) in support of the Single European Market programme and has or is about to promulgate a number of regulations on risk capital to be implemented within EC members. The relevant EC initiatives are:

- the *Solvency Ratio Directive* (Council Directive 89/647/EEC) governing the minimum capital adequacy requirements on commercial banks to cover default risk: this largely follows the Basle Agreement;

- the *Second Banking Co-ordination Directive* governing the initial minimum capital requirements on commercial banks;

- the *Directive on Own Funds* (89/298/EEC) governing the definition of risk capital for commercial banks: this also largely follows the Basle Agreement;

- the proposed *Directive on the Capital Adequacy of Investment Firms and Credit Institutions*, which would govern minimum capital requirements for investment banks; and *position risks* (eg, interest rate and exchange rate risks: investment risk in Basle terminology) for both commercial and investment banks; the definition of capital for investment banks largely follows the Own Funds Directive.

Managing credit risk on currency swaps

Netting

The dramatic growth in the size of the swap market has increasingly encouraged swap intermediaries to seek ways of containing their exposure to risk. The imposition by banking supervisors of risk capital requirements on off-balance sheet instruments such as swaps has generated particular interest in the containment of default risk as a way of ameliorating the burden of capital requirements. Proposals to limit default risk have centred on the procedure of **netting**.

Netting is the offsetting of several separate payments outstanding between the same two counterparties and the settlement of the overall difference as a single net amount paid in one direction rather than several gross amounts paid in both directions.

Netting generally occurs *within* individual swaps when interest payments between the counterparties occur on the same dates. Often payment frequencies will be rearranged to allow netting, eg, annual fixed-interest payments will be split and paid semi-annually to match semi-annual floating-interest payments.

Netting *between* separate swaps (which is what the term 'netting' is usually taken to mean) takes place if there is a default by a swap counterparty. It involves the netting of the net interest and principal payments due on separate swaps in the event of default by one of the counterparties. Thus, if two counterparties have transacted a number of swaps with each other and each counterparty has at least one payment due, the opposing net payments due on the separate swaps can be offset against each other if there is a default and only the overall net difference between the individual net amounts actually settled. Netting between swaps can be achieved by:

- **novation** — with each new swap, a single new contract is created incorporating the new swap and all previous still-outstanding swaps: the ISDA master contracts achieve this by adding new swap agreements as appendices[6];

- **close-out** — a cross-default clause nets out all outstanding swaps between two counterparties only in the event of one defaulting.

Market participants have sought to enforce netting in cases of default in order to limit their default risk. Without netting, the receivers or administrators of bankrupt companies can maintain swap contracts which are profitable from their point of view and default on unprofitable swaps, even if these contracts are with the same counterparty: the so-called practice of **cherry-picking**. The problem with netting is that there have been doubts about the ability to enforce it in most major jurisdictions. Netting can be construed as giving swap counterparties superior rights to other creditors and this is generally not possible. Little exists in the way of legislation or legal precedent to clarify the position. Although most swap contracts contain opinion from legal counsel in support of netting and much of the documentation work of ISDA has been directed at establishing the legal enforceability of netting, none of this is a substitute for an actual legal judgement. Ironically, the generally strong credit history of the swaps market has precluded such an opportunity!

In the US, the problem of netting appears to have been partially resolved by the enactment in August 1989 of the *Financial Institutions Reform, Recovery and Enforcement Act* which recognised netting provisions in cases of insolvency involving US domestic banks and thrifts. This Act was clarified in June 1990 by an amendment to the *US Bankruptcy Code* which stated that netting would be enforceable against insolvent corporate end-users and non-bank swap dealers. However, the situation remains unresolved in the case of cross-border swap defaults. In the UK, the Companies Act 1989 explicitly gave precedence to netting, but only through recognised clearing houses and investment exchanges over normal insolvency rules.

Netting and capital adequacy

In view of the residual doubts about the legal enforceability of netting between domestic counterparties and the unresolved doubts about cross-border netting, the Basle-based Committee on Banking Regulation and Supervisory Practices has made only limited concessions to the argument that netting should be translated into lower risk capital requirements. The supervisory authorities distinguish between:

■ **netting** — meaning offsetting between swaps transacted between the same counterparties on the *same* day;

■ **set-off** — meaning offsetting between swaps transacted between the same counterparties on *different* days.

The Basle Agreement allows market risk to be measured for the purposes of calculating default risk after netting by novation (netting between swaps transacted on the same day), but does not recognise any set-off (netting between swaps transacted on different days). The general issue of netting is being studied by a sub-committee on Interbank Netting Schemes, but no recommendations to relax the Basle Agreement to reflect set-off have yet emerged.

Credit enhancement

Credit enhancement is any technique which reduces the default risk on transactions by providing protection against any loss due to default by a counterparty, but without reducing the credit risk (probability of default) on that counterparty. The principal techniques of credit enhancement are:

- *collateralisation*;

- *insurance* by a third party.

Collateralisation

One or both swap counterparties are protected against loss due to a default by the other by:

- the *pledging* of suitable assets (usually government securities or marketable collateralised assets);

- *guarantees* by highly creditworthy third parties.

There are two basic approaches to collateralisation:

- the *weaker* counterparty posts collateral at the inception of a swap and subsequently adds further collateral to cover any increase above this initial amount in the value of the swap to the stronger counterparty;

■ *mutual* collateralisation by both counterparties: usually involving the posting of collateral at the inception of a swap by both counterparties and the subsequent addition by either counterparty of further collateral to cover any significant increases above the initial amounts in the value of the swap to the other counterparty or a significant deterioration in its own creditworthiness.

Collateralisation emerged in the US as a means of allowing thrifts and smaller regional banks to participate in the interest rate swap market. It remains most common in the US and in long-dated swaps. Thrifts, which lend fixed-rate mortgages but usually fund at floating rates, are important natural users of interest rate swaps and have ready access to marketable collateralised assets, like mortgage-backed securities, to use as collateral.

Insurance

In March 1986, the World Bank group arranged an insurance facility with the Aetna Insurance Company of the US to cover up to 30–50% of the credit exposure on specified currency and interest rate swaps with AA and A-rated counterparties. The limited cover is designed to allow the World Bank to replace swaps at current swap rates. The World Bank pays a commitment fee and a variable exposure-related insurance premium. The insured credit exposure is marked to market weekly. The World Bank has subsequently arranged an insurance facility with Deutsche Bank.

The Aetna insurance facility effectively allowed the World Bank to circumvent a restriction imposed by its Executive Board limiting it to AAA-rated counterparties. This permitted the World Bank to diversify its swaps portfolio, which had become concentrated with a very limited number of counterparties. Insurance was anyway cheaper than intermediation by AAA-rated banks (of which there are a decreasing number).

Regulation of the conduct of business in swaps in the UK

Bank of England Wholesale Markets Supervision

The trading of currency and interest rate swaps in the UK banks is regulated by the Bank of England under its **Wholesale Markets Supervision** regime. The Bank's area of responsibility is part of a wider supervisory framework: the transacting of swaps with end-users is governed by this wider framework. From 29 April 1988, *investment business* in the UK has been subject to the *Financial Services Act 1986 (FSA)*. This legislation was intended to establish a comprehensive framework of investor protection in the UK and investment business includes all forms of non-credit financial intermediation: dealing in, arranging, advising on and managing investments. All financial intermediaries must be authorised and supervised by the *Securities and Investment Board (SIB)* or an authorised *Self-Regulatory Organisation (SRO)*. Credit activities (traditional commercial banking) continue to be supervised by the Bank of England under the *Banking Act 1987*. The FSA is enforced by sanctions under criminal law, a civil law framework under which intermediaries can be sued by investors, if they breach the Act and the threat of exclusion from investment business. The FSA, although designed to protect small investors, encompasses some professional markets such as that in Eurobonds. However, it was eventually decided that certain *wholesale* markets — in 'treasury' products such as foreign exchange, bullion, money and related instruments (including interest rate swaps) — do not need the degree of investor protection offered by the FSA and could be exempted from the FSA, as they are composed of professional intermediaries fully aware of the risks to which they are exposed and have been traditionally supervised by the Bank of England. A special clause, *Section 43*, was drafted into the Act. Despite this exemption, however, the FSA indirectly forced the Bank of England to impose a more formal framework of supervision on the wholesale markets in the UK, in order to stop Section 43 being seen or becoming a regulatory loophole, particularly as some instruments are used both in investment business and in the wholesale markets.

Prior to the FSA, the Bank had exercised informal authority over the traditional foreign exchange, bullion and money markets, and had monitored the development of markets in related derivatives such as FRAs, futures, options and swaps. Following the FSA, the Bank developed a formal (but non-statutory) wholesale markets supervision regime under a special *Wholesale Markets Supervision Division* (separate from its Banking Supervision Division). The regime was elaborated in the so-called *Grey Book*, formally entitled **The Regulation of the Wholesale Markets in Sterling, Foreign Exchange and Bullion**, which was published by the Bank in April 1988. The wholesale markets supervision regime can be broadly divided into two functions:

■ *designation* of institutions eligible for exemption from the FSA under Section 43 and for supervision by the Bank of England (Chapter I of the *Grey Book*);

■ *conduct of business rules* (Chapter II of the *Grey Book*):

   — *capital adequacy* requirements;

   — the *London Code of Conduct*.

Designation for exemption from the FSA

No institution can be unconditionally exempted from the FSA, given the diversity of instruments traded by most financial institutions. Some instruments traded in the wholesale market are also defined as investments by the FSA. Exemption from the FSA is therefore limited to particular transactions. The Bank of England developed a set of criteria to distinguish when transactions are wholesale (and therefore eligible for exemption from the FSA). The transactional criteria are twofold:

■ identity of *instrument*;

■ *size* of transaction.

The Bank offered three categories of transaction based on its two criteria:

- transactions in **wholesale designated** instruments, which are all exempted from the FSA on the assumption that the type of institution transacting will automatically be wholesale and which are:

  — sterling wholesale deposits

  — foreign currency wholesale deposits

  — spot and forward foreign exchange

  — spot and forward gold and silver

  — commercial bills

- transactions in **investment designated** instruments, which are listed in the table below, for which exemption from the FSA depends on the *size* of the transaction.

Instrument	Minimum transaction size (£ '000)
London CDs	100
short-term commercial paper	100
short-term non-London CDs	100
other short-term debentures	100
local authority debt	100
short-term public sector	100
OTC currency options	500
OTC interest rate options	500
gold and silver options	500
FRAs	500
SAFEs (ERAs and FXAs)	500
interest rate swaps	500
cross-currency swaps	**500**
repos	100

Using the criteria above, the Bank of England classifies *institutions* for the purpose of judging eligibility for exemption from the FSA into:

- **listed institutions** — specifically listed by the Bank of England for exemption from the FSA as being 'fit and proper' (by reason of its capital, management and operational resources, standards of business conduct and high reputation and standing) to act on a regular basis as either *market-makers* or *brokers* in one or more wholesale designated instruments: listed institutions have no protection as investors under the FSA for any transactions in wholesale designated instruments;

- **wholesale market counterparties** — unlisted institutions having undertaken transactions in wholesale designated instruments in amounts recognised by the Bank of England as wholesale and within the previous 18 months: these institutions have very little protection for investors under the FSA for transactions in wholesale designated instruments or in investment designated instruments in wholesale amounts;

- **investment customers** — unlisted institutions transacting wholesale designated instruments, but not in wholesale amounts; or listed or unlisted institutions transacting investment designated instruments or undesignated instruments, whatever the amount: these institutions have considerable protection as investors under the FSA.

London Code of Conduct

The Bank of England's revised *Grey Book* of May 1992, formally entitled *The London Code of Conduct: a guide to best practice in the wholesale money markets*, sets out Codes of Conduct for (1) 'traditional' sterling money market, (2) swaps, (3) bullion, (4) foreign currency assets and (5) other wholesale markets. The sections specifically concerning interest rate swaps are:

- *Deals at non-current rates* (page 3). As a general rule, the Bank cautions against the use of off-market rates. It accepts their use in swaps, but advises that management should be satisfied that proper controls are in place to ensure that off-market rates are not used to conceal illegal activities and that the overall terms of off-market swaps (including fee payments) should be in line with par swaps.

■ *Know your customer* (page 4). When entering into transactions in swaps, the Bank recommends as good practice the sending of pre-deal telexes to inexperienced counterparties outlining key terms and strongly recommends the preparation of checklists for use when negotiating and finalising arrangements for swaps. A sample checklist is provided (this was set out in *Part One*).

■ *Procedures: firmness of quotation* (page 5). The Bank notes that considerable use is made in the swap market of 'indicative interest' quotations and that an unconditional firm price is only to be given where a principal intermediary deals directly with a counterparty or when such a principal has received the name of a counterparty from a broker. It states that a principal who quotes a price as 'firm subject to credit' is bound to deal at that price if the counterparty is in a category of counterparty previously identified as acceptable for this purpose. The only exception is where an intermediary has reached its credit limit for a counterparty. It is not acceptable practice to revise a price which was 'firm subject to credit' once the counterparty has been named. Brokers and principal intermediaries are advised to establish ranges of institutions for which prices quoted to brokers are firm subject to credit.

■ *Terms and documentation* (page 8). The Bank encourages the use of standard terms and conditions such as BBAIRS and ISDA Interest Rate and Currency Exchange Agreements. In the case of the latter, the Bank advises that all material options and/or modifications allowed for in Schedule A, and/or choices offered via the Interest rate and Currency Exchange Definitions, must be clearly stated before dealing. Firms should make clear at an early stage, if they are not intending to use standard terms and where changes are proposed. In swaps, the Bank argues that institutions should treat themselves as bound to a deal at the point where the commercial terms of the transactions are agreed and that making swap transactions subject to agreement on documentation is not best practice. It states that counterparties must make every effort to finalise documentation. The Bank believes it should be possible for this to be accomplished within two months of the deal being struck and regards longer than three months as excessive.

■ *Assignments and transfers* (page 8). Counterparties which enter into a swap with the intention of shortly afterwards assigning the deal to a third party are advised to make clear their intention to do so when initially negotiating the deal. It is also recommended that the confirmation sent by counterparties should specify any intent to assign and give details of the procedure that will be used. The subsequent documentation should also make provision for assignment. Consent for the assignment must be secured from the other counterparty before releasing its name to the third party. The other counterparty is obliged to provide sufficient information to enable the assignment to be conducted in accordance with other provisions of the Code, in particular, details of the type of credit acceptable as a new counterparty and reimbursements required to cover administrative costs. Finally, it is noted that proper and clear documentation is just as important for the assignment of swaps as for their origination.

Notes

1. For example, Global Credit Analysis published by IFR in co-operation with Moody's Investors Service.

2. Formerly known as the Cooke Committee after its first chairman, Peter Cooke of the Bank of England.

3. Consisting of the representatives of the banking supervisory authorities in the US, the UK, Japan, Germany, France, Canada, Italy, Netherlands, Belgium, Sweden, Luxembourg and Switzerland. This is in fact a group of 12 rather than 10!

4. Prior to the Basle Agreement, risk was generally calculated as a percentage of a bank's assets and often ignored off-balance sheet exposures.

5. The Organisation of Economic Co-operation and Development (OECD) is composed of the US, the UK, Japan, Germany, France, Canada, Italy, Netherlands, Belgium, Luxembourg, Switzerland, Austria, Sweden, Denmark, Finland, Norway, Iceland, Spain, Portugal, Australia, New Zealand, Ireland, Greece and Turkey. For the purposes of the Basle Agreement, Saudi Arabia is included.

6. In strict legal terms, *novation* is a process involving three parties, one taking over the obligations of another to the third (typically, a clearing house).

Self-Study Exercises: <u>Questions</u>   Part 5

Assume in all questions that all interest rates are quoted on the same basis in terms of day count, annual basis and compounding conventions.

Question 5.1:   What are the key differences between the impact of a default on a currency swap compared to that on an interest rate swap?

Question 5.2:   What is replacement cost?

Question 5.3:   Take a sterling/dollar currency swap (fixed-against-fixed) with an exchange of principal at maturity. Assume that, since the swap was transacted, UK interest rates have fallen and US interest rates have risen, while sterling has appreciated against the dollar. If the payer of sterling defaults and the affected counterparty arranges a replacement swap, who pays the replacement cost?

Question 5.4:   Take the following dollar/Swiss franc currency swap (fixed-against-fixed):

life	= 6 years
dollar fixed interest rate	= 3%pa
Swiss franc fixed interest rate	= 8%pa
dollar principal	= $10m
Swiss franc principal	= SwFr12m
$/SwFr exchange rate	= 1.2000

Assume there is a default by the counterparty which pays dollars and receives Swiss francs, after exactly three years. The parameters of the swap are now:

life	= 3 years
dollar fixed interest rate	= 6%pa
Swiss franc fixed interest rate	= 6%pa
$/SwFr exchange rate	= 1.4000

Assume a replacement swap is transacted with a new counterparty at the original interest and exchange rates. What is the replacement cost and who pays whom?

Question 5.5: Take the following sterling/dollar cross-currency coupon swap (fixed-against-floating):

life	= 4 years
dollar floating interest rate	= Libor
sterling fixed interest rate	= 7%pa
dollar principal	= $37.5m
sterling principal	= £25m
£/$ exchange rate	= 1.5000

Assume there is a default by the counterparty which receives dollars and pays sterling, after exactly two years. The parameters of the swap are now:

life	= 2 years
sterling fixed interest rate	= 10%pa
£/$ exchange rate	= 1.4500

Assume a replacement swap is transacted with a new counterparty at the original interest and exchange rates. What is the replacement cost and who pays whom?

Question 5.6: Why does the Basle Agreement apply higher residual maturity weights to currency swaps compared to interest rate swaps?

Question 5.7: What is the Basle risk weight attached to a two-year currency swap transacted with a Singapore-based bank?

Question 5.8: What is the minimum risk capital requirement under the Current Exposure Method of the Basle Agreement for the currency swap in Question 5.4 at the date it was transacted, if the counterparty is the bank in Question 5.7?

Question 5.9: What is *cherry-picking*?

Question 5.10: What is the minimum transaction size for a currency swap to qualify a counterparty for supervision by the Bank of England?

Self-Study Exercises: <u>Answers</u>   Part 5

Answer 5.1:   The impact of credit risk on currency swaps compared to interest rate swaps differs in two key respects:

- whereas derivatives like interest rate swaps involve exchanges of interest only, *non-derivative* off-balance sheet instruments like currency swaps involve exchanges of *both* interest and principal;

- currency swaps create an exposure to both *interest rate* and *currency risk*, whereas interest rate swaps create an exposure to interest rate risk only.

Answer 5.2:   The **replacement cost** of a currency swap is the upfront cash fee which, in the event of default by a counterparty to the swap, must be paid by the **affected counterparty** in order to induce a new counterparty to transact a replacement swap which is an exact replica of the defaulted currency swap and which restores the status quo before default. As interest and exchange rates will have moved since the defaulted swap was originally transacted, the replacement swap will be priced at what are now historic (or so-called off-market) rates. If the replacement counterparty has to pay above current interest through the replacement swap or receive below current interest, or has to pay a higher exchange rate at maturity, it will require compensation for the difference between the original and current rates before it will transact the replacement swap. The replacement cost will cover the immediate loss due to both interest and exchange rate changes over the life of the defaulted swap, in other words, *current market risk*. The replacement cost of a currency swap should be equal to the value of its replacement, priced at the original interest and exchange rates.

Answer 5.3:   If the counterparty affected by the default (the payer of dollars and receiver of sterling) arranged a replacement swap at current market rates, compared to the defaulted swap, it would have to pay dollars at a higher interest rate and receive sterling at a lower interest rate, as well as pay more dollars per pound in the exchange of principal amounts at maturity. In practice, the affected counterparty would transact a replacement swap at the (now historic and off-market) interest and exchange rates which applied to the defaulted swap. The counterparty to this replacement swap would therefore pay above current sterling interest rate through the swap and receive below current dollar interest, and receive less dollars per pound in the exchange of principal amounts at maturity. The *affected counterparty* (receiver of sterling/payer of dollars) should therefore have to pay the replacement swap counterparty a compensatory cash payment in order to induce it to transact the replacement swap.

Answer 5.4:   The replacement cost of the defaulted swap is equal to the value of the replacement swap, which is in turn equal to the difference between the NPV of the dollar cash flow stream and the NPV of the Swiss franc cash flow stream, where the Swiss franc NPV is translated into dollars.

The NPV of the *dollar* cash flow through the replacement swap (which replicates the dollar cash flow through the defaulted swap) can be calculated, using a bond calculator, from the following data:

```
n           = 3 years
i           = 6%pa
PMT         = 3%pa
FV          = 100        (= $10m)
```

which gives an NPV of:

PV = 91.98 (= $9,198,096)

The NPV of the *Swiss franc* cash flow through the replacement swap (which replicates the Swiss franc cash flow through the defaulted swap) can be calculated, using a bond calculator, from the following data:

```
n          = 3 years
i          = 6%pa
PMT        = 8%pa
FV         = 100  (= SwFr12m)
```

which gives an NPV of:

PV = 105.35 (= SwFr12,641,523)

At the new \$/SwFr *exchange* rate of 1.1000, the NPV of the SwFr cash flow translates into:

SwFr12,641,523 / 1.4000 = \$9,029,659

The difference between this and the NPV of the dollar cash flow is:

\$9,198,096 − \$9,029,659 = \$168,437

The value of a new generic swap priced at current market rates should be zero. The replacement swap has a non-zero value because it is priced at historic off-market rates. Because the NPV of the dollar cash flows is greater than the NPV of the Swiss franc cash flows, the payer of dollars and receiver of Swiss francs — which is the replacement counterparty — needs to be compensated in order to induce it to transact the replacement swap at historic off-market rates. This compensation, in the form of a replacement cost of $168,437 is paid *by* the affected counterparty *to* the replacement counterparty.

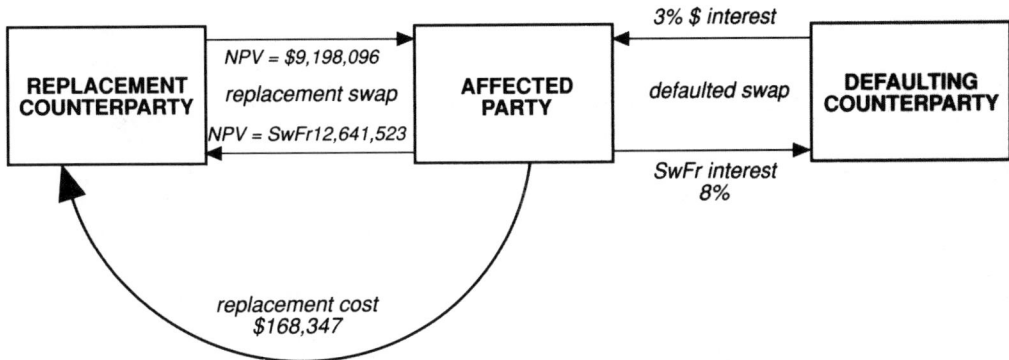

Answer 5.5: The replacement cost of the defaulted swap is equal to the value of the replacement swap, whch is in turn equal to the difference between the NPV of the dollar cash flow stream and the NPV of the sterling cash flow stream, where the sterling NPV is translated into dollars. As the dollar interest rate is floating, only the dollar principal exchanged at maturity (and not the interest) is included in the value of the swap.

As explained in *Part Four*, the NPV of a cash flow composed of floating interest and a principal amount is equal to the nominal value of the principal amount itself. Therefore, the NPV of the *dollar* cash flow through the replacement swap is $37.5m.

The NPV of the *sterling* cash flow through the replacement swap (which replicates the sterling cash flow through the defaulted swap) can be calculated, using a bond calculator, from the following data:

n   = 2 years
i   = 5%pa
PMT   = 7%pa
FV   = 100 (= £25m)

which gives an NPV of:

PV = 103.72 (= £25,929,705)

At the new £/$ *exchange* rate of 1.4500, the NPV of the sterling cash flow translates into:

£25,929,705 x 1.4500 = $37,598,073

The difference between this and the NPV of the dollar cash flow is:

$37,500,000 − $37,598,073 = $98,073

The value of a new generic swap priced at current market rates should be zero. The replacement swap has a non-zero value, because it is priced at historic off-market rates. Because the NPV of the dollar cash flows is greater than the NPV of the sterling cash flows, the payer of sterling and receiver of dollars — which is the replacement counterparty — needs to be compensated in order to induce it to transact the replacement swap at historic off-market rates. This compensation, in the form of a replacement cost of $98,073 is paid *by* the affected counterparty *to* the replacement counterparty.

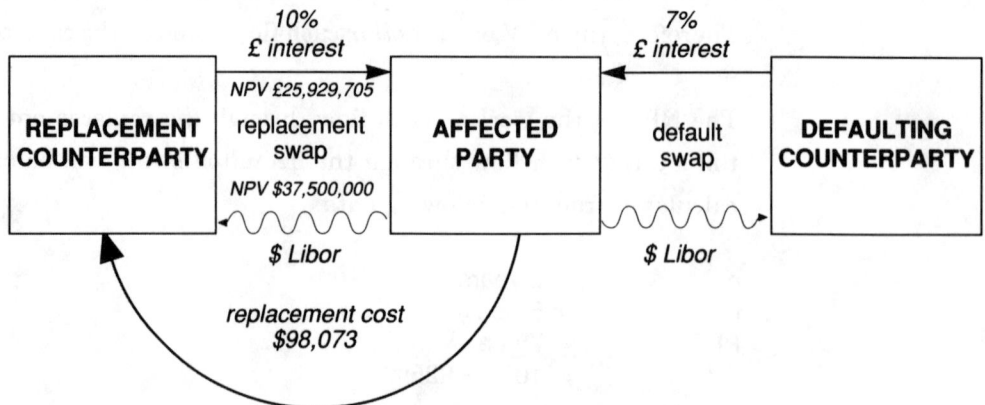

Answer 5.6: The risk weights prescribed by the Basle Agreement for currency swaps (and other currency instruments) are much heavier than for interest rate swaps (and other interest rate instruments) because currency instruments usually involve an exchange of principal amounts. This increases the **delivery risk**, which is the magnitude of the risk that one counterparty to a currency swap might make a payment before detecting a default by the other on the counterpayment.

Answer 5.7: As Singapore is not a member of the OECD and as the transaction is long-term, the risk weight would normally be 100%. However, for interest rate and exchange rate instruments, including swaps, 100% risk weights have been reduced to 50%.

Answer 5.8: At the time it was transacted, the $/SwFr currency swap in Question 5.4 would have zero current market risk. However, the future market risk under the Current Exposure Method is represented by a residual maturity weight of a flat 5% of the principal amount of $10m, which is $500,000. This exposure is then multiplied by the risk weight of 50% for the Singapore bank to give a risk-adjusted exposure of $250,000. The minimum risk capital requirement is 8% of this, which is $20,000.

Answer 5.9: *Cherry-picking* is the practice where the receivers or administrators of bankrupt companies maintain swap contracts which are profitable from those companies and default on unprofitable swaps, even if these contracts are with the same counterparties.

Answer 5.10: The minimum transaction size for a currency swap to qualify a counterparty for supervision by the Bank of England is £500,000 in terms of its principal amount.

Glossary

Affected counterparty

The counterparty to a transaction like a currency swap on which the other counterparty has defaulted.

Alternate performance

The payment of a net settlement amount in a currency swap instead of an exchange of principal. This payment is made by the counterparty paying the currency through the swap which has appreciated. In a currency swap with an exchange of principal at maturity, this counterparty foregoes the exchange rate profit by having committed to pay the appreciating currency at an exchange rate fixed at the start of the swap (prior to appreciation). In a currency swap without an exchange of principal at maturity, this gain must be foregone by payment of a net settlement amount.

Arranger

An intermediary which arranges a swap between two end-users without actually directly participating in the transaction. An arranger performs the same function as a *broker*, but differs in that it participates in swaps on other occasions or in other markets as a principal counterparty. Typically merchant banks or investment banks. Arrangers charge fees rather than take a dealing spread.

As of basis

The documentation for interest rate swaps is often exchanged after confirmations. Such deals are said to have been made on an *as of* basis.

Asset swap

Where the cash flows exchanged through a currency swap are funded with cash flows received on specific assets, particularly where the assets are bought and sold as part of the same package with the swap. It is important to note that an asset swap does not involve any change in the swap mechanism itself. The term simply identifies the purpose of the swap, rather than its structure. It is therefore possible to have asset swaps which are also coupon or basis swaps. Where an asset swap is sold as a package with assets, the swap and the assets themselves remain otherwise separate instruments in that they can, and usually are, contracts between different sets of counterparties.

Assignment

The sale of a currency swap by one of the counterparties (the assignor) to a third party (the assignee). The assignee effectively substitutes for the assignor. Assignment requires the agreement of the other counterparty. The value of the swap is exchanged between the assignor and the assignee in a cash payment.

Back-to-back loan

A precursor of the currency swap, designed to overcome the deficiencies of the parallel loan. (See also footnote 2 in *Part One*.)

BBAIRS

British Bankers' Association Interest Rate Swap. The name applied to the BBA's *Recommended Terms and Conditions for London Interbank Interest Rate Swaps*; and to the *Interest Settlement Rate* published daily on behalf of the BBA by *Telerate* on screen pages 3740–50 for use in resetting the floating interest rate in swaps in several major currencies, for a range of tenors between one and 12 months.

Broker

An intermediary that arranges swaps between end-users without actually directly participating in the transaction. Brokers perform the same function as arrangers, but differ in that they specialise in arrangement. Brokers charge fees related to the size and maturity of the swap rather than taking dealing spreads between transaction prices: this is to ensure that they are impartial between the swap counterparties in terms of price and are interested only in matching two couterparties at mutually satisfactory terms so that a deal is consummated.

Cash swap

A currency swap involving an initial exchange of principal amounts of currencies.

Circus swap

A circus swap is a simple form of *cocktail swap*, composed of a *cross-currency coupon swap* (fixed-against-floating) and a single-currency coupon swap, where both floating interest streams are calculated at the same Libor. These swaps are combined to replicate either:

- a *currency swap* (fixed-against-fixed)

- a *cross-currency basis swap* (floating-against-floating)

For example, a circus swap might consist of a cross-currency swap between Swiss franc fixed interest and US dollar six-month Libor on the one hand and a US dollar coupon swap on the other hand. This produces a Swiss franc/US dollar currency swap.

Cocktail swap

In cases where it is difficult to swap non-dollar floating interest, the desired swap is achieved indirectly by going through a series of swaps involving intermediate currencies. The composite structure is called a **cocktail swap**. It is similar to the way in which illiquid 'cross rates' (exchange rates between two non-dollar currencies) are constructed in the foreign exchange market: one non-dollar currency would be bought against dollars and then the dollars sold for the other non-dollar currency, with the dollar providing a common link, which cancels itself out. The link in currency swaps is typically *six-month US dollar Libor*, reflecting the fact that, in the markets in Eurodeposits which ultimately provide floating-rate funds, Eurodollars are very liquid, whereas the markets in Eurodeposits in most other currencies are generally illiquid. There can be a very considerable number of legs to a cocktail swap. These might include both currency and (single-currency) interest rate swaps. Cocktail swaps are also often created by swap intermediaries hedging their exposure to less liquid currency swaps.

Cross-currency basis swap

A contract which commits two counterparties to exchange, over an agreed period, streams of **floating** interest payments in different currencies and, at the end of the period, the corresponding principal amounts of currencies.

Cross-currency coupon swap

A contract which commits two counterparties to exchange, over an agreed period, a stream of **fixed** interest payments and a stream of **floating** interest payments, both in different currencies and, at the end of the period, the corresponding principal amounts of currencies.

Currency swap

Generic definition. A contract which commits two counterparties to exchange, over an agreed period, two streams of interest payments in different currencies and, at the end of the period, the corresponding principal amounts of currencies.

Specific definition. A contract which commits two counterparties to exchange, over an agreed period, two streams of **fixed** interest payments in different currencies and, at the end of the period, the corresponding principal amounts of currencies.

Derivative instrument

An off-balance sheet financial contract whose performance is derived from the behaviour of the price of a physical or financial commodity, but which does not actually require that commodity to be bought or sold. Not all off-balance sheet instruments are derivatives, as some involve a future impact on the balance sheet (eg, currency swaps and forward foreign exchange contracts).

Differential swap

Sometimes known as a **diff swap** or **quanto swap**. This is a very special type of *cross-currency basis swap* (floating-against-floating) which does not involve any exchange of principal, even at maturity. Both streams of interest payments through a diff swap are calculated with reference to the same notional principal amount of the same currency and both streams of interest are actually paid in this currency. For example, a $/DM diff swap would typically involve an exchange of interest at six-month Deutsche mark Libor for interest at six-month US dollar Libor. Both Libor indexes would be applied to the same notional principal amount of, say, Deutsche marks and both interest streams would also be paid in Deutsche marks. In other words, the swap would exchange six-month US dollar Libor paid in Deutsche marks for six-month Deutsche mark Libor also paid in Deutsche marks. If six-month US dollar Libor was fixed at 5% per annum and six-month Deutsche mark Libor at 10% per annum, a diff swap for a notional principal amount of DM150m would entail an interest payment, for a period of 182 days, of:

182/360 x 5/100 x 150,000,000 = DM3,791,667

against a counterpayment of:

182/360 x 10/100 x 150,000,000 = DM7,583,333

Generic swap

Generic is a term used to describe the simplest of any type of financial instrument. Also called **straight** or **plain vanilla** versions. The term is not as widely used for currency swaps as for interest rate swaps, but is equally valid. Specifically, a generic currency swap has:

- a constant *notional principal amount*;

- an exchange of *fixed-against-floating* interest: in other words, a generic swap is a simple type of *cross-currency coupon swap*.

- a constant *fixed interest* rate;

- a flat *floating interest* rate (ie, no margin over the index): typically, the floating interest rate would be *US dollar Libor*;

- regular (but not necessarily simultaneous) *payment* of fixed and floating interest;

- an immediate (or spot) *start* to the swap;

- no special *risk features* (eg, a combination with an option).

ISDA

International Swap Dealers' Association. A New York-based organisation, established in March 1985, representing market-makers in interest rate and cross-currency swaps. Its most tangible achievement has been the production of standardised contract documentation for swaps.

Market-maker

An intermediary which is committed to quote firm buying and selling (two-way) prices for swaps in all trading conditions. Market-making is very rare in currency swaps.

Marking to market

Revaluing swaps and other instruments by calculating the profit or loss — or *replacement cost* — which would be required if a replacement instrument had to be transacted at current market prices.

Master contract

A document which sets out standard terms and conditions for a swap transaction and only has to be updated with details specific to a new transaction, such as price, maturity, notional principal amount, etc. This allows dealers to avoid lengthy and complex negotiations for simple swaps, by limiting agreement to a few key details. Other terms and conditions are settled by reference to the master contract. The master contracts drafted by ISDA work by novation: each new deal is added as an appendix to the master contract and becomes part of a single integrated contract, together with all previous deals under the master contract. This technique is intended to assist in enforcing the netting of swaps in the event of a default.

Netting

In the event of default by a swap counterparty, the ability of individual creditors to offset the value of outstanding swaps which are profitable to the defaulter against the value of swaps which are unprofitable to it. This reduces the loss in the event of default by an active user of swaps by avoiding *cherry-picking*.

New issue arbitrage

Arbitrage between a new borrowing (typically a Eurobond issue) and a currency swap. Where such an arbitrage opportunity exists, the borrower will receive fixed interest through the swap at a rate higher than it pays on its borrowing and end up paying subsidised floating interest.

| **Off-balance sheet instrument** | A financial contract which is not recorded on the balance sheets of the counterparties, although it may be scheduled to appear on the balance sheet at a known future date (eg, a currency swap or forward foreign exchange contract). |

Off-balance sheet instrument — A financial contract which is not recorded on the balance sheets of the counterparties, although it may be scheduled to appear on the balance sheet at a known future date (eg, a currency swap or forward foreign exchange contract).

Off-market — A swap which is priced at other than a current market rate.

Par — A swap which is priced at a current market rate.

Parallel loan — A precursor to the currency swap. This instrument originated as a means of circumventing exchange controls in the UK. (See also footnote 2 in *Part One*).

Par forward — A special type of outright forward foreign exchange transaction, which is actually a series of outright forwards packaged into a single transaction with each exchange of currencies at a single average (par) forward exchange rate. As such, par forwards produce a constant stream of cash flows up to maturity, just like a currency swap.

Price — The interest rates and exchange rate at which a currency swap is transacted.

Because the market convention is to assume the floating interest rate index is six-month US dollar Libor, unless otherwise specified, *cross-currency coupon swaps* are quoted in terms of the fixed interest rate only.

Replacement cost	The difference between the net present value of an existing swap and the net present value of a new swap at a current market rate. The amount which would be gained or lost if the counterparty to the existing swap defaulted and the other counterparty negotiated a new replacement swap. The usual measure of the current credit risk on a swap.
Reversal	A new currency swap of the same type as an existing swap, but opposite in terms of the direction of interest and principal payments, and therefore a hedge to the existing swap. Also called a **matching swap**.
Termination	The cancellation of a swap contract. One counterparty pays the other the value of the swap as a cash payment to compensate for the loss of expected profit over the remainder of the life of the swap.
Warehousing	The temporary hedging of currency swaps until a *reversal* can be agreed, typically using government bonds.

How to mark the self-study questions

Each of the questions has been awarded between 1 and 11 marks. The marks are set out in the table. Where questions have more than one part, fractions can be awarded. When all the marks have been added up, the results should be assessed against the distribution curve below.

Question	Part one	Part two	Part three	Part four	Part five
1	2	4	6	3	2
2	2	4	6	1	4
3	2	4	8	2	5
4	2	2	2	4	5
5	2	4	4	1	5
6	5	6	1	4	1
7	2	6	4	11	2
8	10	10	4	4	4
9	6	10	4		1
10	2	10	6		1
Total	**35**	**60**	**45**	**30**	**30**

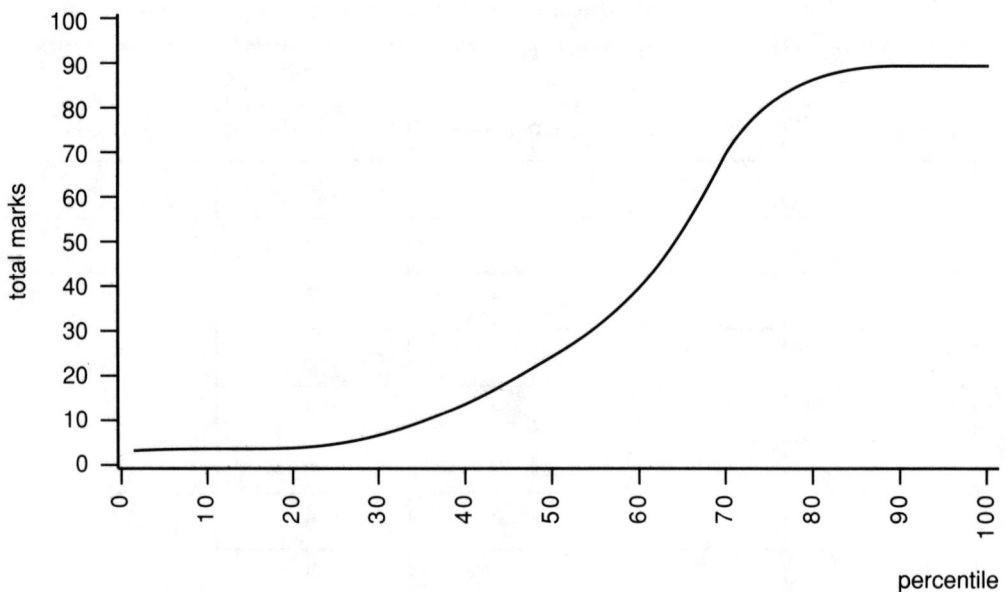

Percentile	Assessment
0—50%	You should start the Workbook again. Check that you work through it more methodically than before and in an environment conducive to study.
50—60%	You should think about re-reading the Workbook to reinforce your understanding of swaps. If you have lost marks in just one or two chapters, there is probably no need to re-read the whole Workbook, but you should go through the worked answers with care.
60—80%	A good result. You should think about skimming through the Workbook again to consolidate your knowledge.
80—100%	An excellent result. You should be able to progress quite easily to more specialised texts on swaps.

Coopers & Lybrand offices

ustralia
Prothero
oopers & Lybrand Tower
0 George Street Sydney
ew South Wales 2000
l: (03) 606 4500

ustria
Wirth
stfach 161
1092
enna
l: (1) 31377 0

hamas
ohnson
Box N 596
ssau NP
l: (809) 322 1061

hrain
Ruttonsha
Box 787
nama
: (0973) 53007

lgium
eckhout
rcel Thirty Court
enue Marcel Thirty 216
200 Brussels
: (02) 774 42 11

rmuda
Iolmes
Box HM1171
nilton
rmuda HMEX
: (809) 295 2000

zil
araldi
xa Postal 3168
01060
Paulo
Brazil
(11) 530 0200

ada
id Atkins
na Canada Centre
King Street West
onto
rio
I 1V8
(416) 869 1130

nnel Islands
rrell
Motte Chambers
elier
y
(0534) 602000

rus
padopoulos
3ox 1612
sia
(02) 453053

mark
lladsen
3ox 1443
500
tebro
(97-42) 19 88

Finland
M Tervo
PL 1015
00101
Helsinki
Tel: (0) 658 044

France
K Pilgrem
BP 451-08
75366 Paris
Cedex 08
Tel: (1) 44 20 80 00

Germany
H Wagener
Treuarbeit AG
Postfach 120
D-W 1000
Berlin 15
Tel: (030) 884 2020

Germany
K Lührig
Truehand-Vereiningung AG
Postfach 170 552
D-W 6000
Frankfurt am Main 1
Tel: (069) 71100

Hong Kong
R Chalmers
Sunning Plaza
10 Hysan Avenue
Hong Kong
Tel: 839 4321

Hungary
A Romer-Lee
PO Box 694
1539 Budapest
Tel: (1) 135 0140

Isle of Man
C Talavera
12 Finch Road
Douglas
Tel: (0624) 626711

Italy
P Barone
Via del Quirinale
00187 Rome
Tel: (0) 6 4744896

Japan
N Yamakoshi
Shin-Aoyama Bldg
Twin West 20F
1-1 Minami Aoyama 1-Chome
Minato-Ku
Tokyo 107
Tel: (3) 3475 1722

Leichtenstein
R Silvani
PO Box 1113
9490 Vaduz
Tel: 2 90 80

Luxembourg
M Chèvremont
BP 1446
L-1014
Luxembourg
Tel: 49749 1

Malaysia
M Abdullah
PO Box 10184
50706
Kuala Lumpur
Tel: (3) 441 1188

Malta
J Bonello
PO Box 61
Valleta Malta
Tel: 233648

Mexico
H Lara Silva
Apartado Postal 24-348
Col Roma
06700 Mexico
DF
Tel: (5) 208 1277

Netherlands
H Schaper
PO Bix 4200
1009 AE
Amsterdam
Tel: (20) 568 6666

New Zealand
R Hill
GPO Box 243
Wellington 6000
Tel: (4) 499 9898

Norway
E Westerby
Havnelageret
0150 Oslo 1
Tel: 02 40 00 00

Poland
D Thomas
Iwonicka 19
09-924 Warsaw
Tel: (22) 42 87 66

Portugal
C Bernardes
PO Box 1910
1004 Lisbon Codex
Tel: 793 0023

Rep of Ireland
B Cunningham
PO Box 1283
Dublin 2
Tel: (01) 610333

Rep of South Africa
R Barrow
PO Box 2536
Johannesburg 2000
Tel: (011) 498 4000

Russia
S Root
Ulinska Schchepkina 6
Moscow 129090
Tel: (095) 281 9466

Saudi Arabia
G Karaman
PO Box 2762
Riyad 11461
Tel: (01) 477 9504

Singapore
D Compton
Orchard PO Box 285
Singapore 9123
Tel: 336 2344

Spain
JJ Hierro
Apartado de Correos
36-191
28080 Madrid
Tel: (1) 572 0233

Sultanate of Oman
N Ferrand
PO Box 6075
Ruwi
Tel: 5637 17

Swedan
Johan Hafstrom
PO Box 27318
S-102 54 Stockholm
Tel: (8) 666 8000

Switzerland
R. Tschudi
Postfach 4152
CH 4002
Basel
(060) 277 5500

Thailand
N Charoentaveesub
GPO Box 788
Bangkok 10501
Tel: (2) 236 5227 9

Turkey
M Clarke
Buyukdere cad No 111
Kat; 2-3
Istanbul
Tel: (1) 175 2840

United Arab Emirates
H Nehme
PO Box 990
Abu Dhabi
Gayrettepe 80300
Tel: (02) 21123

United Kingdom
P. Reyniers
P.Rivett
London EC4A 4HT
Tel: (071) 583 5000

United States of America
C Jenkins
One Post Office Square
Boston
Massachusetts 02109
Tel: (617) 7574 5000

United States of America
W Van Rijn
1301 Avenue of the Americas
New York
NY 10019-6013
Tel: 259 7000